The Cinema
A History

Keith Reader was born in Kent in 1945, and educated at the Universities of Cambridge and Oxford and in the cinemas of Paris. He lectures in French at Kingston Polytechnic where he is jointly responsible for a course on the French cinema, an area in which he has also written articles and papers.

TEACH YOURSELF BOOKS

The Cinema
a history

Keith Reader

TEACH YOURSELF BOOKS
Hodder and Stoughton

This edition 1979

Copyright © 1979 Keith Reader

Published in the USA by David McKay & Co. Inc., 750 Third Avenue, New York, NY 10017, USA

British Library CIP

Reader, K
    History of the cinema. – (Teach yourself books).
    1. Moving-pictures – History
    I. Title   II. Series
    791.43'09'04 PN1993.5.A1

ISBN 0 340 22631 5

Printed and bound in Great Britain for Hodder and Stoughton Paperbacks, a Division of Hodder and Stoughton Ltd, Mill Road, Dunton Green, Sevenoaks, Kent (Editorial Office: 47 Bedford Square, London WC1 3DP) by Richard Clay (The Chaucer Press) Ltd, Bungay, Suffolk

Contents

Abbreviations

MGM Metro-Goldwyn-Mayer

NASCAP National Association for the Advancement of Coloured People

OAS Organisation de l'Armée Secrète (French neo-Fascist movement that waged guerilla war to keep Algeria French)

RCA Radio Corporation of America (leading sound-recording company)

RKO Amalgam of RCA and Keith-Orpheum cinema chain – leading Hollywood production company 1921/1953

UFA Universum Film Aktiengesellschaft – German state-sponsored film production company in 1920s and 1930s

Acknowledgements

I should like to take this opportunity to thank the Library and Information Services of the British Film Institute for their helpfulness and patience, and also Chris Cook and Eleonore Kofman, for personal help and kindness.

The author and publisher would like to thank the following for permission to use the photographs: Cinegate Film Distribution for Plates 6 and 14; Columbia-Warner for Plate 13; Connoisseur Films for Plate 10; Contemporary Films Ltd for Plates 2 and 11; Gala Films for Plate 12; Metro-Goldwyn-Mayer Inc for Plates 4 and 8; Transit Films for Plate 3; Still from the film *Bus Stop* by courtesy of Twentieth Century-Fox Film Company Limited; United Artists Corporation Ltd for Plates 5 and 9.

Introduction

This book aims to provide a history of the most important developments in the eighty-two years of the cinema's existence. It is neither a checklist of films and directors (though I have tried to include the most important), nor a full-scale work of reference like Cawkwell and Smith's indispensable *World Encyclopedia of Film* (my source for the dates of films here listed). Its object is to survey film developments, whether in the making of, writing in, or writing about film, in such a way as to show that these areas are closely connected with one another and with the wider social and cultural factors that go to determine them. My hope is that the (putative) reader approaching this work with a vague general interest in, but few systematic ideas about, the cinema will leave it aware, not only of who the 'big names' are, but of why they became big, how they operated, and how their work is part of the society that produced it.

The 'big names' will in this text tend to be those of directors rather than stars or executive producers. This should be taken to mean, not that I endorse the auteur theory (ref. p. 131–32) whereby a director is seen as the primary 'creative' force of a film, but that this theory has come to dominate historical writing on the cinema to such an extent that it is very difficult to dissociate oneself from it entirely. But it should constantly be borne in mind that directors have no automatic right to be considered the 'authors' of the films discussed for convenience under their names.

To this end I have devoted some attention to the evolution of theories of cinema, and in particular to cinema seen as a *language*, a means of expression and communication on a par with (though very different from) the written word. The view that the cinema is at best a diversion, at worst a source of depravity on the one hand and pseudo-intellectual posturing on the other, exists now only in certain isolated pockets of resistance; it would be agreeable if this book could help to wipe them out, but even more so if it could clarify not only why cinema is an art, but *how*.

I have tackled vexed problems of dating by reference to Cawkwell and Smith, and of translation by giving a film's title in English. The exception to this is French films, which are given in the original with a translation appended except when the original is self-evident to those with no French (example: *Lancelot du Lac*), or known hardly, if at all, by an English label. This is due partly to Francophone arrogance, but also to a feeling that it is as arrogant and snobbish, in reverse, to bracket *Crazy Pete* after *Pierrot le Fou* as it would be to refer to *The Silence* as *Tystnaden*.

Actors and the parts they play have occasionally been conflated where no ambiguity is likely to arise, with a view to saving space (thus, on p. 145 it should be perfectly plain that 'the sexual insecurities of Donald Pleasance and Françoise Dorléac' relate to the characters they play . . .).

I hope that there are no major oversights, inaccuracies, or omissions; to those slighted or offended by any that do arise, I take this opportunity of apologising in advance.

KEITH READER
London 1978

1 The Beginnings: Up to 1918

The cinema as a commercial undertaking began on 28 December 1895, at the Grand Café, Paris, where the Lumière Brothers from Lyon gave the first public showing of films for entrance money. Less than eight weeks later, on 2 February 1896, the first commercial screening in England took place at London's Regent Street Polytechnic; the new art-form was already giving evidence of the prodigious capacity for spreading internationally that it has never since ceased to display. This introductory chapter details the technical, social, and aesthetic development of the medium, in Europe and America, in the years up to the end of the First World War.

Moving pictures: the prehistory

'Moving pictures' of various kinds had been a source of entertainment for many years before, and the invention of the photograph in the 1820s had given an impetus to the evolution of the medium. Optical toys, another popular form of entertainment, also exploited one of the main principles on which the cinema depends, that of the persistence of vision, whereby still images in rapid succession give the illusion of movement because the retina retains each image for a brief moment after its disappearance. Victorian children delighted in such toys as the Stroboscope and Zoëtrope (literally, 'Wheel of Life'), in which a band carrying a succession of 'action' pictures was wound along inside a drum in which slots were cut; the discontinuity between the images and the persistence of vision combined to give the illusion of movement.

But the cinema could not arrive until a way was discovered of breaking down and resynthesising movement by means of the camera, which was first achieved by the émigré English photographer Eadweard [*sic*] Muybridge. Rumour has it that the Governor of California wanted to settle a bet about whether his champion trotter, Occident, ever had all four feet off the ground at once, and that in 1878 Muybridge devised a system of cameras distributed along the race-track and operated by trip-wires as the horse sped past. The resulting photographs (in which the horse appeared with all its feet in the air) showed that artists had hitherto given unrealistic portrayals of animals in motion, and Muybridge extended his methods to analyse and reproduce the movements of human beings.

At much the same time, the French physicist Étienne Marey was developing a similar technique to analyse the motion of birds in flight, with a single gun-shaped camera whose compactness and portability gave it a clear advantage over Muybridge's multi-camera system. The race was on. Among the principal competitors were the British photographer William Friese-Greene, whose disorganisation so offset his inspiration that he died unrecognised and penniless in the middle of a cinematic congress; Louis le Prince, whose mysterious disappearance on a train between Dijon and Paris prematurely removed him from the running; and the versatile Thomas Alva Edison, who decided that moving pictures would provide an appropriate supplement to his newly-invented phonograph. Accordingly, in 1890, he devised the Kinetoscope, not strictly a movie projector since the film rotated in a continuous loop behind an illuminated aperture (rather like a What-The-Butler-Saw machine), and began making commercial films for it in 1894.

The first 'real film'

But it was in France, on 10 March 1895, that the first celluloid film was projected, and the device used given the name of cinematograph by its inventor, Louis Lumière. The facilities he had at his disposal make it far from surprising that he was the first to show moving pictures commercially; he directed the largest photographic factory in Europe (whose workers leaving for home unwittingly 'starred' in one of the short films projected at the Grand Café), and his subject-matter is typical of the amateur photographer – a boat leaving harbour, a train arriving in a station (the shot which made audiences at the first showings leave their seats in fright), a baby being fed, a group of delegates arriving at a photographic congress. The films and apparatus were registered in the names of Louis and his elder brother Auguste, though most of the credit belonged to Louis. Their father, Antoine, ran the Paris showings with considerable professionalism, and in 1896 there were up to twenty daily projections of a programme of twelve short films. One of these, *L'Arroseur Arrosé* (*The Waterer Watered*), was the first slapstick picture. It depicted a gardener watering a lawn as the dupe of an urchin who trod on his hose to interrupt the flow of water and then removed his foot so that it restarted abruptly when the puzzled gardener looked to see what was wrong. Law and order, however, triumphed in the end, when the gardener gave the urchin a taste of his own medicine. Humour was also evident in *La Charcuterie Mécanique* (*The Mechanical Pork-Butchery*), in which a pig was fed into a sausage-machine and then 'reassembled' by running the film backwards. In the self-conscious middle-class scenes they depict, and in their 'family-photograph' camera-perspective, these films reflect eloquently the bourgeois social order which produced them. The top-hatted photographer delegates disembarking from the steamer for their congress are French counterparts to George Grossmith's Mr Pooter, who was writing his *Diary of a Nobody* at about the same time.

By 1898 there were a thousand films in the Lumière catalogue. Whether or not Louis Lumière ever told his colleague Georges Méliès that the cinema was 'an invention with no future', he certainly described it as 'a peddlar's trade', and he saw himself first of all as an industrialist with products to sell that his films could publicise. This they did with such success that in 1905 he was able to sell out to Pathé and concentrate on the development of colour photography, graduating successively to membership of the Legion of Honour and a comfortable retirement on the French Riviera. He had provided the cinema, not only with its first 'realist' works, but with the first examples of the home movie and the advertising film that were to be among its most widespread later manifestations.

The father of fantasy

When Tsar Nicholas II visited France in 1896, four firms competed to film his visit. Two of these remain household names, Pathé and Gaumont, and two are key figures in early film history: Lumière and the man who is often cited as his complement or 'opposite', Georges Méliès. Méliès remained all his life, as he started out, a conjuror, and his initial interest in the cinema was as an additional entertainment for his theatre. It was in 1897 that he built the first true film studio, near Paris, from which over a thousand films emerged in the next sixteen years. His best-known work, *Voyage dans la Lune* (*Journey to the Moon*, 1892), characteristically combines Jules Verne-like science-fiction (the fantastic space-rocket) with contemporary theatrical elements (the line of chorus-girl Moon-dwellers) and a reassuring anthropomorphism (when the rocket crashes on the face of the Moon, a tear trickles from its eye). This may suggest why Méliès's success was short-lived. His fairy tales, science-fiction fantasies, and excursions into Gothic grotesque (as in *Les Quat'Cent Farces du Diable* – *The Devil's Four Hundred Pranks*, 1906), for all their visual imaginativeness and the trick photography they pioneered, show little conception of how film could be used as a kind of language and even less of internal development or progress. Blatant pirating of his ideas by American firms contributed to his decline, to such an extent that in 1909 he was President of the International Congress of Film Editors, yet by 1913 had been forced to sell out completely. It was already becoming impossible for a small-scale enterprise such as his to compete with the well-equipped concerns that were making their appearance in the United States. His films are heavily theatrical, in their reliance on static tableaux, their plethora of conjuring-tricks (a favourite is Méliès inflating his own head with an enormous pair of bellows), and their unvarying camera angle and position. *A la Conquête du Pole* (*The Conquest of the Pole*), made in 1912, is contemporary with the first major works of D. W. Griffith and Charlie Chaplin, in comparison with which it must already have begun to seem anachronistic.

After the First World War, Méliès was widely believed to be dead, until in 1928 he was discovered running a toy-shop in draughty and tiring conditions on Montparnasse Station in Paris. Belatedly, a fund was set up which enabled him and his wife to live in reasonable comfort in a house outside Paris until his death in 1938 – the first cinematic victim of the large trusts, and the first man to show that the cinema could be almost literally a magic lantern.

Other French pioneers

Far more commercially successful than Méliès, and more directly influential in the development of the new industry, was Charles Pathé, who established the first producer–director collaboration with Ferdinand Zecca. The French film historian Georges Sadoul sees Zecca's work as influenced by George Smith and the other British directors whom he dubbed 'the Brighton School'. To the latter he attributed the first use of *montage* and the splicing together of discontinuous shots to form a filmic 'sentence' – a fundamental stage in cinematic evolution. Zecca's studio near Paris produced such diverse works as *Les Victimes de l'Alcoolisme* (1902), which condensed Émile Zola's 400-page novel *L'Assommoir* into five minutes, and a series of chase films featuring the first great silent comedian, André Deed. Pathé developed so fast and so adaptably that by 1914 it was the largest company in the world. One of its major assets was Max Linder, 'Gentleman Max', Deed's successor as leading comedian. Linder's elegant and withdrawn style in such films as *Max Professeur de Tango* (*Max the Dancing-Master*, 1912) and *Voyage de Noces en Espagne* (*Spanish Honeymoon*, also 1912) advanced film comedy beyond simple chasing and falling around to the nuances of movement and facial expression characteristic of the great American silent comedians. Ill during the First World War, he made propaganda films as an attempt to compensate for being unable to fight. Poor health, depressive tendencies, and American distribution problems led to his suicide, along with his wife's, in 1925.

Intellectual interest in the cinema began early; the Société du Film d'Art adapted a number of celebrated stage-plays from 1908 onwards, using leading Comédie Française personnel in this first attempt to make the cinema culturally respectable. Pathé added this string to its bow in 1909, a reaction typical of the skill that by 1914 led it to distribute twice as much film in the USA as American-based companies.

One of Pathé's most profitable investments, carried over wholesale from popular magazines, was the 'cliff-hanger' serial, which in such incarnations as *The Perils of Pauline* did roaring business and was surrealistically adapted by Louis Feuillade in *Fantômas* (1913/1914) and its wartime successors. These films continue to have a direct influence far beyond the others discussed in this section (Feuillade's *Judex* of 1916 was refilmed by Georges Franju forty-seven years later), and their blend of black comedy and dream-imagery, their protracted and fantastic plots, and their prophetic townscapes, give them a strikingly modern quality. French intellectual interest in the cinema took a turn far more significant than filming the classics when the poets Guillaume Apollinaire and Max Jacob founded a kind of Fantômas 'fan-club', at a time when outside France the cinema was variously regarded as a passing curiosity or a threat to Western civilisation.

The other European industries

If France led European cinema production up to the First World War, Denmark was not far behind, hard though it may now be to believe that the Nordisk distribution company was in 1913 the second-largest in the world. Actresses such as Asta Nielsen (directed by her husband, Peter Urban Gad) exuded self-destructive passion amid a wide range of city locations in a way that looked forward to much major German cinema. The traditionally high quality of Scandinavian acting, and the ready availability of top stage personnel for filming, gave these industries a favourable start over most of their competitors.

The major Scandinavian directors of this period were Swedish. Victor Sjostrom came to the cinema from a stage-acting career in 1912, and right from his earliest works set the tone often thought of as characterising the Swedish cinema – gloomily intense, to be sure, but also periodically shot through with sunlight and deeply involved with landscapes, like Ingmar Bergman in the very *Wild Strawberries* in which Sjostrom was to star forty-five years later. *Ingeborg Holm* (1913) tells of a widow forced to sell her children and sent to the workhouse, where she has a mental breakdown before being reunited with the one surviving child. The workhouse where Ingeborg is confined and the farm where she finds her child are settings of considerable symbolic force, like the sea on which the fisherman *Terje Vigen* (1916) defies the blockade during the Napoleonic Wars because his family are starving. Beneath the metaphysical gloom is an acute awareness of social injustice, as in the work of the great Scandinavian dramatists Ibsen and Strindberg.

Sjostrom's colleague, the Finn Mauritz Stiller, worked with similar material and many of the same actors, but to quite different effect. It is unlikely that Sjostrom would have made a film about film-making like Stiller's *Thomas Graal's Best Film* (1917), and even more unlikely that had he done so the result would have been so poised and ironic – Stiller was altogether a more urbane director. We shall see how Sjostrom and Stiller migrated to the USA with very mixed success. The difficulty of the Scandinavian cinema was to be simply holding on to its leading performers.

The other major European industry to make a significant contribution to the pre-war development of the medium was in Italy, where both contemporary and classical stories were filmed in grandiose, quasi-operatic style. Giovanni Pastrone's *Cabiria* (1914) combined elaborate studio-built sets with location filming, and made what was for its time an extensive use of the tracking-shot (where the camera moves in a horizontal sweep), besides prefiguring the American Griffith in its interweaving of an individual story with massive historical events.

Many of the main lines along which the cinema was to develop were already plain by 1918: large international trusts (such as Pathé) had emerged, producing comedies, dramas, and thrillers for a mass market, studio sets were being used and even contrasted with location filming (a synthesis implicit in the contrast drawn by Georges Sadoul between the studio-bound Méliès and the location work of Lumière), and it was beginning to be realised how well-adapted the cinema was to telling the story of an individual against a wider social background.

The United States

In 1900, a strike of vaudeville artistes was successfully broken in many parts of the United States by the use of film as alternative entertainment. . . . This realisation of the medium's commercial potential was aided by inadequate patenting of new equipment (Edison being particularly careless), so that in the first decade of the century over 8000 cinemas (or 'nickelodeons') were opened. The prehistory of the American industry is characterised by a running battle between the large trusts (notably Biograph and Vitagraph), and the independent producers and distributors. The General Film Company (representing the trusts) compelled exhibitors to buy licences from it and conform to restrictive terms and conditions, and the independents either sold out or – often successfully – fought back. Ferocious lawsuits and attacks by bands of hired thugs punctuated a story worthy of a Hollywood movie.

Already in 1902 and 1903, when the former Edison cameraman Edwin Porter made his *Life of an American Fireman* and *The Great Train Robbery*, the American cinema was displaying far more narrative sophistication than anything by Lumière or Méliès, with quite complex editing, use of cross-cutting (movement from one scene or action to another and back again), and – in the second film – an open-air chase scene. But the man whose career most accurately and vividly crystallises the conditions in which early American films were produced, and who remains a monument in film history, was David Wark Griffith.

Griffith was a 'resting' actor when, in 1908, he took up a friend's suggestion by approaching the Edison production company with some scripts. At that time he knew next to nothing about the new medium; yet within the next five years he made 456 two-reel shorts for Biograph, which he established firmly as the leading American pre-war producer. Milestones in his early career include his discovery of Mary Pickford in 1909 and, in 1911, *Enoch Arden*, the first film to be made in two parts shown separately.

In the winter of 1910, Griffith went to film in California. This marked the beginning of Hollywood as a geographical entity, shortly to be followed by the burgeoning of the star-system. Up to that year, performers had remained anonymous, which helped to keep salaries down and reassured actors anxious about compromising their theatrical future. It was only when star actress 'The Biograph Girl' defected to the Independent Motion Picture Company, who announced that her name was Florence Lawrence, that fan-magazines, glossy postcards, and the other accoutrements of stardom began to appear.

Griffith was an entirely self-taught director, omnivorous to a fault in his enthusiastic experimentation with his own ideas and plagiarisation of others. He broadened the cinema's syntax and story-telling capacity by cutting between close-ups and long-shots as the action required. He justified a cut in an early film from a woman's face to the castaway husband of whom she was dreaming by analogy with the narrative methods of Dickens.

By 1913, when he left Biograph and signed for Majestic, Griffith was the number one American director, whose work was influenced by the Frontiersman attitude, the unending preoccupation with scale, and the epic sweep of the emergent capitalist society. Not surprisingly, it was also blighted by the crude racialism, the maudlin familiocentric sentimentality, and the obsession with fresh-faced girlish virginity also characteristic of such a society, so that it is singularly appropriate that this most American of directors' most successful work should be entitled *The Birth of a Nation* (1915).

This film relates episodes from the American Civil War from a partisan Southern point of view. It caused protests from the National Association for the Advancement of Coloured People, and fights at many screenings – justifiably so when the Negro is portrayed as a grimacing monster to flee from whose loathsome embraces Mae Marsh is obliged to commit suicide, and when the last-reel charge to the rescue is carried out by the Ku-Klux-Klan. . . . Not that this worried the film's backers, whose $100 000 investment brought them $20 000 000. In nine months the film was shown 6266 times in New York alone, to audiences stirred doubtless by its flamboyant chauvinism and its fervent advocacy of nubile virtue, but also by its powerful sense of the interrelationship between the individual and history, achieved by the most grandiose techniques of juxtaposition that the cinema had yet seen. The cross-cutting between different scenes and levels of action had a profound effect on spectators who could feel themselves to be part of the history of this great country of theirs.

After the boom, the slump. Most of Griffith's share of the *Birth of a Nation* profits went into *Intolerance* (1916), made with the backing of the Triangle Company (co-directors Griffith, Mack Sennett, and Thomas Ince). This started as a melodrama (*The Mother and the Law*), and expanded into a simultaneous relating of the Passion of Christ, the destruction of Babylon by the Persians, the Massacre of the Huguenots, and a modern tale of unjust condemnation to death (the only one to have a happy ending). These were linked by a recurring shot of a woman rocking a cradle. The statistics are part of film legend: 200 000 feet of film (eventually cut to under 12 000), 60 000 actors, costs of $2 000 000 – and no shooting script. . . . *Film Daily* opined after the opening that *Intolerance* 'was without question the most stirring experience that has ever been presented in the world', a statement certainly correct from a financial point of view. Realism in its most literal sense has never been carried so far. When Griffith wanted to show a vast army storming a walled city, he built a real walled city and hired 16 000 extras to storm it. The film did good business for five months and then lost money, leaving Griffith a backlog of debt he was never to discharge. This seems puzzling; the ponderous sententiousness of the titles, the carefully-engineered happy ending in the modern episode contrasted with the barbarism of the others, and the Mom-and-kiddie sentimentality must surely have appealed to a public already predisposed in Griffith's favour by *The Birth of a Nation*. But the failure becomes more comprehensible when we consider the speed of cutting between one episode and the next, which baffled audiences in 1918, and the hostile reception of the film outside the United States (during the First World War it was banned virtually everywhere in Europe, and the Huguenot section was never authorised for public screening in France). It is hard nowadays to avoid the feeling that *Intolerance* marks the end of a line rather than the new departure it was so enthusiastically hailed as. Its literal-mindedness and emotional naïvety have dated, and in a way emphasise rather than off-set its narrative scale (the Soviet directors were able to learn the lessons of the latter while avoiding the former), and the 'spare-no-expense' approach was never fully credible in Hollywood again, as directors like Stroheim and Welles were to discover.

Griffith turned out an amazing number of films after *Intolerance*, including the war propaganda essay *Hearts of the World* (1918), and the visually beautiful tear-jerker *Broken Blossoms* (1919), in which Lillian Gish delivers to her Oriental protector the immortal line: 'Why are you so good to me, Chinky?' 1921 marked his last commercial success, *Orphans of the Storm*; ten years later, he had made his last film. To see him as a martyr to the system he had helped to bring to birth is partially, but misleadingly, true. Even without the financial burden of *Intolerance*, it is unlikely that he would have been able to maintain his earlier success through a string of melodramas that even undiscriminating audiences must eventually have begun to find emotionally monotonous (even W. C. Fields, in his one Griffith film *Sally of the Sawdust* (1925), has moments that verge on the maudlin). The reputation he acquired for autocratic inflexibility, coupled with a penchant for emotional involvement with his leading actresses and bouts of heavy drinking, cannot have helped. He outlived his success, an embarrassment to the industry that gave him a special citation in the Academy Award presentations for 1936 and a retrospective at the New York Museum of Modern Art in 1940, yet for his last seventeen years could find him no employment.

Thomas H. Ince, a partner of Griffith's in the Triangle Consortium, is a name rarely heard today, yet his organisational techniques were far more prophetic of later producers and directors than Griffith's. His legendary 'personal supervision' of his films in practice amounted to delegating the everyday business of direction to a variety of subordinates (including William S. Hart, whom he later made famous as the first major Western star), whose labours he then edited ruthlessly. Beside Griffith's all-embracing romantic conceptions, this sounds prosaic to a degree; yet, when he died in 1924 aged only forty-two, Ince was far more prosperous than Griffith, and several of his 'apprentices', such as Frank Borzage, went on to become successful directors in their own right. In the same year as the racist incitement of *Birth of a Nation*, Ince gave leading roles in two films to the Japanese actor Sessue Hayakawa and his wife Tsuru Aoki, a pioneering venture. While his *magnum opus Civilisation* (1916), a mythical parable of pacifist inspiration, lacks the acuteness and breadth of Griffith's epic, he spotted and exploited the potential of the Western with a far shrewder eye to the market than Griffith ever showed.

The third member of Triangle, Mack Sennett, also adopted techniques of stringent editing and delegation to teams of sub-directors that enabled him to remain financially successful throughout the silent era. His place in film history is a special one, as the presiding genius of the silent comedy and the man who elevated the custard-pie to mythical status. In reality, custard-pies were only one of the humorous devices that made up the stock-in-trade of Sennett's comic empire; vats of dough, unlikely animals, kicks up the backside, and car-chases were equally common, linked together by fluent camera-work and nightmarishly rapid editing. There is a cruelty to much of this humour that clearly accounts for its continued appeal to children, and that evokes the brash, brusque, pitiless society in which it was produced. The settings are realistic enough – the streets and slums of Los Angeles; the action is reversed, stopped, double-exposed, and – above all – speeded up to suggest both the manic exhilaration of a child playing with a new toy and the brutal, bewildering carousel that the cities of the time must have appeared to new settlers in them. Many of these were Europeans with little or no English for whom films – particularly such as the Sennett comedies for which understanding of the sub-titles was optional – were one of the few available sources of entertainment. So well suited were these films to their time that Sennett's Keystone organisation was turning out four half-reelers a week only a year after its foundation, and could barely keep up with the demand thereafter.

The first superstar

The earliest Sennett comedies had none of the mannered grace of Max Linder; their principal prankster was the gross Roscoe ('Fatty') Arbuckle, whose subsequent spectacular disgrace largely overshadowed his earlier prominence. In 1913, a young stage comedian from Kennington in London accepted a contract with Keystone; Charlie Chaplin had embarked upon one of the longest careers in cinema history. He remained with Keystone for only just over a year, making thirty-five short films, the last fifteen of which he wrote and directed himself; the tramp character that was to become his trademark appeared as early as *Mabel's Strange Predicament*, his second film. Even in such a brief stay he had a considerable influence on the Keystone comedies, introducing subtle sight-gags and nuances of facial expression.

In November 1914, Chaplin signed a contract with the Essanay company for $1250 per week as against the $250 he had been earning with Sennett. What a 'superstar' is has never been precisely defined, but if the rapid creation of a lucrative mythical persona is accepted as a criterion then Chaplin was one for over sixty years. Two years after his début Chaplin statuettes and mementoes were on the market – by 1917 he was the first screen millionaire. His fourteen Essanay films (1914/15) mark the emergence of the lovesick little man who finds fulfilment in dreams (as in *The Bank*, about an abortive romance with a cashier), or consolation in stoicism (as in *The Tramp*, where at the end Charlie the lover shrugs his shoulders and walks off with determined jauntiness). Chaplin was to continue moving from one remunerative contract to another for some years, displaying a business acumen at odds with the bemused and outflanked persona of his films, but not at all with the manipulative skill that lay behind it. David Thomson's assertion that 'the history of bisexuality in the movies begins with Chaplin' is borne out by the tremulous, winsome expression so characteristic of Charlie in love.

But the coy and artful creation of complicity that nowadays makes Chaplin's films appear mannered and strained beside those of Buster Keaton should not blind us to the harshness of the décor and the pointedness of the social comment that we find first in the films he made for Mutual in 1917. *Easy Street* has him as a down-and-out who joins the police in a squalid city area, encountering thugs and even a drug-addict; in *The Immigrant*, he is one of a group of passengers whose cramped and sordid treatment rises to a climax as their boat sails past the Statue of Liberty. . . . If Chaplin incarnated the 'Age of the Common Man', this was because he recognised the conditions in which many 'common men' were forced to live, as well as because of his skill at playing upon audience response.

The rapidity of Chaplin's contract changes gives some idea of the speed with which consortiums were formed to exploit the expanding industry. One of the most significant was Lasky's Feature Players, formed in 1913, with Jesse Lasky and Samuel Goldfish (later to be known as Goldwyn). In 1916, they merged with Adolph Zukor's Famous Players, which, with Cecil B. de Mille as director-in-chief, went in for longer, 'quality' productions using leading stage actors. Short-lived though the alliance was, it reflected clearly the financial and social expansion that took place as the nickelodeon evolved into the movie-palace, as well as the early drive towards a theatre-influenced cultural respectability that we have seen in the French cinema too.

Lewis Jacobs characterises the dominant attitude in the immediately pre-First World War American cinema as the 'Pollyanna philosophy'[2], whose fundamental ingredients were homely loving-kindness and a cheerful, freckled acceptance of poverty. The expansion of the cinema to cater for a more middle-class market combined with the outbreak of the First World War to jolt the industry out of this sugary complacency. Sexuality was no longer, as with Griffith, a matter of virginal potential fending off brutish appetite, and its various social implications began to emerge in references to divorce, birth-control, and the 'woman of the world', exemplified by the first American screen-vamp, Theda Bara. Probably the first American film in which women were depicted as having strong social and political views was Herbert Brenon's *War Brides* (1916), made just before America entered the First World War, in which the heroine leads a strike to stop the fighting and eventually commits suicide as a pacifist protest.

American involvement in the First World War unleashed a barrage of propagandistic, and often unashamedly jingoistic, films. Many were directed by Vitagraph's J. Stuart Blackton, who had begun making films with such titles as *Safe for Democracy* and *The Glory of the Nation* even while the United States was neutral. *War Brides* was banned, and Hollywood flung itself into the First World War effort. Cinemas were used for rallies, Mary Pickford and Douglas Fairbanks embarked on cross-country fund-raising tours, and even Fatty Arbuckle was filmed frantically striving to lose weight in order to conserve food supplies. Anti-German films with titles like *The Prussian Cur* were pumped forth for troops on service. The immense political and ideological potential of the cinema was realised as swiftly in the United States as in the Soviet Union, albeit with rather less subtlety. H. J. Heinz, of baked-bean fame, had built his own cinema in the grounds of his Pittsburgh factory for his employees (rather as Italian motor-manufacturers were later to sponsor football teams as a 'bread-and-circuses' distraction for potentially truculent employees), and his example was copied in Army cantonments.

By 1918, the United States cinema was a financially (if not always aesthetically) sophisticated industry. It moulded and adapted itself to changing public taste, tackling a variety of themes and areas that mirrored the rise in American self-confidence – for the ten years ahead at least.

2 The European Cinema: From 1918 to 1927

The decade immediately following the First World War was perhaps the single most productive one in the cinema's history (possible exception made for the fifties). It signalled the emergence of important new industries in the Soviet Union and Germany, both producing crucial theoretical work to complement the films made within them. It also marked a further and deeper interplay between the movies and other art-forms, and brought the silent film to a peak that caused many of its leading practitioners and theoreticians to abhor the coming of sound.

Much of this productive activity, paradoxically, was thanks to the First World War. This provided irrefutable evidence of the medium's value as propaganda. By forcing individual industries back on their own resources, it contributed to the emergence of cinematic trends, often intimately connected with the industry in one particular country but fertilised by intellectual and aesthetic developments in other fields. The immediately post-war period was known in Germany as the *Aufbruch*, or 'upsurge', because of the intellectual and artistic ferment that characterised it. This phenomenon, marked in other countries as well, combined with the increasingly obvious economic and political potential of the medium to make this period one of great financial expansion and intellectual innovation.

The new Soviet cinema

Nowhere was this truer than in the post-revolutionary Soviet Union. Until 1917, the Russian industry had produced a predictable diet of costume-drama and farce, but important innovations had taken place in other fields that were to influence the Soviet cinema. The Futurist movement, initiated by the Italian Marinetti, aroused a great deal of interest in Russia with its enthusiasm for technological advance and ferocious rejection of symmetry and grace in art. The Soviet futurists shared Marinetti's interest in the cinema as an art-form admirably suited to the new industrial age, and became influential when they threw in their lot with the Bolsheviks shortly after the October Revolution. At the same time, the theatre director Meyerhold was striving towards a stylised theatre, characterised by an aggressive anti-naturalism and by the system he called 'bio-mechanics'. This was based on then widespread ideas of the body as a precisely-engineered machine, which to produce effective acting required only intense physical and psychological training – a view that had much in common with the Futurists. Where Marinetti saw in machines the art of the future, Meyerhold looked for the underlying principles of art in the machine.

The ground had thus been prepared for the innovatory development of Soviet cinema well before the Bolshevik Revolution. Crucially important were the experiments conducted by the film-director and teacher Lev Kuleshov in the assembly of narrative and communication of emotion, an area relatively little explored by directors hitherto with the key exception of Griffith. How elements were combined became as important as what the elements were.

The most significant of Kuleshov's experiments was one in which the same shot of an actor's face was juxtaposed in turn with other shots and then shown to an audience. The results were striking; when the face was shown in conjunction with a bowl of soup, the audience concluded that it expressed hunger, with a coffin, that it expressed bereavement – yet it was the same face each time. Clearly, the creative possibilities of editing were greater than had hitherto been suspected.

External factors also contributed to the development of editing. Faced with nationalisation, film-companies either destroyed stock and equipment or smuggled it out of the country, and the economic situation made it impossible to produce replacements. Old scraps of pre-Revolutionary film were therefore used, carefully spliced together to tell a story or draw a conclusion quite different from the original. Arrangement again became as important as what was arranged.

Montage, dialectic, and Marxist aesthetics

The manipulative possibilities of editing and juxtaposition had evident points in common with Marinetti's bio-mechanics and Meyerhold's theatrical stylisation. Consequently, when the young engineer Sergei Eisenstein joined the Proletkult Theatre in 1920, and a year later became a pupil of Meyerhold's at the newly-founded State School for Stage Direction, the intellectual and political climate was right for the concept of montage to be further developed. In 1919, against all odds, a print of *Intolerance* had somehow reached Moscow, sparking off an interest comprehensible when we remember that it was the first full-length film seen in the Soviet Union in which the possibilities of creative editing had been exploited. Eisenstein's practical interest in the cinema began in 1923, when he made a short film for inclusion in his first stage production, and it was in the same year that he first formulated the concept of the montage of attractions. The 'attractions' in question were those which in Eisenstein's words could be 'verified and mathematically calculated to produce certain shocks'[1], to be combined by skilful editing into a whole greater than the sum of its parts.

The principle of montage had close affinities with Karl Marx's theory of dialectical materialism, on which the Bolshevik régime – in its early years at least – was based. Marx believed that the struggle between social classes for the control of the means of production was the dominant motor of history, and that this struggle followed the pattern known as the dialectic. According to this, one phenomenon or thesis entailed its converse or antithesis, and their fusion or synthesis became in its turn the starting-point or thesis in another dialectical process. Marx saw this matrix as the course of history, seen not as a random amalgam of personalities and events, but as the working-out, via a series of struggles and inherent contradictions, of a process that would eventually abolish the distinction between social classes. There are obvious similarities between this theory and Eisenstein's ideas on montage – the belief that emotional and political response (the behaviour of an audience as of a society) was governed by ascertainable laws, the stress on collision and contradiction where earlier theorists had tended to emphasise continuity, and connected with this the notion that the collision of two images or two classes would lead to more than a simple sum of their parts, to a qualitatively different result.

Eisenstein's first feature film, *Strike* (1924), was made under the auspices of Proletkult as one of a projected series of eight films called *Towards the Dictatorship*. The film tells the story of an eventually unsuccessful strike, ruthlessly put down by the employers, in a qualitatively new way. The traditional conception of individual character was replaced by that of type; the bosses are cigar-smoking, card-playing caricatures, and the agents provocateurs they employ to break the strike are shown leaping out of barrels set in the earth. What individuals happen to be like, Eisenstein suggests, is less important than the social forces they represent. The film makes impressive use of metaphorical montage, notably in one sequence that alternates between oxen being killed in a slaughter-house and strikers being butchered – a pointed piece of de-humanisation that still has immense force. It comes as no surprise that Eisenstein spoke in connection with this film of the 'montage of shocks', or that he was later to proclaim a belief in 'ciné-fist', the aggressive force of the camera.

Much of the film is very funny; each police spy as he appears turns into a different animal (successively monkey, bulldog, fox, and owl). The humour, whose propaganda value is obvious, also helps to prevent us from simply absorbing the film as a quasi-documentary record of 'real' events. The question posed, through the narrative method as much as through the subject-matter, is not 'What were the parties to this particular strike like?' but 'How does a strike work?'

Eisenstein followed *Strike* in 1925 with *The Battleship Potemkin*, the film that was to make his name internationally. This was also begun as part of an ambitious sequence, this time planned to celebrate the twentieth anniversary of the 1905 uprising. Eisenstein decided to concentrate on one event from the original scenario, the mutiny on board the battleship in the port of Odessa. Sailors who refuse to eat rotten meat (shown in close-up teeming with maggots) are sentenced to be shot. The resulting mutiny attracts the townspeople of Odessa onto the steps overlooking the sea, where they shout encouragement to the mutineers until the Tsarist militia descend the steps, shooting and killing. The film ends as the mutiny spreads to other ships, a precursor of the coming revolution.

Potemkin's continuing power to excite audiences cannot be accounted for simply by its explicit political content. Its visual conciseness is masterly, as in the sequence where the mutineers mourn their shot leader, Vakulinchuk; the fog that shrouds the harbour and cloaks the scene in mourning is also the haze before the daybreak of revolution. The sequence showing three stone lions in different positions, shot to resemble one beast rising up and roaring in fury at the massacre, is one of Eisenstein's most pregnant uses of montage, incorporating the animal and mineral worlds into the coming uprising.

The climax of the film is the massacre on the Odessa steps. The camera sweeps up the cheering crowd; a title ('Suddenly. . . .') heralds the inexorable downward movement of the soldiers' feet, which is then contrasted with the upward movement of a mother carrying her dead son. The contrast between up and down governs the whole of the sequence, which is remarkable for the cogency of the overall structure as well as for the telling eye that Eisenstein and his cameraman Tisse displayed for visual detail. A pram (whose occupant remains invisible) dangles perilously over the edge of one of the steps, punctuating the rush of movement, and then rushes downwards, restarting the movement at what seems twice the speed. A bespectacled woman seen near the beginning of the sequence reappears with her spectacles broken and her face covered in blood; we never see the actual wounding. It is easy for a modern viewer to take for granted the narrative economy and condensation of this passage, and its assumption that what we are not shown may be as important as what we are. Editing and narrative here become one.

Eisenstein made *October* (1927) as part of the tenth anniversary celebrations for the Bolshevik Revolution. It relates the two uprisings of 1917, ridiculing the Menshevik leader Kerensky who is likened to a strutting peacock. It also emphasises the world-wide importance of October by the use of a clock Eisenstein had found in the Winter Palace in Leningrad, whose dials showed the time in various capitals throughout the world. The dials are seen rotating faster and faster until they apparently merge in what Eisenstein called 'the sensation of one single historic hour' [2].

For *October*, Eisenstein carried further than ever before his use of typage, rigorous type-casting which involved his assistants in hunting through offices, bars, and doss-houses for suitable faces. Physiognomy was all, acting ability and training of zero or secondary importance, in accordance with Eisenstein's stress on the type as against the individual. This reached its apogee with the use of Alexandrov to play the part of Lenin, simply because his facial features were exactly the same. Yon Barna in his biography of Eisenstein tell us:

'. . . nothing in the world could hide the poor man's inner emptiness and primitive intellect. Despite this, he was drilled into walking and behaving like Lenin, down to his last characteristic gesture.' [3]

This was a triumphant vindication of Eisenstein's belief in the malleability of actors and audiences, and also an instance of his unwillingness to trust or cooperate productively with either which was to impede the later development of his contribution to cinema.

Eisenstein's great rival, Vsevolod Pudovkin, came to the cinema from a scientific career and was also instrumental in developing the theory of montage. Where Eisenstein saw it as a process of collision and shock, Pudovkin saw it as one of linkage; Jay Leyda describes his first film, *Mother* (1926), as 'not shot, but built'[4]. *Mother*, based on a play by Maxim Gorki, tells the story of a peasant woman who becomes imbued with revolutionary fervour thanks to her son's example. Its most famous use of montage juxtaposes the son in prison, the workers' uprising, and an ice-floe breaking up on the river – not unlike Eisenstein's *Potemkin* lions in its politicised version of the Romantic 'pathetic fallacy', whereby the natural and inanimate worlds were supposed to show sympathy with human – here social – emotions.

Mother was followed by *The End of St Petersburg* (1927), which was like *October*, made for the anniversary celebrations. Then came *Storm over Asia* (1928) which was about a Mongol fur-trapper condemned to death during the Revolutionary War, reprieved when the British invaders discover him to be a descendant of Genghis Khan and try to use him as a puppet ruler, and finally triumphant as a rebel-leader. Despite moments of great visual excitement, these films in their more linear and less dialectical use of montage now strike many audiences as blander and less stimulating than Eisenstein's.

Eisenstein and Pudovkin shared a preoccupation with the art (or science) of staging a film. The neurology student Boris Kaufman, self-styled Dziga Vertov ('Spinning top'), was initially more concerned with documentary observation, and with the camera as roving eye and/or probing revolutionary rifle-barrel. His career began with the foundation of the Kino-Eye group in 1918 which launched a vast newsreel programme with a new edition almost every week. Right through to 1924, Vertov remained active in the production of newsreels. His conception of montage was at once more radical and more free-wheeling than either Eisenstein's or Pudovkin's.

His best-known film, *The Man with a Movie Camera* (1929), juxtaposes apparently unconnected incidents and people to build up a picture of city life. The film's delight in camera virtuosity (accelerated motion, frozen shots, split-screen) blends with a delight in the way people are, at work or at rest, and at the same time undercuts any facile assumptions that what we see 'just happened' to be going on in front of a neutral and unselecting camera. This is done, partly through shifts and doublings-back that deny the viewer any 'safe' place from which to contemplate the film (one literally often does not know where one is), and partly through regular punctuating shots of a film editor at work in the cutting-room. Here we are reminded, both that under socialism the film-maker is a worker like any other (a healthy piece of self-demystification), and also that, what we have just seen and periodically been tempted to accept as 'real' has in fact been produced by his efforts. The reminder that 'film is film' – unlike its tedious and woolly echoes in the work of later directors – stimulates a reflection on the social role of the artist and the nature of 'realism' in art. This probably has more to do with later cinematic developments than do the theories of Eisenstein, even though its intellectual baggage is less outwardly imposing.

The Teutonic frisson: Germany

The other national industry to expand dramatically after the First World War was that of Germany, which up to 1917 had been rudimentary. Here the closing of the frontiers and the wartime demand for escapism helped the development of light comedies, directed notably by Ernst Lubitsch. *Carmen* (1918) and *Madame Dubarry* (1919), starring Pola Negri, enjoyed considerable success at home and in the USA, thanks to their fluid, free-ranging camera-work and the performance of Emil Jannings – the foremost German silent actor – as Louis XV in *Madame Dubarry*. This film details the rise and fall of the celebrated courtesan with apparent dedication to an individualistic and atomised view of history. If she opts for a rich rather than a poor lover, it is because of the number of buttons on her dress; if she is guillotined during the Revolution it is because of the vengefulness of her cheated lover rather than because by her actions she has betrayed her class – conceptions a whole world away from the Russians or even Griffith. . . . At all events, the film was immensely successful, and paved the way for the profitable career Lubitsch was to enjoy in Hollywood after he left Germany in 1923.

A key event in German cinematic history was the setting-up in 1917 of the UFA Combine (UFA = Universum Film Aktiengesellschaft, Universal Film Company Ltd). A third of its shares were publicly owned, and it was intended to act as a government-directed propaganda agency for Germany. After the First World War, UFA expanded rapidly (on the distribution rather than the production side), and was certainly Europe's most successful film-exporting company. Its financial *contretemps* (most acute after 1926, when German currency was stabilised) survived thanks to humiliating agreements with American financiers, and then to an effective take-over by right-wing backers.

UFA gave the German industry an opportunity unique in Europe to produce films with guaranteed international distribution. Many of the films made during the 1920s were influenced by the Expressionist tendency in art and the theatre, which turned its back on naturalism and sought in heavily stylised geometrical sets and intense, hallucinatory contrasts of light and shade parallels for the torments and convolutions of the human psyche. There is a great deal of obscurantist nonsense talked about the dark mysteries of the Teutonic soul breaking through the cinema of this period. However, as Siegfried Kracauer points out in *From Caligari to Hitler*, much of the cinema's morbidity and grotesquerie was anchored in the unstable political and financial situation of the time, and in the middle-class tendency to nihilistic withdrawal from political life after the abortive Communist revolution of 1918. Nowhere in the German cinema of this period do we find anything resembling the sensitivity of a Griffith or a Pudovkin to the interrelationship of the individual and history.

Paul Wegener, an actor who had worked for the leading Expressionist stage director Max Reinhardt, acted in and co-scripted the first major German film, Stellan Rye's *The Student of Prague* (1913), and followed it with *The Golem* (1914, remade 1920), which he codirected. The latter was a film entirely studio-made amid fantastic settings, and told of the protection of Prague from an anti-Jewish pogrom by the bringing to life of a clay statue (the Golem of the title). The fascination with the mystical animation of dead matter, and its converse, the taking away of life, were obsessively frequent concerns; no better example could be found than Robert Wiene's *The Cabinet of Dr Caligari* (1919).

We first see Caligari as a fairground showman animating a somnambulist, Cesare, who slinks forth at night to murder, and is eventually denounced. Caligari turns out to be the mad director of a lunatic asylum, in which he is eventually confined. Or rather, this is the *denouement* in the original script; the film as shot incorporates a framing-sequence which changes its emphasis entirely, revealing Caligari to be sanely doing his job and the man through whose eyes we have seen the story to be an inmate of his asylum. . . . David Thomson regards this as the most effective part of the film, making it 'one of the first films to exploit the resemblance between watching a film and dreaming'[5], and hence questioning the realist status of the celluloid image. But its sociopolitical implications are deeply disturbing. The all-trustworthy, all-powerful authority undermined in the original script is now rehabilitated, and Teutonic subservience to those in charge triumphantly vindicated. Kracauer views Caligari as a precursor of Hitler in his hypnotic persuasiveness and horrific misuse of power, and if we take this view it becomes extremely difficult to see the ending as other than a pernicious apologia for authoritarianism.

The sets for *Caligari* feature vast gables and rooftops of Baroque complexity; none have been so angular. Today, the film seems often laboured, in some ways as much a grotesque museum-piece as its mad (? sane) protagonist. Its principal claim to fame is that it popularised the term Expressionism throughout Europe and the United States.

Morbidity is inseparable from the German silent cinema, though not always so ponderously stylised as in *Caligari*. Fritz Lang's *Der Müde Tod* (= 'Tired Death', but usually known in English as *Destiny*), made in 1921, shows the figure of Death disillusioning the young girl who tries to bargain with him for the life of her lover by telling her three stories. It is really one parable set successively in Islam, medieval Italy, and China, illustrating the inexorable power with which he is cursed. Lang's Death is a weary, mournful figure, and the nightmarish quality of the film comes largely from his own powerlessness over the forces he incarnates. A similar preoccupation with demonic forces outstripping individual control is manifest in Lang's *Die Nibelungen* (1924), which retells the Siegfried legend in grandiose Wagnerian set-pieces, and *Dr Mabuse the Gambler* (1922), introducing the master-criminal Mabuse, preying on the despair and insecurity of the inflationary era.

Lang's most influential film, *Metropolis* (1926), greatly impressed Goebbels, who was no doubt more attracted by the futuristic city of the title, and the ant-like regimentation of the workers in their nightmarish subterranean conditions, than by the workers' revolt and the final reconciliation of Capital and Labour in a welter of brotherly love. The film nowadays seems worrying through its very visual power, as manipulative and regimented as the society it portrays, and its utter failure to demonstrate any insight into the mainsprings of industrial society.

Contemporary with the Expressionist cinema of which Lang was the greatest practitioner, films were being made that conformed more closely to naturalist criteria. The Austrian scriptwriter Carl Mayer conceived the idea of the *Kammerfilm* or 'chamber film', a term readopted some forty years later by Ingmar Bergman, and was the scenarist for *Der Letzte Mann* (1924) ('The Last (or Lowest) Man'), one of the films by which its director Friedrich Wilhelm Murnau is best remembered.

Murnau's first major feature, however, was *Nosferatu* (1922), an adaptation of the Dracula story, largely shot on location in Bremen. Those who look everywhere for reflections of the Germanic soul find fertile terrain in this film, with its preoccupation with bloodsucking and diabolic possession, and its stress on the all-conquering power of love (the vampire is defeated through the heroine's willingness to sacrifice herself for her lover). But its importance really lies in the suppleness and fluidity of its camera-movements (the antithesis of Eisensteinian montage), and the supernatural intensity with which natural settings are invested. The vampire's coach voyages through a landscape that is clearly a normal piece of European countryside, which makes the skeletal riders and other ghost-train paraphernalia that swoop past far more frightening than the most elaborately-designed Expressionist set could have done. Nosferatu (copyright problems prevented the use of the name Dracula) arrives in Bremen on board a galleon whose material solidity emphasises the sepulcharal ghastliness with which he moves.

The Last Laugh concentrates on just one character, making it even more of a 'chamber film' than *Nosferatu*. This is the arrogant head-porter of a luxury hotel (Emil Jannings in his second-greatest performance), whose age and weakness lead to his demotion to lavatory attendant. Such a tale would have yielded either broad farce or soft-hearted situation comedy from a British director, but in post-Prussian Germany with its obsessive status-consciousness provides material for the blackest tragedy. The story is told entirely without the use of titles; the camera moves with such precision, and Jannings ladles on the sentiment so powerfully, that further precision becomes unnecessary. The happy ending that box-office considerations forced Murnau to tack on functions as a merciless parody of the very idea of the happy ending. The celebration of Jannings's unexpected inheritance takes place *à deux*, Jannings with the one friend who has remained loyal to him throughout – a jibe at obsession with the position rather than the man that leaves a sour taste in the mouths of an aware audience.

The use of fluctuating contrasts of light and shade, marked in Murnau's work, was common in the German cinema of this time, for example in E. A. Dupont's *Variety* (1925), which made a star of Emil Jannings's back resolutely hunched against the camera for most of the film. The plot is a melodrama of sexual jealousies among circus acrobats, enlivened by heavily theatrical presentation and audacious camerawork in the circus scenes.

Melodrama was an inescapable ingredient of the inter-war German cinema, whether sexual, supernatural, or social, as in the so-called *Strassenfilme* ('street-films'). These, of which the prototype was Grune's *Die Strasse* (*The Street*, of 1923), saw the street as the scene of exotic, and potentially dangerous, adventure. Grune's umbrella-toting bourgeois leaves home in search of adventure, is framed for the murder of a prostitute, and is grateful to return to the safe refuge of his domestic hearth and reviving tureen of soup. As in *Caligari* and *Variety*, order triumphs, and the message is clear that excitement, like insanity and crime, does not pay.

Better remembered today is *Joyless Street* (1925), by George W. Pabst, if only because it gave Greta Garbo her first starring role after her début for Mauritz Stiller the previous year. This was one of the first European films to convey the grim desolation of the Depression. Pabst's most important work was to come after sound, but already here many of its most characteristic qualities were manifest – a fascination with the atmosphere of urban poverty, a not always justified faith in his own powers of psychological insight, and – like Griffith before him and many more after – a capacity for seeing his leading actresses as obsessive, inspirational *anima* figures.

The 'street-film' produced documentaries as well as features; the best-known of these is *Berlin: Symphony of a Great City* (1927), edited by Walter Ruttmann from 'candid-camera' footage shot on the streets of Berlin. The editing style, radically different from Dziga Vertov's, stresses patterns of movement, and at the same time suggests a vacuous, scruffy urban reality typified by the garbage that litters the streets. Formalist visual precision coexists with a world of amorphous chaos – an amalgam of aestheticism and nihilism which makes Ruttmann's evolution into a Nazi propagandist hardly surprising. However closely their makers may have thought they were transcribing the social reality of their day, German films of this period rarely do so without falling into one of the two traps exemplified in Ruttmann's work. The street is either a place from which to cull striking images or a sinister whirlpool from which one is lucky to escape with honour and wallet intact.

The German cinema after 1918, one of the most exciting periods in the development of the art, all too often displays in its handling of contemporary themes an atomisation that reflects the political confusion and nihilism which culminated in the Nazi régime.

French intellectual influences

The Russian and German industries had expanded from their modest pre-war scale to become among the most important in the world. What of those that were well-established before 1918? The intellectual interest we have already noted in France expanded with the formation of the first ciné-clubs, under the aegis of the critic Louis Delluc. Delluc made films himself, but his greatest importance lies in the discussions he led and stimulated, stressing the importance of the 'photogenic', the poetry of the image, and in the films he and his collaborator Léon Moussinac brought to Paris. Eisenstein, Wiene, Sjostrom were all premiered there thanks to the efforts of the Ciné Clubs of France, and Paris has been unchallenged as the world capital of cinema art ever since.

Part at least of the reason for this lies in the central position that intellectuals have always occupied in French public life, manifested in polemical groupings and the overt taking-up of positions. So it is not surprising that the French film-makers of the 1920s were the most assertively cinematic in Europe, given to flamboyant innovation, and at the same time strongly influenced by developments in the other arts. The Dadaists, and their successors the Surrealists, advocated in poetry and painting the overthrowing of realist conventions and the evocation of dreamlike, irrational states. Their influence, and that of the Symbolists, is plain in such films as Germaine Dulac's *La Souriante Madame Beudet* (*Smiling Madame Beudet*, of 1923), about a woman trapped in soporific bourgeois surroundings that render her latently homicidal, or Marcel L'Herbier's *L'Inhumaine* (1924), whose implausible plot features a fake suicide, a poisoned coma, and a final emergence into consciousness – a metaphor of the Symbolist view of poetic creation as a delving into uncharted spiritual areas. The French avant-garde cinema of this period rarely 'tells a story' as we have seen the Russians and Germans doing; even Jean Epstein, attracted to such surroundings as the wild seascapes of Brittany and committed to the documentary, is far more concerned with the dreamlike power of such images as a man reaching out for the face of his beloved superimposed on the sea (in *Coeur Fidèle/Faithful Heart* of 1923), than with the conventional development of narrative.

Dream in the above films is tragic or melodramatic; in more overtly surreal cinema it inclines towards the violently farcical. René Clair's *Entr'acte* (1924) substitutes for any pretence of coherent narrative a string of expectations aroused and systematically disrupted. The 'interval' of the title punctuates a ballet called *Relâche* (*No Performance Today*), in which the voluminously-bloomered ballerina, up whose skirt the camera perpetually glances, turns out to be a no less voluminously-bearded male, and the coffin involved in the farcical funeral procession disgorges a young man in perfect health. . . . For all the film's frenetic zaniness, it offers little real challenge to or onslaught upon the spectator and his world.

Such a criticism could never be levelled at *Un Chien Andalou* (*An Andalusian Dog*, 1928) or *L'Age d'Or* (*The Golden Age*, 1930), the two films which Luis Buñuel, backed by the French aristocrat the Vicomte de Noailles, made in collaboration with Salvador Dali. Both films were the source of scandal (Fascist rioting broke up the premiere of *L'Age d'Or*), and both have retained an unfortunate aura of affectionate notoriety.

The slitting-open of the girl's eye at the beginning of *Un Chien Andalou* and the debauchees emerging from the '120 Days of Sodom' at the end of *L'Age d'Or*, led by a double of Jesus Christ, have acquired a classic status that rather obscures what Buñuel described as their 'desperate, passionate call to murder'. Buñuel conducts the slitting in *Un Chien Andalou* – a clear warning of what he proposes to do with our complacent vision. Raymond Durgnat has shown[6] that *Un Chien Andalou* can be read as a Freudian text of sexual development and uncertainty, and *L'Age d'Or*, following on from this, dramatises as it parodies the clash between sexuality and the bourgeois social order that is a recurrent theme in the work of the Surrealist poets. The lovers entwine passionately in a bath of mud and bring a starchy orchestral concert to a halt with their passion. Forty-six years of cinema have produced nothing more powerful.

The French silent films described up to now make little *overt* reference to social and historical developments. The one major director of this period who deals with them explicitly is Abel Gance. *J'Accuse!* (*I Accuse!*) of 1918 demystifies the chauvinistic fervour of the War, with a somewhat embarrassing compensatory exaltation of the poet-hero Jean, whose descent into blindness and insanity has much in common with Romantic conceptions of the accursed artist. The combination of rapid, rhythmical cross-cutting, contrasts of light and shade, and a Romanticism that contrives to be simultaneously pompous and simplistic is characteristic of Gance's whole *oeuvre*.

Napoléon (1926) has earned a place in cinema history as the first film to split the screen in three, a device rather obviously used to illustrate Napoleon's sway over his armies by placing him in the middle of the triptych flanked by two advancing columns. More striking, and more prophetic, are the childhood scenes – the snowball fight and the skirmishes in the dormitory – which endorse another Romantic commonplace, that the man of genius is marked out from infancy as a man alone. Sequences such as the cross-cutting between the revolutionary Convention and a storm-tossed sea bear a superficial resemblance to Griffith or Eisenstein; the superficiality lies in the fact that Gance's view of history is an uncritically epic one, in which powerful 'natural' forces (Napoleon or the Revolution) surge up *ex nihilo* for our admiration and visual delight. Griffith, even at his clumsiest, has a far surer grasp of how historical events are produced, which is why his films still excite where Gance's merely dazzle and invite admiration.

It would be false to suppose that the French industry was nothing but a hive of avant-garde experimentation; the big-studio formula of costume melodrama was as successful as elsewhere, enlivened by the presence of numerous Russian emigrés. The actor Mozhukin filmed the life of another actor, *Kean*, in 1924, incorporating scenes of roistering and dancing in taverns that were to influence Eisenstein's *Ivan the Terrible*; it was suitably ironic that a refugee from Bolshevism should have provided a stimulus to its greatest-ever artist. . . . By and large, however, the big-studio productions were uninspiring, though many of the young directors whose careers were just beginning at the advent of sound were to alter this situation in the 1930s.

Scandinavia and Britain

The Scandinavian industries early encountered what was to be an insuperable problem – the plundering of their leading performers by better-off industries. Greta Garbo and Mauritz Stiller left for Hollywood via Berlin in 1925; Victor Sjostrom had taken up his contract with Samuel Goldwyn a year earlier. Even Carl Theodore Dreyer, one of the two best-known Scandinavian directors of all, made his best-known film, *The Passion of Joan of Arc*, in France in 1928.

Joan of Arc pushes the silent close-up as far as it could go, with a performance from Renée Falconetti in her only film role whose overwrought intensity is still unparalleled. Montage is the stock-in-trade of Dreyer's film syntax just as much as it is of Eisenstein's, but it is of a very different kind, composed almost exclusively of close-ups that separate the action into its component parts. The image invariably, and often sadistically, centres on Falconetti's face even when it does not actually occupy the screen. The complex social interaction of Eisensteinian montage here gives place to an attempt to produce a film language of emotion, perhaps the first example of what Ingmar Bergman was to describe with reference to some of his own films as 'chamber cinema', or of Jean-Luc Godard's attempt to film 'what goes on between people, in space'[7].

What of the industry in Britain, where only one film in every twenty shown was 'home-made'? Spectaculars, literary adaptations, and wartime reconstructions, it goes without saying; so too, given the pragmatic distrust of theory that has long bedevilled British intellectual and artistic life, does the absence of any body of theoretical work or experimentation comparable to what we have seen in the other major countries. Cecil Hepworth had made the earliest successful British film in 1905, *Rescued by Rover*, and the Hepworth company continued until its demise in 1923 to turn out simple, but by all accounts not unentertaining, tales of the English countryside. Far more significant, though, were the débuts of Anthony Asquith, son of the former Prime Minister, and Alfred Hitchcock, chilling spines with *The Lodger* in 1926 and exploring a boxing milieu with *The Ring* in 1927.

Britain was, as she was to remain, something of an offshore island; Sweden and Denmark suffered through importing too many films and exporting too many performers; the Italian industry stagnated in – literally – spectacular decline (*Quo Vadis?* and *The Last Days of Pompeii*, major successes of 1913, were both remade thirteen years later, an index of the industry's sluggishness). There was no question but that, at the advent of sound, France, Germany, and the Soviet Union were the dominant film-making countries on the European continent.

3 The American Silent Cinema: From 1918 to 1927

During the dizzy and artificial prosperity of the twenties 'boom' years, Hollywood became the unquestioned capital of the American industry, a glamour-factory of competing carnivorous trusts catering to an increasingly affluent audience, and attracting talent from all over the world. The political value of the medium, proved conclusively in the war, was recognised by President Harding, who secured a gentleman's agreement with the industry to present Bolsheviks in an unfavourable light; thus the novel *Comrades* turned up in a screen adaptation entitled *Bolshevism on Trial*, and few could have been in any doubt what the verdict would be. Otherwise, political and social issues were trivialised by the cinema just as surely as by the popular press which also enjoyed record expansion in this period. It would not have been in the big companies' interest to permit any explicit reference to the hysterical mushrooming of the stock-market, from which they profited as much as anybody else. Bootlegging and gangsterdom, products of the society on which Hollywood thrived, were rarely off its screens, but hardly ever did the cinema attempt to tackle the underlying causes of these titillating pursuits.

Still, this did not appear to worry the spectators. By 1926 one hundred million Americans per week were attending the cinema, film-stars were among the highest-paid members of the population, and the big trusts had a virtual monopoly of production, distribution, and exhibition. Histories of the European cinema have always tended to be written around directors; in Hollywood, the director in this period became only the intermediate (and not necessarily the most important) member of a triumvirate, flanked by the producer who put up the money and thus

controlled subject-matter and the star(s) who would usually determine
how successful the movie would be. Our survey of this crucially important decade will thus pay as much attention to the production trusts and
their influence over subject-matter and treatment as to the details of
spectacular individual careers.

Trusts, money, sexuality, and prudery

The major trusts of this period are memorable Hollywood names: First
National (swallowed up by Warners when sound came), which built
3000 theatres between 1919 and 1921, Adolph Zukor's Paramount, spear-
headed by Cecil B. de Mille, and Goldwyn which amalgamated with two
other companies in 1924 to form Metro-Goldwyn-Mayer. They needed
to be doubly adroit, in assessing the vagaries of what was still a largely
unformed public taste as well as those of the stock market; their success
is adduced by their survival.

Let it not be thought, however, that these companies were concerned
solely with profit, at the expense of social responsibility. They gave
splendid proof of the latter in setting up the Motion Picture Producers
and Distributors of America, under the presidency of the Harding minister
Will H. Hays, in 1922. This was in reaction to a string of scandals that
hit the industry in the early twenties. The most notorious of these – still
the archetypal Hollywood scandal – was the Fatty Arbuckle case. Arbuckle
co-hosted a Hollywood party in 1921, in apparent ignorance of the recent
introduction of Prohibition. After two drunken days the starlet Virginia
Rappe died, allegedly as a result of Arbuckle's thrusting ice-cubes into
her vagina in an attempt to revive her after she had fainted in his embraces. He was eventually acquitted of manslaughter, but the jury need
not have bothered. He was blacklisted from the movie industry (Hays
being a prime mover), and although he directed a few films under the
aliases of William Goodrich and Will B. Goode his career was swiftly
and ruthlessly terminated.

The Press outcry was so gleefully indignant that the industry decided
something had to be done to cosmeticise its image. The result, the
Motion Picture Producers and Distributors Association, advocated a
three-wise-monkeys' morality ('see no evil – hear no evil – speak no
evil') which became enshrined in the notorious Hays Code of 1930,
governing what could and could not be referred to in films.

The wonder is that, in spite of the dual political and puritanical
stranglehold under which it laboured, Hollywood during this period still
produced many exciting, and a few great, films. Probably the key

director was Cecil B. de Mille, a name still synonymous with the spectacular. Subject-matter appears to have been indifferent to him: British
social comedy (*Male and Female*, 1919), Biblical spectacular (*The Ten
Commandments*, 1923), and patriotic drama (*Whispering Chorus*, 1918),
were all grist to de Mille. His extravagance is often prevented from
appearing merely silly by the energy behind it and his impressive
technical skill. *The Ten Commandments*, which shows the continuing
influence of Griffith in its juxtaposition of a Biblical and a modern story,
remains an important film for an understanding of the conflicting codes
that ruled Hollywood in the twenties. The quarrel between the fiercely
pious mother and her maverick, eventually syphilitic architect son in the
contemporary part of the film parallels the kind of conflict exemplified
in the Arbuckle scandal and the industry's reaction to it.

It was under de Mille that Gloria Swanson's career as one of the first
cinematic sex-symbols was launched. In such films as *Male and Female*
and *Don't Change your Husband* (1919), she played the newly-married,
prematurely sophisticated woman in search of adventure, espousing the
kind of ideas that the English scriptwriter Elinor Glyn was to popularise
– the importance of 'it', a sexual magnetism independent of conventional
good looks, and the even greater importance of using 'it' skilfully to get
the man of your choice and dominate him. Small wonder that there was
conflict between de Mille's underlying Christianity and the erotic
imperialism Swanson deployed in the films she made for him.

Equally successful as a silent star was Mary Pickford, whose curly-
headed innocence belied her immense business shrewdness. In 1919 she
had come into United Artists with Chaplin and Griffith, and married
Douglas Fairbanks as her second husband; it was not long before such
films as *Daddy Long Legs* (1919) and *Pollyanna* (1920) earned her the
title of America's Sweetheart. She chose the directors for whom she
would star, rather than the other way round, and collaborated with
cameramen she had also chosen to preserve her adolescent appearance
well beyond its natural term.

On the male side, there is no doubt who was Sex Symbol Number One.
Rudolph Valentino's blatant inability to act, the posthumous revelation
of his homosexuality, and the sham exoticism of his most successful films
generally contrive to send present-day audiences into hysterics of a
rather different kind from those that marked his funeral in 1926, when
weeping women attended his lying-in-state and lined Broadway as his
cortège glided past. Valentino's first success was *The Four Horsemen of
the Apocalypse*, made for Rex Ingram in 1921; the outbreak of war
transforms him from dance-hall sybarite into unlikely military hero, and

this dual identity (again exemplifying the moral contradictions of Hollywood may well have accounted for the wide popularity the film enjoyed. Today he is better remembered for the 'Sheik' films – *The Sheik* made for George Melford in 1921 and *Son of the Sheik* for George Fitzmaurice in 1925 – in which violent sexuality smoulders extravagantly before its eventual domestication. 'Sex-symbol' though he may have become, Valentino's Latin aggression is a veneer; his wives and the MGM executive June Mathis had little difficulty in dominating him, and androgyny is much more in his line than the *machismo* erroneously attributed to him.

Vying with Valentino for female approval was the original swashbuckler, Douglas Fairbanks, who produced and took an active interest in the scripts of the adventure films that made his name. He was successively, between 1921 and 1925, one of *The Three Musketeers*, *Robin Hood*, *The Thief of Bagdad*, and *Don Q, Son of Zorro*, leaping gracefully around from one setting to the next, the debonair smile never out of place. The directors for whom he worked most successfully were Allen Dwan, for whom he made *Robin Hood*, and Albert Parker, who directed his best-remembered film, *The Black Pirate* of 1926. The toothy candour of his smile is further removed from modern ideas of the erotic than Valentino's epicene langour; what both have in common is a careful process of construction, the engineering of a screen persona in which scriptwriter, cameraman, set designer, and lighting crew all played their parts, and for which the resources of a big studio were an indispensable precondition.

It would be wrong to suppose that the American cinema at this time was exclusively devoted to the studio-bound cultivation of star images. One of the main reasons for the original move to Hollywood was the climate, which permitted location shooting throughout the year; and the genre which has consistently taken most advantage of this is the Western, as popular in the twenties as it has been ever since. Tom Mix and William S. Hart were its first stars, though neither survived the coming of sound. Nor did James Cruze, the son of Danish immigrants, who became the most successful silent director of the most potent native American myth with such titles as *Ruggles of Red Gap* and *The Covered Wagon* (both 1923).

The other major name in the silent Western proved to have better powers of survival. The Irish-American John Ford made a tremendous impact with *The Iron Horse* of 1924. The film tells of the building of the Union and Central Pacific Railway across America – a railway whose tracks converge endlessly towards the horizon in accordance with the

ceaselessly advancing 'frontiersman' mentality that lies at the heart of
the Western genre. But the progress is not without problems or grief.
The chief engineer's father is revealed to have been killed by Indians
while carrying out a preliminary survey, a martyr to 'savages' in the
cause of progress as white men killed by Indians in Westerns have
invariably been. . . . The film's mixture of brutality and sentimentality
(in its subsidiary love-intrigue) foreshadows the great Ford Westerns of
the sound era; the use of the railway as a metaphor for the progress
of 'civilisation' contrasts illuminatingly with its use in the Gance
film discussed earlier (p. 28), in which it figures as a menacing theatre
of emotional conflict. Few images crystallise more succinctly one of the
major differences between European and American movie cultures of
this period.

The other major arena for action pictures was, not surprisingly, the
war. The industry that was so prompt to champion the offensive was
equally willing to sing its praises afterwards. In the year after *The Iron
Horse*, one of the major American directors, King Vidor, made his first
real impact with *The Big Parade*, about an ordinary American soldier's
service in France. The title is significant, for the First World War is
treated precisely as a parade, in which Jim is forced to participate but
which he is too ordinary and nice a guy to question. His victories are in
getting his French girl-friend to understand him and in returning home
with one leg at least intact.

The melting-pot

Hollywood had helped to create the Frontiersman myth by its very
foundation as well as by the films it produced. In much the same way,
its omnivorous absorption of acting and directing talent from all over
Europe provided one of the best illustrations of another founding
American myth, that of the melting-pot. Victor Sjostrom became Sea-
strom for MGM, who allowed him scope to take the melodrama out of
the studio into the outdoor locations he had exploited in Sweden. He
was responsible for Lillian Gish's most successful vehicles after her split
from Griffith in 1921, *The Scarlet Letter* (1926) and *The Wind* (1928). Two
years after this, he returned to Sweden, to concentrate on an acting career.

Mauritz Stiller was not so lucky. MGM from the start displayed a
greater interest in his protégée Greta Garbo than in him, to such an
extent that he returned to Sweden in 1928 (only three years after arriving)
and died in the same year. Garbo's silent films for MGM had meanwhile
begun the process of her elevation to a pinnacle of stardom reached by

no previous actress. Basil Wright described Mary Pickford as 'the hearth goddess' and Garbo as 'the moon goddess'[1], epithets which nearly capture another Hollywood split – between the traditional woman whose virgin countenance Mr Moviegoer was expected to dream of leading to the altar and the 'new woman' who would provide a – presumably vicarious – escape from domesticity, at once soulful and sexy. *Flesh and the Devil* (1926) and *A Woman of Affairs* (1929), two of Garbo's films for Clarence Brown, encapsulate in their titles the sexuality of the escape; Garbo's lonely eyes and matchless hinting at a perpetually enigmatic vulnerability provided the soulfulness that was to culminate in her much-publicised wish to be alone. It is deplorable, but hardly surprising, that Hollywood should from the first have operated the classic sexist division of women into wives ('nice girls') and courtesans ('vamps'). A production machine which viewed society as an affluent and patriotic status quo periodically enlivened by episodes of spicy exoticism could hardly do otherwise. The 'new woman', far from being free, was but the obverse of her prissy predecessor.

Not all the European performers who made it in Hollywood had been enticed from their home-country industries. Erich von Stroheim had lived in the United States for twelve years, acting as factotum to Griffith among others, before making *Blind Husbands* for Universal in 1918. Already in 1921 he was running into the kind of trouble with production companies that was to lead to his downfall; *Foolish Wives* was heavily cut at studio insistence, which did not prevent it from losing money. There is little doubt that Stronheim's conceptions were both tyrannical and grandiose, and that Irving Thalberg (in charge of his budget at Universal as he was later to be at MGM) was, in his own terms, right to curb his extravagance. Equally, there is little doubt that Thalberg's prime concern was with order and economy, originality coming a poor third. The clash between the two men reached its peak over the filming of *Greed* (1923), a new departure from the social satires Stroheim had directed up to then. *Greed* adapted Frank Norris's novel *McTeague* into forty-two reels, which were reduced first to twenty-four and then to ten on Stroheim's dismissal in 1925. The film is a terrifying evocation of lower-middle-class avarice, whose scenes at the wedding-breakfast (where a funeral passes ominously outside) and in the California Desert's Death Valley have lost none of their power to shock, and whose implicit challenge to the accumulative values on which Hollywood was based must have alarmed Thalberg almost as much as its production costs. *Greed* was the first major film to make extensive use of deep-focus, shots plunging deep into the 'third dimension' of the screen, permitting the development of narrative in depth as well as in breadth; this is how it relates the wedding-breakfast to the funeral, which passes 'behind' as well as outside.

Having prised Stroheim away from his mammoth original conception, MGM turned him towards safer territory with *The Merry Widow* (1925), a commercial success despite renewed threats of dismissal for extravagance. He was to direct only three more films, none of them for MGM; the *coup de grâce* was *Queen Kelly* (1928), made in collaboration with Gloria Swanson and Joseph Kennedy, still notorious for the scene in which the convent-girl (Swanson) throws her pants into a visiting prince's face. Extravagance (again), wrangles with his partners, and the coming of sound midway through shooting ensured that the film was never completed.

In the year in which *Greed* was finally released, the Austrian Josef Stern made his feature début under the name of Josef von Sternberg. *The Salvation Hunters* was an inexpensive location melodrama whose reputation for social realism was to be belied by Sternberg's later works. Far more prophetic was *The Last Command* (1928), which subjected Emil Jannings to the same kind of titanic humiliation he had undergone in *The Last Laugh*. Jannings plays a derelict who is cast in a bit-part as a White Russian general in a Hollywood epic about the Revolution; his claims to have been just that in Russia are mocked, but turn out to be true. The last charge in which the director orders him to lead his troops also turns out to be just that, for Jannings dies of a heart-attack while the scene is being shot. At the beginning, a true statement dismissed as 'bit-playing'; at the end, part-playing erupting into 'life', and Jannings dying before the cameras the kind of death he might have wished to die in a real battle. Sternberg's films are of interest, not only as exercises in masochistic degradation, but also as reminders that realism in the cinema is not reality, an oblique comment on the power of the image (our own of ourselves and the celluloid one on the screen).

The Hollywood career of Friedrich Murnau, cut short by a fatal car accident in 1931, was marred with disputes with William Fox's production company and by the commercial failure of the love story *Sunrise* (1927), far more open and less gloomy than his German films. *Sunrise* counterpoints the big city – a flashing whirl like the fairground which stands as a microcosm of it – with the open country, all sunlight on water – an all-American contrast on which Murnau's camera thrives as though liberated from German restraints. Murnau's two subsequent films also flopped, and his last work was *Tabu* (1931), shot in the South Seas with Robert Flaherty.

The alliance of Murnau, a director cramped by the social structure at home and the financial structure in America, and Flaherty, the man apropos of whose work the term 'documentary' was first coined, in the year in which Griffith directed his last film (and poor Fatty Arbuckle had been wasting away in disgrace), lends credence to the view of Hollywood as a Moloch which not only devoured its own children, but also let them rot when devouring would have been far more merciful. Flaherty did much filming in the Arctic, which reached its apogee with *Nanook of the North* (1922), a film about the Eskimo community starkly and simply shot, and imbued with a liberal belief in the noble savage amusing to a modern public, but progressive in the chauvinistic context of its time.

Flaherty followed *Nanook* with *Moana* (1926), which introduced panchromatic film, much more sensitive to wide colour-ranges than the orthochromatic which had hitherto been the norm. *Moana* is visually beautiful in its evocation of Samoan initiation-ceremonies, but displays little insight into social organisation. Aesthetic admiration stands bail for the failure to grasp the ways in which the community functions. The film did not succeed financially, and Flaherty's subsequent Hollywood career was episodic and troubled (he may share the nominal credit for *Tabu*, but the major part of the film is Murnau's). In 1930, he left for Britain, for an intermittently successful collaboration with John Grierson.

The comedians

One area of the silent cinema remains uncovered in this chapter so far, yet its productions are among the most abidingly successful of all. The prodigious spate of Chaplin's pre-First World War comedies was tempered after he joined First National in 1917 with finicky perfectionism, which sometimes resulted in thirty feet of film being shot for every one used. The 'little man' moved through such 'little-men' situations as war service (*Shoulder Arms*, 1918) or child-minding (*The Kid*, his first feature, 1921), with happy endings sometimes self-deflating (in *Shoulder Arms* his heroic capture of the Kaiser is only a dream), sometimes merely sub-Dickensian (the mother of the abandoned waif in *The Kid* becomes an opera-star, and the three are reunited after a separation in which Chaplin finds escape in a dream of Paradise). The bewilderment and ambiguity of certain critical reactions to Chaplin can be traced to the evident skill with which, especially at his most forlorn, he manipulates audience reactions. He is without question the genius of tear-jerking. The result is an uneasy feeling of complicity in escapism – uneasy because after all the escapism knows itself for what it is and thereby invites mockery; but even so ... To what extent Chaplin's later pro-Communism can be reconciled with the tendency present throughout his work to open a hatch in unpalatable reality and disappear (with a broad wink) into the Land of Dreams is a highly pertinent question.

The Gold Rush (1925), filmed without a script, for much of its length gently derides Charlie's dreams and delusions. One of two struggling prospectors in the Yukon, he invites a girl to dinner; needless to say, she doesn't come, so he dreams she is there, just as when food runs short he cooks and eats an old boot, treating the laces as spaghetti and enjoying a candle sprinkled with salt as an hors-d'oeuvre, celery-fashion. At the end, however, he strikes it rich and gets the girl. The film is dazzling in its ingenuity and comic choreography, as well as disturbing in its adroit engineering of a passion against which it is impossible to vaccinate oneself entirely.

Buster Keaton, on the other hand, unblinkingly refused pathos. Like Chaplin's, his films are superbly crafted, but the crafting takes place anywhere but on Keaton's deadpan face – in the sets, a paranoiac world forever ganging up or falling down on him, in the acrobatic grace of his movements, in the exploitation of the distance between performer and camera that reaches its apotheosis in *The General* (1926). It was Fatty Arbuckle who gave him his start in 1916, and by 1920 he was an established star, guaranteed $1000 per week plus 25 per cent of the profits.

His first features were made in 1923, *The Three Ages* (a parody of Griffith) and *Our Hospitality*, about feuding families in the South. David Robinson has cited[2] Keaton's expressed dislike of the 'ridiculous' in comedy (he was to have little time for the Marx Brothers), in connection with this latter film's carefully-assembled 'realist' narrative which makes explanatory titles largely superfluous. *Sherlock Junior* (1924) appears to move right away from such cinema; Buster plays a projectionist whose dream-self penetrates the screen on which he is projecting, there to dominate comic action which includes some splendid locomotive gags and a crossbar ride on a driverless motor-cycle. Few films have so distilled one of the main sources of our pleasure in the fantasy of film – the fact that (just like Sherlock/Buster) we the spectators are simultaneously outside the film (which is 'up there' on the screen) and inside it because its images are orientated towards us and open out for us a point of view on and within its action. At the same time, Keaton's insistence on performing the gags as shot and not faking them in the studio, which was to cost him a good few injuries in his career, indicates the continuance of that interest in 'realism' that motivated his careful choice of location in his other films and underlay his phobia for the ridiculous.

The Navigator, made in the same year, was Keaton's biggest box-office success, but not the film by which he is best remembered. That distinction belongs to *The General* (1926), the best possible vindication of Nicholas Ray's statement that the movies are 'the biggest, most expensive electric train-set anybody could be given to play with'. The train-chase had been a standard part of the comic repertoire since Sennett, but no film has ever made such varied and agile use of it. Our perspective on the train, and the distance between it and the camera, are constantly altering. Sometimes we are with Buster in the driver's cab, but unlike him aware of disaster looming along the track; sometimes outside a tunnel, wondering whether and in what state driver and train will emerge; sometimes we watch from a distance, as in the final cataclysm when the bridge is blown up and the train plunges down into the river, where according to movie myth it still lies. Potential sentimentality in the framing love-story is defused by Keaton's poker-faced refusal so much as to recognise its existence. He is a desultory individual to whom emotional and physical events 'just happen', and this greatest of silent film comedies thereby becomes also one of the most eloquently ambiguous individualist films.

Keaton's solo career was already drawing to a close when *The General* was made. His last independent production was *Steamboat Bill Junior* (1928), famous for its climactic typhoon-sequence. In the same year he joined MGM, and the resulting loss of autonomy combined with the advent of sound (which judging by the verbal wit in many of his titles he would have been well able to cope with in more propitious circumstances) and marital and drink problems to bring about a slide in his fortunes cruelly evoked in his brief cameo in Billy Wilder's *Sunset Boulevard* of 1950. He dried out in 1956 and died ten years later, after farewell appearances in *A Funny Thing Happened On the Way to the Forum* and a Samuel Beckett short. When I saw *Sunset Boulevard* at the Paris Cinémathèque in 1972, the capacity audience burst into spontaneous and prolonged applause on Keaton's appearance – ironic since he was called in precisely to play himself as a fallen Hollywood giant, but also a richly-deserved tribute to the greatest American silent director of them all.

Harry Langdon underwent an even more total commercial eclipse as a result of sound. Far more than Chaplin's or Keaton's, his face, baby-like in its distracted roundness, was his fortune. Figures involved with his best-known films survived into the sound epoch far better than he did; in the delightful cross-Continent walking-gag of *Tramp, Tramp, Tramp* (directed by Harry Edwards in 1926), the girl he gets is a twenty-year-old Joan Crawford, and *The Strong Man* of the same year was the feature début of Frank Capra whose career was to be highly important in the early sound days.

Harold Lloyd – an established director of shorts as early as 1919 – hardly needed to adapt to sound or be destroyed by it. His commercial shrewdness enabled him to enjoy a comfortable California retirement, sustained by the release of two feature-length packages of his best work. The classic Lloyd pose shows him dangling desperately by one hand from a clock-face; his is the slapstick of urban paraphernalia, but it is a paraphernalia of which he is well in control. David Thomson describes him as 'not just the "college boy" – fresh-faced, neat, bespectacled – but the budding executive of Comedy Inc.'[3]. Such a combination of two classic American stereotypes could hardly fail to be successful. Lloyd's films are certainly less funny than Langdon's or Keaton's, but his career, just because it was so unperturbed, reads eloquently beside theirs as an exemplar of the qualities the Hollywood silent cinema most consistently rewarded.

4 The European Cinema: From 1927 to 1939

Al Jolson's 'You ain't heard nothing yet', in *The Jazz Singer* of October 1927, was the death-knell of silent cinema. But there was at first much serious and vehement opposition to sound. Chaplin was bitterly hostile through most of the thirties, Delluc and Germaine Dulac were condemnatory, and Paul Rotha, a leading British theorist later active in the documentary movement, castigated dialogue films as 'a degenerate and misguided attempt to destroy the real use of the film'[1]. The French film theorist Christian Metz has suggested as a possible explanation for this an over-literal interpretation (clearest in much of Eisenstein's work) of the cinema as a language. As Metz says: 'Compared to a *subtle* language (verbal language), it defined itself unawares as a coarser double'[2]; if the silent cinema was indeed a 'language' in the strict sense of the word, capable of setting a scene or telling a story with images as the poem or the novel could do with words, then clearly speech was a superfluous addition, encroaching upon rather than widening its scope.

These debates were to remain largely theoretical, for the commercial potential of sound was too immediately apparent for its future to be in any real doubt. Theatre and radio stars became available to the cinema; areas of social reality previously hinted at, or laboriously exposed in titles, could now receive precise and naturalistic treatment; and both European and American companies adapted sufficiently quickly for the sound movie to be the norm within two years, a providential bulwark against the worst effects of the Depression. This chapter will examine European sound-films up to the outbreak of the Second World War with special attention to the creative uses of sound that were made almost from the moment of its invention, as well as to the various effects of its sudden popularisation on the market and the major individual figures and companies.

The first impact

Certain of the early results of sound now seem grotesque, notably those in films made by personnel imported lock, stock, and barrel from the theatre. Actors continued to make the lavish gesticulations that had characterised silent cinema, as though sound had not been invented. Fears that the language barrier would halt the growing internationalisation of the industry led to numerous films being shot several times over in different languages, until dubbing or subtitling took over for economy reasons. Partially-shot silent films were dragged into the sound era via frequently incongruous superimposition of dialogue. Many studios and directors concentrated on what were little more than filmed theatre-plays and variety performances, ignoring the mobility of the camera. The large production companies reinforced their stranglehold over the international market by their ownership of sound-system patents; the German Tobis Klangfilm was the only major European patent-holder, and other industries were forced to pay its royalties or those of the two principal American companies, RCA and Western Electric.

At the same time, serious interest in the medium grew. The magazine *Sight and Sound* made its first appearance in 1932, to be followed the year afterwards by the setting-up of the British Film Institute. Henri Langlois in 1936 founded the Cinémathèque Française, the first and still the most important film archive and museum, and French literary interest in the medium developed with the involvement of Jean Cocteau and André Malraux, who filmed his Spanish Civil War novel *L'Espoir* (*Hope*) in 1938. The first film festival was organised in Venice in 1932, under the aegis of the Mussolini government, who perverted it into such a transparent political farce that in 1938 the British and American members of the jury resigned in protest. The still-thriving Cannes Festival was planned as a less corrupt (!) alternative, but war intervened to delay its launching.

The French industry was particularly hard-hit by American and German cinematic imperialism. The Paramount studios near Paris were the scene of the multi-lingual shooting mentioned above (some films went through as many as fifteen different versions), and Tobis also moved in, building large and well-equipped studios at Épinay.

It was with Tobis that René Clair developed into the only major

European director of musicals, with *Sous les Toits de Paris* (*Beneath the Rooftops of Paris*, 1930), a folksily gentle comedy-drama set in a poor area of Paris, *Le Million* (1931), a wild yet precisely-choreographed chase after a lost lottery ticket, and *A Nous la Liberté* (*Freedom for Us*, 1932). The last-named is an anarchistic satire on mass-production which compares factories to prisons, and whose tycoon central character (an escaped convict) reacts with gleeful regression to the arrival in his factory of his old cell-mate, pelting a large paternalistic portrait of himself with handfuls of food and turning the factory over to the workers in it before setting off with his friend down the open road to the strains of the title-song. Clair's Paris, the setting also for *Quatorze Juillet* (*July 14th*, 1933) and *Le Dernier Milliardaire* (*The Last Millionaire*, 1934), is a studio construction in which bravely-smiling flower-girls and impeccably ragamuffin accordionists adorn every street-corner; what is exhilaratingly childlike in *A Nous la Liberté* has in these other films a tendency to become irritatingly childish.

The Surrealist cinema launched by Buñuel continued to thrive through its various mutations in the thirties. Buñuel himself returned to his native Spain to make *Las Hurdes* (*Land without Bread*, 1932), a fiercely angry documentary about a poverty-stricken region of the country, and to produce films in the new Republican industry before leaving for New York, and then Mexico, after the Fascists took over. In France, Jean Cocteau put his convoluted, egocentric literary imagination at the service of the cinema with *Le Sang d'un Poète* (*The Blood of a Poet*, 1930), whose Freudian imagery (it gets off to a resounding start with the collapse of a phallic chimney-stack) is considerably heavier and less witty than Buñuel's. The film is now of interest primarily as a 'dry run' for the mystical, dreamlike style Cocteau was to perfect in his post-war films.

Far more satisfyingly dreamlike, because unafraid of the ludicrous aspects of nightmare, is the brief output of Jean Vigo. Son of a prominent anarchist murdered in a Paris prison during the First World War; from the age of twenty plagued by the tuberculosis that was to kill him nine years later; making his films on money scraped together with immense difficulty, and seeing his best work *Zéro de Conduite* (1933) banned; such a career would undoubtedly have led, in Hollywood, to compensatory mythical canonisation and a plethora of biographical movies. . . . His total *oeuvre* consists of two short films and two extraordinary features, *Zéro de Conduite* (the French school system's equivalent of 'detention') and *L'Atalante* (1934). *Zéro de Conduite*, shot under conditions of extreme constraint, is an anarchistic account of an uprising by boys at a regimented boarding-school against their headmaster, who is only four feet tall and speaks in a squeaky-voiced parody of every procrastinating bureaucrat, and his sidekick 'Pet-Sec' (Dry Fart). The ending has the boys on the roof, pelting the pompous prize-ceremony beneath, not with bullets as in Lindsay Anderson's *If* thirty-five years later, but with cushions and cotton-wool – far more absurdly dreamlike missiles, recalling also the slow-motion pillowfight in the dormitory about half-way through the film.

There are similarities between the liberating glee of *A Nous la Liberté* and that of *Zéro de Conduite*, but on a superficial level only. Vigo's adolescents are aware of the tense and grotesque elements that Clair's bourgeois ignores as he shrugs off adulthood for a carefree Arcadia. These elements achieve central importance in *L'Atalante*, titled after the barge on which it is set, and onto which the captain brings his young wife. The marriage begins to disintegrate under the pressures of waterway life, and the wife runs away to the temptations of the big city, but is found and brought back by the first mate, Père Jules, an early major role for the faun-like Swiss actor Michel Simon. What is striking about the film is not just the surrealistic river-poetry or the social acuteness of the scenes on land, outside the church, and in the barge-company's office, but the way in which the disorder on board (notably in Père Jules's cabin, teeming with stuffed animals and other nautical relics) is contrasted to that, far more sinister, of Paris. Père Jules keeps a pair of preserved hands in a jar, from which the bride recoils in horror, but they are much less dangerous than the disembodied hands which steal her bag at the station booking-office in Paris. Nightmare, for Vigo, is not to be contained within an explicitly fantasy world, it is omnipresent; and it is this that makes *L'Atalante* a frightening as well as a funny and lyrical film.

The most commercially successful French directors of the period under discussion made a habit of cooperating on one another's films. Jacques Feyder acted as scriptwriter for Julien Duvivier (himself a former assistant to Feuillade and L'Herbier), and in his turn gave the first opening, as camera assistant, to Marcel Carné, regarded in the immediately pre-war and Occupation period as the leading French director. Such interconnections help to account for the homogeneity of much of the output of the period, and hence in part for its success.

Feyder returned to France in 1931 after ten not particularly happy years with MGM in Hollywood, to direct *Le Grand Jeu* (*The Big Game*, 1934), and *La Kermesse Héroïque* (1935), about a siege during the Spanish occupation of the Netherlands lifted when the Dutchwomen 'entertain' their would-be conquerors – innocently bawdy enough to a modern audience, but enough to provoke riots when the film was shown in Belgium and Holland.

Duvivier sprang to fame with *Poil de Carotte* (*Redhead* – a 1932 remake of a 1925 silent), about a boy whose estrangement from those around him culminates in attempted suicide, and followed this in 1937 with two great successes, *Un Carnet de Bal* (*A Ball Programme*) and *Pépé le Moko*. The former is a heavily nostalgic account of a widow's disillusioning search for the man she danced with on one night in her youth, the latter gave Jean Gabin one of his first major roles in a tale of a gangster trapped in Algiers, and unwittingly betrayed to the police by the woman he loves.

This somewhat schematic account should at least emphasise the heavy atmosphere of pessimism that hangs about many French films of the immediately pre-war period, much as decadence does about many films of the Weimar Republic, and is especially characteristic of the work of Marcel Carné – a director now so far fallen out of fashion that most of his films are currently commercially unavailable in the United Kingdom (though there are signs of a revival).

Carné started as assistant to Feyder and Clair, and in 1936 began his eleven-year partnership with the poet and scriptwriter Jacques Prévert. This was responsible, before the war, for *Drôle de Drame* (*An Odd Drama*, 1937), a bizarre comedy set in a no less bizarre stylised Dickensian London, and two melodramas featuring the craggy, weary-eyed Jean Gabin, the working-class hero of a sordid urban environment. In *Quai des Brumes* (*Misty Quay*, 1938), he is a deserter on the run, attempting to protect Michèle Morgan from the toadlike attentions of a toyshop owner (Michel Simon); in *Le Jour se Lève* (*Daybreak*, 1939), he is caught between an ingenuous flower-girl and a world-weary conjuror's assistant (Arletty), all three manipulated to his own destruction and Gabin's suicide by the conjuror (Jules Berry). Today, much about these films seems dated (the heavy, throbbing music, the remarkable but inexorably studio-bound sets, the malignity of the villains pitted against Gabin's stolid loyalty that comprehends nothing, least of all in either film his own death), and there is a tendency to write them off as historical curiosities, manifestations of pre-war malaise. This is less than fair to the acute theatrical sense Carné displays, in his choice and direction of actors, and in the structuring of *Le Jour se Lève* as a three-act tragedy punctuated by flashback, or to the laconic wit of Prévert's dialogue, an astringent contrast to the films' sentimentality which subtitling largely obscures.

Quai des Brumes and *Le Jour se Léve* both take place in gloomy Northern settings (fog-bound Le Havre and an unidentified industrial town respectively). The playwright Marcel Pagnol showed that studios could just as successfully mock up sunnier locales, in his Marseille-based trilogy *Marius* (1931), *Fanny* (1932), and *César* (1936), the first directed by Alexander Korda, the second by Marc Allégret, and the third by Pagnol himself. Warmth that rarely becomes heat, and affectionate indulgence of Provençal whims, are qualities that ensured considerable success and periodic revival of the trilogy and *La Femme du Boulanger* (1938), in which a village is plunged into despair when the 'baker's wife' of the title runs off with a young shepherd – not for moral reasons, but because the baker refuses to bake any more bread until she returns.

It was Pagnol who provided the backing for Jean Renoir to film *Toni* in the South of France in 1935, for which he is more deserving of remembrance than for his own films. Renoir, son of the painter, was for many years a greatly neglected director, whose films were felt to lack the polish of a Clair or a Carné. It was not until after the war that his full importance came to be realised, thanks *inter alia* to the work of the critic André Bazin who acclaimed Renoir's 'respect for the continuity of dramatic space and, of course, duration'[3]. The contrast between a film by Eisenstein or Robert Wiene and one by Renoir will make clear what Bazin means; it is the contrast between a world of metaphorical juxtaposition and dislocation and one of apparent organic continuity, between the camera as obvious organising presence and as transparent 'window on the world', between in Penelope Houston's words 'shooting out towards a world existing beyond the camera' and 'filming a scene put on for its benefit'[4]. An illusory contrast, obviously; whatever we see on the screen has been organised by the camera and (except in certain kinds of *cinéma-vérité*) 'put on for its benefit'. But Renoir was largely responsible for a mode of organisation radically different from much that had gone before him, visible already in such early silents as *Nana* (1926).

His first major sound films were the magnificent drama of jealousy *La Chienne* (*The Bitch*, 1931), and the Maigret detective-story *La Nuit du Carrefour* (*Crossroads Night*) and *Boudu Sauvé des Eaux* (*Boudu Saved from Drowning*), both made in 1932. The disreputable tramp Boudu (Michel Simon), rescued from attempted suicide by drowning at the beginning of the film, throws the household of his benefactor, the liberal bookseller Lestingois, into a disarray of which Groucho Marx would not have been ashamed, before at the end swimming happily away down the river (now, as often in Renoir, seen as a kind of natural 'life-force'). *Toni* is even more remarkable, not least because it was shot entirely on location at a time when studio-bound sets were the rule. Renoir filmed this drama of jealousy (based on the newspaper report of a real murder case) with a totally non-professional cast, and the result is a far cry from Pagnol's cosy Southern warmth; the scene where the migrant worker Toni sucks poison from a bee-sting on Josepha's neck has extraordinary sensual power.

To have told such a story about migrant workers using a migrant-worker cast was itself a political act, as the Popular Front alliance of Left-of-Centre parties must have realised when they commissioned Renoir to direct *Le Crime de Monsieur Lange* in 1935. This was scripted by Jacques Prévert, and the villain Batala, director of a pulp publishing firm who fakes his own death and absconds with the proceeds, was played by Jules Berry; but the evil here, unlike that in Carné, has a clear socio-economic basis, and a coherent attempt is made to resist it when the workers, headed by the absent-minded author Lange, set up a publishing cooperative.

The originality of Renoir's mode of visual organisation is apparent in the Christmas-banquet scene in the works after Batala's disappearance, in which the camera's long circular pan apprehends the scene – and hence the cooperative – as a whole disturbed only by the recrudescence of Batala from the (literal and figurative) shadows. In much the same way, the migrants in *Toni* are presented, in an entirely unforced and un-patronising manner, as a community bounded – both constrained and defined – by the railway, the river, and the surrounding hills. It is this perception (and the consequent use of tracking-shots and deep-focus rather than Eisensteinian montage) that led Bazin to appreciate Renoir for being 'more concerned with the creation of characters and situations in which they could express themselves than with a story'[5]. Conflict and contradiction are an integral part of the characters and situations, as well as of the images – nowhere more so than in Renoir's two best-known films, *La Grande Illusion* (1937) and *La Règle du Jeu* (1939).

Class and barriers in war and 'peace'

The 'great illusion' of the first film's title is (approximately) that the enforced camaraderie of war can ever break down the barriers of class (and, as a recent British critic has argued[6], sex). The aristocratic French commanding-officer de Boeildieu (Pierre Fresnay) sacrifices himself to permit the escape of his fellow-prisoners, the engineer Maréchal and the wealthy bourgeois Rosenthal, yet Charles Spaak's dialogue makes it quite clear that he has far more in common with his German opposite number, von Rauffenstein (Erich von Stroheim).

Maréchal and Rosenthal escape, via a romantic idyll between Maréchal and a German peasant-woman, across the Swiss frontier – another great illusion, but this time a providential one since although invisible in the snow the frontier prevents a group of German snipers from firing on them. The film was originally scheduled to end with a projected rendez-vous between Rosenthal and Maréchal, on the first New Year's Eve after the war, at Maxim's restaurant in Paris; the camera was to have shown two empty places. . . . Bourgeois and proletarian are no less aware of the inexorability of class divisions than the dying aristocracy, whose particled members are brought together by nothing so much as a common aware-ness that their class is doomed.

Renoir's filming is fluent and unobtrusive, in a way that elicits from many students viewing the film such comments as 'you hardly notice the technique'; you do, though, for it is precisely that that produces for us the sense of a fugitive, contradiction-torn whole, which we half-watch, half-participate in (as in the scene where the English officers dress up in drag for the camp concert-party, and the camera follows the gaze of the other prisoners towards them, mocking and incredulous yet at the same time imprinted with unmistakable eroticism).

All of which is true, only more so, of *La Règle du Jeu*, greeted with incomprehension by audiences when first shown, released in a cruelly abbreviated version when Renoir left for America at the outbreak of war, and not seen in its original form until 1958. The class conflicts here lack even the tenuous cement of wartime to hold them together. During a house-party in the French countryside near Orléans, the unhappy wife of the host (like de Boeildieu an aristocrat, like Rosenthal a Jew – evidence of how traditional barriers are crumbling), hesitates between eloping with the passionate aviator André Jurieu and the brotherly attentions of Octave (played by Renoir himself), whose magnanimous stepping-down in favour of Jurieu leads to the latter's death amid a tangle of mistaken identities. The aristocratic characters attempt to manipulate the title's 'rules of the (social) game', much as the Marquis does his collection of mechanical toys, so as to achieve their desires – or, more complicated, articulate them as a preliminary to their achievement – while remaining within the bounds of the social structure. But the structure is so worm-eaten, so rotten with its own contradictions, that only a supreme collective act of hypocrisy at the end can disguise the fact that it has collapsed altogether. When the Marquis, in the last sequence, speaks of Jurieu as 'this wonderful friend, this excellent companion', the old order rallies *in extremis* to agree on the truth of this statement – a last desperate attempt to bend rules we know have already been shattered beyond repair.

Below stairs, nobody tries to bend the rules. The gamekeeper Schumacher, boringly besotted with his vain and frigid wife, adheres to them with a literal ferocity which ensures that it is he who at the end fires the shot that kills Jurieu; the poacher-turned-servant (Julien Carette as a splendid spiv) disregards them altogether so that when he is extruded from château society at the end it really matters little to him.

La Règle du Jeu was initially able to establish itself as a 'cinema classic' largely because it is particularly susceptible to a literary reading such as the above, so that at a time when the artistic status of the cinema was still in question such problems could be evaded by situating the film in a specifically French literary tradition of ironic social analysis. Such a reading is clearly important and indispensable, but does not take the measure of the film as cinema. The long rabbit-hunting sequence is important, not only because it is echoed at the end when Jurieu's death is compared to that of a rabbit, but also because of the way in which we move from one point of view to another, back and away again. We are periodically invited to identify ourselves with the hunted rabbit, just as later in the final tragic-comic chase-scene through the château corridors camera movements and perspectives ensure that we may at any moment be identifying ourselves with one character, or several, or none, and find a secure refuge only in the imperturbable comment of the butler Corneille when he is told by the Marquis to 'stop this farce' and replies: 'Which one?' The plot, written down, schematised as literature, has a perfect, closed symmetry in which the status quo alone triumphs. Viewed as cinema, this security too breaks down and dissolves into fluid camera-movements. The disturbing openness of the film, our inability to settle the visual and emotional issues it raises, is both a product of the time at which it was made (the year the Second World War broke out) and an exploration of the ambiguous possibilities of the cinematic medium.

Germany

The development of the early German industry was dominated by the UFA combine, and by the Tobis syndicate which monopolised European sound patents, so that from 1929 the industry was the most prosperous in Europe, churning out a stream of lucrative operettas and pseudo-historical spectaculars. There coexisted with this a 'social-realist' tendency, taking its subject-matter from the lives of poorer people. Jutzi's *Mutter Krausens Fahrt ins Glück* (*Mother Krausen's Journey to Happiness*, 1929), about a working-class mother whose 'journey' is her suicide after her son is branded as a thief, is a good early example of this. But the economic slump (2 500 000 unemployed by January 1930) and the UFA stranglehold restricted the development of this type of cinema. The Marxist playwright Bertolt Brecht collaborated on the film *Kühle Wampe* (or *Whom does the World belong to?*, 1932), funded by working-class organisations and directed by Slatan Dudow, about a poor city family who vainly try to escape oppression by moving into a utopian rural community (contrasted in the last reel with an urban clubroom and sports festival). The presentation of the Communist-sponsored workers' activities is somewhat idealistic, but the stress on the need for cultural and political organisation within the cities is unmistakable.

Brecht's contribution to cinematic theory and practice (although *Kühle Wampe* is the only film with which he was involved) is immense. His conception of *Verfremdung* (best translated as 'distanciation') – the presentation of situations and actions, not as 'realities' with which we are invited fully to identify ourselves, but in the words of Roland Barthes as 'a tableau for the spectator to criticise'[7] – has been a major influence on much recent cinematic work (the theory and practice of Christian Metz, Jean-Luc Godard, and Danièle Huillet/Jean-Marie Straub will provide evidence of this). That Brecht's influence should have taken such a delayed and mediated form, despite his interest in the cinema, is indicative of the difficulties under which progressive workers in the medium at that time laboured.

Brecht's name is probably most familiar to film-goers through the adaptation G. W. Pabst made of his *Threepenny Opera* (1931), which gave rise to a protracted and acrimonious lawsuit between the two men. The film's enduring popularity is largely due to the superb performances of Lotte Lenya as Jenny and Erst Busch as the street-singer whose songs provide an ironic commentary between scenes. It is questionable whether the film's departures from the original lessen or intensify its revolutionary impact. In the book, Peachum (the beggars' leader who threatens to wreck the Coronation procession with a demonstration by his men) finishes by joining the archetypal crook-cum-capitalist Macheath in an early variety of fringe banking, whereas in the film he carries out his threat and thus breaks apart the cosy entente between Macheath and the corrupt police chief Tiger Brown. The film's settings are characteristic of German cinema of this period – jumbled, cluttered, for Siegfried Kracauer in *From Caligari to Hitler* the very stuff of decadence.

Pabst's other German sound films include the pacifist *Westfront 1918* (1930), and *Kameradschaft* (*Comradeship*, 1931), in which German miners help trapped French comrades in a disaster that takes place just after the Treaty of Versailles which caused so much bitterness between the two countries. In 1933, like so many other German artists, he left for France.

Fritz Lang's outstanding German film of this period was *The Testament of Dr Mabuse* (1932), a superbly gripping tale of a mad scientist who, although dead, holds on to his criminal empire and plans world conquest through the hypnotic power he exerts, from beyond the grave, on the asylum psychiatrist Dr Baum. The film's foresight goes beyond its figuration of Hitler's malign hypnotic techniques, into an early realisation that the psychiatric process is a two-way one, that it is not a simple question of sanity curing madness – a realisation skirted, but finally avoided, in *Caligari*. . . . The monstrous social lunacy of the sets for *Metropolis* can be read as the complement of the charged private lunacy of Mabuse's cell-confined world; it is no accident that it was the Nazi reaction to these two films in particular that was to precipitate Lang's departure. In *M* (1931), with Peter Lorre as a tortured child-murderer who finally faces a court, not of the judiciary, but of his own criminal peers, he had prefigured the social chaos and collusion that was to drive him into exile within two years.

The best-known of all the pre-Hitler German films was in fact the only one its director made in Germany. Josef von Sternberg was lent to UFA by MGM/Paramount as part of an exchange, whose result was *The Blue Angel* (1930). The film marked the effective end of one career and the beginning of another; Emil Jannings, as the authoritarian school-master ruined by his infatuation with a night-club singer, coped very badly with the English-language version (his accent is far too guttural), and Marlene Dietrich, in her first major role, upstaged him, in popular impact at least, so much that his pride and reputation never recovered. Sternberg insisted on casting Dietrich against the advice of his collaborators, and the result is now show-business legend to an extent that obscures it as a cinematic coup. Dietrich's two renderings of 'Falling in Love Again' rely for their effect, not only on the vocal contrast, but on the way in which lighting enhances and complements it, emphasising her beguiling availability when Unrath first meets her and her chilling sadism when he is a broken man at the end. The artful confusion and clutter of the nightclub sets (in which careful lighting again plays its part) and the harshly disciplined world of the schoolroom contrast, not merely order and disorder, but licence and repression; one world is the necessary condition of the other. Unrath's accession to sexuality after years of celibacy (to a form of childhood after years as repressively repressing father-figure) takes the cataclysmic form it does as a direct result of this rigorous bottling-up, exploding into the fetichistic proliferation of stocking-tops and suspenders in the club-scenes. The film is condemnatory of the Nazi repression to come as much as of the decadence that preceded it.

What remains terrifying is the thoroughness with which Jannings's humiliation unfolds, from the pernickety ritual of his getting-up at the beginning to his insane cock-crowing, attempted murder of Dietrich, and death at his old desk at the end. If Dietrich is sadistic, then we, enthralled spectators of this remorseless degradation, are likewise; no film leaves me with a worse conscience. . . . Dietrich may have eclipsed Jannings when the film was released, but Jannings's is at least as great a performance.

Those performers who remained in Germany after the Nazi takeover in 1933 found themselves forced into propaganda films, the most successful of which took over and utilised already popular genres. Arnold Fanck's 'mountain films', relying on a mysticism of snow and ice, lent themselves particularly well, as did the historical dramas already referred to.

The outstanding name of Nazi cinema, Leni Riefenstahl, was a protégé of Fanck's, and responsible for the most important documentary film ever made, *The Triumph of the Will* (1936). The film remains unviewable outside film-societies, which is perhaps due less to fear that it will turn people into Nazis than to a general sense of inability to handle it. What does one do – physically and critically – with a film whose opening shot (of Hitler's plane descending from the clouds before the Nuremberg Rally) deifies a human being with more pernicious skill than any shot before or since, which plays off leader and admiring masses in a satanic parody of Eisensteinian montage? Part of the answer might be to treat it as neither documentary nor propaganda, but as a particularly dangerous blending of the two, of a kind now common but nonetheless tyrannical in its implications. The 1934 rally, with its immense 'Cathedral of Light' in which the night-time scenes take place, was planned and organised around Riefenstahl's camera; what we see was not specifically staged for her, but neither would it have occurred as it did had she not been there. The film is a striking early instance of the media's power to control events by the very fact of being there to record them.

Even edited down to two hours, it also shows how tedious the iconography of Fascism becomes after a while – an impression reinforced by *Olympic Games, 1938*, whose interminable lissom supermen rapidly bore to distraction. *Triumph of the Will*, however, is enough to stamp Riefenstahl as one of the cinema's greatest directors; that she should have developed that gift in the service of a régime that oppressed women more than any other is a major contradiction.

Russia

Eisenstein, Pudovkin, and Alexandrov (scriptwriter for *October*) cosigned a Manifesto on the implications of sound for the cinema in 1928. The danger they foresaw was the degeneration of sound films into 'photographed performances of a theatrical sort', and the means of forestalling it an extension of the principles of montage, via deliberate non-synchronisation of sound and visual images (a device much used at this time by René Clair), so that one should not (as they saw it) superfluously double the other. The document is interesting because it shows a speed of theoretical (as well as practical) adaptation to sound unmatched elsewhere; Eisenstein's view of the cinema as the supreme art of synthesis ensured that he welcomed sound as a major addition to the medium's vocabulary, and even contemplated turning his partially-finished *The General Line* (1929) into a sound film. The film deals with agricultural collectivisation (decreed by Stalin while it was being made), but not always in a way that met official approval. Its satirisation of the bureaucracy was largely responsible for the title's being changed to *The Old and the New*, thus dissociating it from Party policy.

The Ukrainian Alexander Dovzhenko, in the silent *Earth* (1930), expressed no such reservations about Stalin's approach. Unlike Eisenstein, Dovzhenko had a genuine love and feeling for the countryside, in evidence in *Earth*, inspired by a rural pantheism that never becomes bland or folksy. The sequence after the leader of the farming cooperative has been killed by a young kulak (heavily mutilated by the censor and not shown in complete form until after Stalin's death) is an erotic *tour de force*, in which the killer's frenzy in the graveyard is paralleled by that of the murdered man's lover, thrashing about on her bed. Montage here has a metaphorical function, emphasising the similarity between apparently opposed states; it is as though, in their madness, killer and bereaved become one.

Dovzhenko's sound career produced as its most significant work *Aerograd* (1935), about Japanese attempts to stop the building of a modern city in Eastern Russia. During the war, as director of the Kiev studios, he concentrated on the making of newsreels.

While *Earth* was being made, Eisenstein was out of the country, on the journey which marked the beginning of the end of his career. Uppermost in his mind when he left for a 'world tour' in 1929 was the idea of filming in America; at the end of 1930, he signed a contract with the Left-wing novelist Upton Sinclair to make a film in Mexico. *Que Viva Mexico!* was plagued from the start, by climate, financial and script problems, and harassment from Stalin. When the contract was broken off in 1932, with the film still a long way from completion, Eisenstein returned to Moscow, amid troubles with his health and the increasingly constricting Soviet bureaucracy. *Bezhin Meadow*, which was to have been his first Russian sound film, was begun in 1935, and abandoned at censorial insistence in 1937; Eisenstein's self-rehabilitation came with *Alexander Nevsky* in 1938. He was commissioned to retell the story of the defeat of the thirteenth-century German armies by the Russians under Nevsky, for propaganda reasons that show embarrassingly in the film (the 'Teutonic' troops wear medieval Nazi uniforms, the nationalistic fervour of the scenario is contrived), and caused the film to be shelved in a hurry when the Nazi/Soviet pact was signed.

But the film remains interesting inasmuch as it provided the first opportunity for Eisenstein to experiment with image/music montage. He attempted to get the images (notably in the famous 'Battle on the Ice' sequence) to follow the rhythms and dynamics of the music, a rousing cantata by Prokofiev.

Mark Donskoi's Maxim Gorky trilogy also figures among the outstanding sound films made before the Soviet Union's entry into the Second World War. The first two parts in particular, *The Childhood of Maxim Gorky* (1938) and *My Apprenticeship* (1939), are remarkable for their evocation of the intelligent and ambitious young man's progress through a malicious and backward society that constantly threatens to drag him down – classic nineteenth-century novel subject-matter given epic cinematic resonance through the recurrent use of the Volga river that irrigates the beloved motherland. The Soviet cinema never at this stage shirked appeals – implicit or explicit – to patriotism, which was to come in very useful when they entered the war in 1941.

Great Britain

Alfred Hitchcock's *Blackmail* was virtually complete in its silent form when sound came along. Despite problems with the Czech actress Anny Ondra's English, which necessitated dubbing, it was rapidly reworked as a sound film and released in 1929. Ms Ondra's heroine inadvertently slays with a bread-knife the loathsome 'artist' who attempts to rape her, whence the blackmail of the title. The film's interest (as often in Hitchcock) lies in the fact that from the beginning we know 'whodunit', and are free to concentrate on a psychological drama which, although often heavy, is enlivened by an imaginative soundtrack, notably in the famous sequence when Anny Ondra at the breakfast-table obsessively hears the word 'knife' repeated over and over again – an early subjective use of sound. . . . Hitchcock worked in Great Britain up to 1940, concentrating mainly on the tense and perverse suspense-films with which his name has always been associated. His most successful films of this period are generally thought to be those he made with the backing of Michael Balcon at Gaumont British. Balcon was throughout his career a firm believer in low-budget productions which would have no difficulty in recouping production costs on the home market; at the same time, the style of 'Englishness' which pervades his films (above all those made at Ealing Studios, of which he became head in 1938) endeared itself to foreign distributors and spectators, so that until decline and monopoly rendered his ideas obsolete at the end of the 1950s he was one of Britain's most successful producers.

The Man who Knew Too Much (a Hitchcock/Balcon film of 1934) stars Leslie Banks in the 'title role', as the father who refuses to panic even though his daughter is being held hostage in an international spy-game. The English cult of the gifted amateur, which via Oxbridge dominated sport and politics between the wars to such an extent that it was often difficult to tell where one started and the other left off, is triumphantly vindicated in this film in Banks's cool, effortless ingenuity, as it is by the absurd heroism of the agents in *The Lady Vanishes* (1938). The deadpan quality that has characterised so much of Hitchcock's filming since is well in evidence here; the upper lip is stiff, the lower one curling in a smile.

Financially, however, the most profitable film of this period was *The Private Life of Henry VIII* (1933), with Charles Laughton, produced and directed by the expatriate Hungarian Alexander Korda. £50 000 invested yielded a return of £500 000, and the first major international success of the British sound cinema. Korda's plans for the industry became more grandiose as a result; Denham Studios in Buckinghamshire was set up as a mini-Hollywood, international talents (including Clair and Sternberg) were eagerly recruited, and the industry overreached itself in the interests of blockbusting prestige, until Korda's London Films went insolvent in 1937. The alleged reason was uncertainty about whether the 1927 quota measures – 'import controls' on foreign films – would be renewed after their initial ten-year period.

It would be possible to sit through the total thirties output of all the directors hitherto mentioned without realising that Great Britain was an industrial country, with a large working-class for whom mass unemployment, appalling housing conditions, and disease were often problems; the big studios turned their back on social problems even more than in the United States. There were very few exceptions to this (ironically, one of the most significant, *The Citadel*, about a doctor with a social conscience, was produced by MGM and directed by the American King Vidor), at least in the feature-film area.

Things were very different – fortunately – in the documentary movement, which began in 1928 when the Empire Marketing Board set up a film unit headed by the Scotsman John Grierson. Grierson in fact directed only one film, *Drifters* (1929), a silent often criticised for its desiccated aesthetic treatment of the fishing industry. But his importance went far beyond this, for at the GPO he was the hub of a unit which unprecedentedly widened the subject-matter and the audience for films. It has been pointed out that politically the unit was hamstrung, by Grierson's severe Puritanism and – less debatably – by the fact that he was working for a government agency; but much about film that we now take for granted, especially concerning its educational use, is directly attributable to the unit's work. Grierson brought to England Robert Flaherty (for *Industrial Britain* (1931) and *Man of Aran* (1934)) and the versatile Brazilian Alberto Cavalcanti, responsible for the sound on *Night Mail* (1936). This, codirected by Basil Wright and Harry Watt, is a good example of the strengths and weaknesses of the documentary unit; it brought together talents from the literary (W. H. Auden) and musical (Benjamin Britten) as well as cinematic worlds, to deal with a subject that the feature cinema would have considered beyond the pale, and no doubt helped thousands to realise that their letters and parcels were delivered by other human beings. But this is in many ways the limit of its realisation; we learn precious little about them, their lives, or the social and economic conditions under which they work. The omnipresent British pragmatism that fights shy of sustained theoretical analysis is perhaps as much to blame for this as either of the other elements mentioned above.

Coalmining, broadcasting, environmental pollution, the Empire – the unit's subject-matter reads like a litany of social concerns, linked together by Grierson's idealism. 'The real internationalism is in the manias we share with each other.'[8] Naïve it may have been, but Grierson, unlike most of his British contemporaries, was at least aware of the need to extend the scope of the cinematic institution.

5 The American Sound Cinema: Up to 1939

It was Warner Brothers, perilously undercapitalised during most of the twenties, who led the way with sound, thereby establishing themselves as one of the industry's major giants. The other major combines rapidly followed suit, which was to stand them in good stead when the Depression came in 1929. It has been frequently observed that spending on entertainment tends to rise during economically grim periods, and this, coupled with the fact that sound was still a novelty, probably accounts for the continued success of the cinema through the worst crisis in the United States' history.

As in Europe, so in America one of the earliest areas in which sound was exploited was in the adaptation of plays from stage or radio to the screen. Greta Garbo was *Anna Christie* in an adaptation of Eugene O'Neill's stage play (1930), James Cagney Bottom in Max Reinhardt's *Midsummer Night's Dream* (1935) (which also featured the three-year-old Kenneth Anger, later to become a leading underground director, as one of the fairies), and W. C. Fields played Micawber in George Cukor's adaptation of Dickens's novel *David Copperfield* (1934).

Of more importance for Hollywood was the introduction of the musical, one of its best-loved genres and one that was never produced with the same consistent success elsewhere. King Vidor made striking use of Negro spirituals in *Hallelujah!* (1929), and Walt Disney right from his earliest sound cartoons made great play with the counterpoint sound and image, but the two most successful musical directors of the 1930s were European. Ernst Lubitsch came from Germany in 1923 and worked for Warners and Paramount, developing what came to be called the 'Lubitsch touch'. The witty and stylish unfolding of imbroglios that formed an important part of this owed much to the theatrical traditions of European farce. His twenties and thirties films featured such importations as Jack Buchanan, Maurice Chevalier, and Greta Garbo. Visual lightness was as important for him as light handling of plot, as in the scene from *Monte Carlo* (1930) where Jeannette Mac-Donald sings 'Beyond the Blue Horizon' from a railway train whistling through Europe.

Rouben Mamoulian came from Russia to the United States as a stage director in 1923, and was directing Schoenberg at the New York 'Met' up to 1931. He has a place in the records of film as the director of the first Technicolor feature, *Becky Sharp* (1935), but will probably be better remembered for his musicals, notably *Love Me Tonight* (with Chevalier, 1932) and *The Gay Desperado* (1936), which superimposes two genres with its gangster parodies.

Lubitsch and Mamoulian welded a European style to Hollywood resources, with results that – apart from a few exceptions such as Charles Laughton's raspberry and V-sign in *If I Had a Million* (1932) – are remorselessly tasteful. Nobody could say the same about William Berkeley Enos or Busby Berkeley, the dance director who became a director in his own right. Berkeley, in a Puritan era when the Hays Code strangled freedom of sexual expression, contrived to turn the innocent musical into a whirl of sexual abstraction. His chorus-girls, probingly photographed from high angles in patterns of dazzling fluidity and precision, form the shapes of sunflowers, violins, or sea-anemones in a way that leaves us in no doubt about the significance of the patterns. Never has Freud marked the commercial cinema more strongly than in the sequence from *The Gang's All Here* (1943) in which each chorus-girl cradles an immense banana. The plot matters little, either to Berkeley or to us; indeed, he was involved with three films based on the same play (*Gold Diggers of 1933/1935/1937*). Far more important is the self-mocking yet perfectly choreographed eroticism of the routines, among the most abiding pieces of cinematic camp.

But the name that incarnates the American musical belongs neither to a director nor – primarily – to a singer, but to a dancer: Fred Astaire. His partnership with Ginger Rogers in the 1930s made him the first musical superstar; films such as *Top Hat* (1935) or *Shall We Dance?* (1937) are still remembered for his debonair gliding grace.

Myths and the American genres

Of the three genres that were uppermost in Hollywood production of this period, the musical has the least obvious and explicit links with American society, which may paradoxically have been one of the major reasons for its success. Astaire's well-dressed effortlessness, the luxuriant sexuality of the Busby Berkeley girls, the blatant escapism of 'Beyond the Blue Horizon', were all ideal post-Depression entertainment (there is a possible parallel here with the upsurge of escapist movies – science-fiction and 'disaster' dramas such as *Jaws* and *Star Wars* – in the late seventies).

The two other dominant genres, however, relied heavily upon, as they contributed to, a myth of the individual very characteristic of America's ultra-capitalistic society. The 'man alone', a law unto himself and a solitary entrepreneur in the world of social and financial relationships, is a key figure here. Gangsters, private eyes, and Western heroes can all be seen as species of this genus, object-lessons in the importance of individualism, of looking after oneself and coping through tough, disillusioned effort with the jungle of a society that yet offered great opportunities for the strong and the determined. This myth, clearly connected with the capitalist ethic of individual effort and work, can be seen in different forms in the two other dominant genres of the period, the Western (in which it is given a nostalgic inflection) and the gangster movie (where it is more contemporary). We shall see that the roughly contemporary rise and dominance of these two genres was not merely coincidental; both chimed in different ways with the needs of between-the-wars America.

The Western

John Ford remained the principal Western director throughout the decade, which he rounded off with three major films in 1939. Most of his work was for Fox, apart from three atypically 'literary' films for RKO. *The Informer* (1935), dealing with the IRA, won particular praise, though nowadays its symbolism seems heavy. The screenplay carefully edited out the wider political references in the novel on which the film was based, and Nolan (Victor McLaglen) is presented as a lumbering oaf in accordance with the 'comic-book Irishman' stereotype. Ford's films after this widened their scope to include historical dramas and vehicles for child stars; *Wee Willie Winkie* (1937) is memorable for the scandal caused when Graham Greene wrote an article alleging that its star Shirley Temple was really an adult midget, leading to court proceedings and the bankrupting of the magazine for which he wrote.

Stagecoach, first of the memorable 'trinity' of 1939, is the archetypal Western. The essential ingredients are all there: John Wayne in one of his most enduring performances, the 'perilous journey' motif (with racist overtones – the journey is in a stagecoach across savage Indian country), the combining of a set of motley wastrels, cowards, and drunks into a cohesive unit under the pressure of danger. *Young Mr Lincoln* remains one of the most striking examples of an important Hollywood sub-genre, the 'biopic' or biographical profile of a major historical figure. Henry Fonda's performance shows how the young lawyer is father to the elder statesman; his uprightness and pertinacity in the small-town courtroom are the qualities which will lead him to the presidency. Honesty is the most successful, as well as the best, policy.

Ford turned to colour for his final 1939 film, *Drums Along the Mohawk*, in a War of Independence setting. A tendency to the sentimental and the maudlin, as frequently in his work, tends to work against his gift for vigorous action; but the use of colour is superb, and Henry Fonda's performance first-rate.

The gangster movie

The gangster film, more than any other single art-form, can be regarded as *the* characteristic product of the Depression years. Its nihilism chimed with the disillusionment and disorientation that affected society, its egotistical creed reinforced the capitalist ethic at a time when reinforcement was sorely needed, and, unlike the Western, it often gave a prominent place to members of European immigrant groups (Rico in Mervyn Leroy's *Little Caesar* of 1930, Tony Camonte in Howard Hawks's *Scarface* of 1932). Many commentators have seen gangsters like these as the first examples of the 'anti-hero', espousing negative values or no values at all in a world they recognise as absurd.

Little Caesar, famous for Edward G. Robinson's dying line at the end ('Mother of Mercy, is this the end of Rico?'), is interesting as an early epic of failure; Rico falls from underworld czar to alcoholic dosser, a fall delineated entirely without moralising. Its commercial popularity prompted a spate of imitations; machine-guns and bootlegging were big business on the screen as well as in real life, getting rich quick, by whatever means, became highly glamorous. James Cagney and Spencer Tracy became household names respectively in

William Wellman's *The Public Enemy* (1931), in which Cagney squashed a grapefruit into Mae Clarke's face, and Rowland Brown's *Quick Millions* (1931).

Scarface – loosely based on the career of Al Capone, and produced by Howard Hawks – was the first major success of Hollywood's most important director. In a forty-five-year career Howard Hawks turned his attention to Westerns, science-fiction, comedies, musicals, and war-films as well as the gangster movie, operating within yet at the same time against each genre with the scrupulous craftmanship implicit in his maxim 'A good director is one who doesn't bother you'. Beneath the differing plots and settings, the structures, the patterns of theme and construction, remain strikingly similar.

It is this deep-lying but acute individuality that caused post-war critics to single out Hawks as the classic illustration of the *auteur* theory, which stresses in Peter Wollen's words 'a core of meanings, of thematic motifs, persisting through manifold surface changes'[1], as the defining characteristic of a film-maker's work.

Many of these characteristic motifs are already in evidence in *Scarface*: the absurdity of human action, inevitably cut short by death, the difficulty of communication (the film is full of abortive telephone conversations), the camaraderie of a male group linked together by the danger to which its actions expose it. All are presented with the terse unpretentiousness and witty dialogue of the Hollywood cinema at its best. In the words of another Hawksism, 'that stuff's good, and that stuff's hard to do'.

Two of Hawks's 'action' films of the thirties are of particular interest for their probing of male camaraderie under stress. *The Road to Glory* (1936), scripted by William Faulkner and shot by Gregg Toland (one of the greatest of Hollywood cameramen), is a gripping drama of trench warfare, but without the sentimentality of, say, a Ford. The platoon's terror as their trench is undermined with explosives turns to callous relaxation as not they, but the relief guard, are blown up; camaraderie, Hawks suggests, has its boundaries, which (as Renoir also suggests in *La Grande Illusion*) cannot arbitrarily be assigned across a national or military group. In *Only Angels Have Wings* (1939), Hawks turned his attention to civil aviators, extracting a superb performance from Cary Grant.

The main gangster actors of the period were Tracy, Cagney, Edward G. Robinson, and Humphrey Bogart. Bogart sprang to fame with his performance as Duke Mantee in Archie L. Mayo's *The Petrified Forest* (1936), and then played the vicious foil to Cagney in Raoul Wash's bootlegging drama *The Roaring Twenties* (1939). The genre's popularity remained undiminished throughout the decade.

The cinema of social conscience

Films were made which demonstrated a slightly less cynical attitude to social and ethical problems than the gangster movies. This was particularly true as a result of the election of President Roosevelt in 1933 and the subsequent 'New Deal' – a series of social reforms including public works, grants to farmers, and a form of social insurance. Often the cinematic transformations were superficial; G-men (federal detectives) were simply substituted for gangsters, the basic pattern remaining the same. But there were films that probed much deeper; Fritz Lang's first American film, *Fury* (1936), begins with Spencer Tracy's wrongful arrest on a kidnapping charge, and a horrifying depiction of the fury of the mob who attempt to lynch him, then operates a devastating reversal as Tracy returns, presumed dead, and proceeds to exert *his* fury on getting the ringleaders brought to trial. . . .

Nobody can accuse Hollywood of the thirties of being short on ethical posturing. The Hays Code was followed in 1934 by the foundation of the Church-inspired Legion of Decency. Neither institution, nor all the tackling of contemporary social themes, prevented gross anti-worker bias in the treatment of strikes, the virtual ignoring of the Negro other than as servant or figure of fun, and the glamorisation of individual initiative – moral, immoral, or amoral – above all else.

The melting-pot

Among emigré directors, Lang had shown great rapidity in adapting himself to Hollywood. *Fury* was followed in 1937 by *You Only Live Once*, in which the flight of the wrongly-convicted Henry Fonda leads to the death of his lover, Sylvia Sidney, as well as his own. It is interesting to compare Lang's style of romantic fatalism with Carné's 'poetic realism' in the roughly contemporary *Le Jour se Lève*. Neither film allows us to feel the least glimmer of hope for characters shown as the victims of a Fate that preys upon their basic honesty, and – secondarily – of a society that oppresses them (Gabin's workplace, the prejudiced employer who denies Fonda a second chance). But their geography is markedly different. Gabin spends the entire film cooped up in his attic, a prisoner of his obsessive memories as much as of the police outside, while the movement of *You Only Live Once* is constantly outwards, from the prison at the beginning to the final despairing flight across country towards the border. Not all, or even most, European cinema of the period is as claustrophobically introspective as the Carné film, nor are most individualist frontier-chasing heroes so obviously foredoomed as Henry Fonda; but the contrast between the two is none the less suggestive, if only because it sheds light on how the fate-theme prominent throughout Lang's *oeuvre* adapted itself to the structures of Hollywood cinema.

Hollywood in the 1930s was just as much of a melting-pot as it had been before sound. Michael Curtiz came from Hungary via Germany, to work uninterruptedly for twenty-seven years for Warners. His record as the most productive director of the decade (forty-four films in all) owes much to Warners' efficient studio mechanism, which brooked no nonsense in its insistence on rapid output. The majority of Curtiz's thirties films turned away from the society of the time towards horror (*Doctor X*, 1932), tropical drama (*Mandalay*, 1934), or historical romance (*The Charge of the Light Brigade*, 1936). His treatment of contemporary themes distils much that is weakest about thirties Hollywood. The Negroes in *The Cabin in the Cotton* (1932) are servile stereotypes, the whites (Richard Barthelmess as a poor sharecropper, Bette Davis as a sizzling sub-Faulknerian belle) little better. A certain sanctimoniousness affects the electric-chair endings of *Twenty Thousand Years in Sing Sing* (1932), in which Spencer Tracy returns voluntarily to the prison to die for a murder committed by his lover, Bette Davis, and *Angels with Dirty Faces* (1938), where James Cagney's gangster fakes terror at the request of a priest who wants him to disillusion his youthful admirers.

None of this is to deny Curtiz's professional handling of a variety of genres, nor his role as a star-builder (Bette Davis, of whom the slogan 'nobody's as good as Bette when she's bad' was coined, is a case in point). But is is important to realise how far the Hays Code, the Legion of Decency, and the big studios' dependence on the economic and political status quo influenced choice and treatment of subject-matter in this period, more than the liberal attitudes embodied in the 'New Deal'.

The career of Columbia's most successful thirties director, Frank Capra, is exemplary in this respect. His heroes are men of bottomless integrity who succeed simply by standing up for their principles and thereby forcing others around them to recognise their own corruption. Clark Gable, the reporter in *It Happened One Night* (1934), woos and wins his runaway heiress (Claudette Colbert), and the fairy-tale received a further twist in reality when both performers won Oscars; Gary

Cooper in *Mr Deeds Goes to Town* (1936) gives away his inherited fortune, and withstands relatives who seek to denounce him as mad; James Stewart in *Mr Smith Goes to Washington* (1939) merely by being honesty incarnate drives a prominent senator to condemn the corruption of the Congress system. All this had something to do, doubtless, with post-New Deal conscience-searching, but a great deal more with the hidebound and frequently Philistine individualism of the 'self-made man'.

The role of women

Sexual topics required even more careful handling than social ones. When Samuel Goldwyn bought the rights to Lillian Hellman's play about lesbianism, *The Children's Hour*, Hays Office pressure led to its botched conversion into a straight triangle film, *These Three* (1936). *These Three* was directed by William Wyler, who like Hawks has ranged omnivorously across a variety of Hollywood genres – but there the resemblance ends. With sound, Wyler moved from action two-reelers to diligent tranposition of stage-plays to the screen, thereby acquiring a solemnity and displaying a lack of imaginativeness neither of which could ever be imputed to Hawks. By transposing *Wuthering Heights* (1939) from a Victorian to a Georgian setting (apparently for no better reason than that the costumes could be more colourful), he destroyed much of the novel's flavour and significance as a social document; and the impact of *Dead End* (1937) was blunted by Goldwyn's insistence on filming it on an elaborate studio set.

Of the three major native American genres we have identified, women were all but excluded from the Western, admitted as brazen molls or tearful lovers in the gangster film, and welcomed in high-kicking splendour in the musical, while with a few exceptions (such as Bette Davis), female sexuality in 'realist' narrative films was thwarted by the Hays Code. Two directors produced work which constitutes a major exception to this general rule – George Cukor and Josef von Sternberg.

Cukor's début as a solo director was also Katherine Hepburn's first film – *A Bill of Divorcement* (1932), with a superb performance from the by now alcoholic John Barrymore as her mentally-disturbed father, to look after whom she cancels her wedding. Most successful among Cukor's pre-war films is *Camille* (1936), with Greta Garbo as the consumptive heroine. The film's main drawback is that it is impossible to believe in Garbo as a whore (or even a courtesan), or in the ability of Robert Taylor's conventional thirties good looks to inspire a *grande passion* in her. Lighting and décor combine to soften Garbo's features far more than in her previous films, and the death sequence ranks among the most consistently successful weepies in Hollywood history.

Cukor's films do little to present woman other than in a conventionally subservient manner; for this, we must look to the Hollywood films Dietrich and Sternberg made together after *The Blue Angel* – *Morocco* (1930), *Dishonoured* (1931), *Shanghai Express* and *Blonde Venus* (1932), *The Scarlet Empress* (1934), *The Devil is a Woman* (1935). These are the last word in studio-bound extravagance – an assertion often made to back up a dismissal of them as romantic nonsense, but in fact the key to their cinematic importance. Nowhere this side of the total abandonment of linear narrative has the cinema so turned its back on naturalism, or so committed itself to the construction of an entirely self-contained world every element in which has a purely metaphorical significance (the fans in *Morocco* and the fronds and beaded curtains in *The Devil is a Woman*, for instance, both suggesting in their absurd proliferation a universe of omnipresent intrigue and concealment). The cinematic image is a pure icon, divorced from any correspondence to an external reality.

The plots are preposterously flimsy and melodramatic, chosen expressly by Sternberg so that his audience's full attention would be focused on the play of light and shade that is the hallmark of his photography. It is difficult to say how far the power of Dietrich's presence is (as Sternberg was later to claim) purely the result of this play. The fact that she was never so effective in other directors' films, and that Sternberg's post-war career was less successful than before, suggests that the use of camera and lighting had a lot to do with it, but was not the whole story.

Sternberg's later career was marked by failures and disappointments (notably his abortive 1937 adaptation of Robert Graves's *I, Claudius*), alleviated by the extraordinary *The Shanghai Gesture* (1941), in which the effete Dr Omar (Victor Mature) and Ona Munson as 'Madame Gin Sling' go some way towards redeeming Dietrich's absence; but the conclusion is inescapable that he, although a greater artist, must have been as dependent on her as she was on him.

The Dietrich persona marked a milestone in cinema history. Women had been explicitly sexual, even sexually aggressive (Jean Harlow, Mae West of 'Is that a gun you're carrying, or are ya just glad to see me?' fame), but never before thus taken the initiative in sadistically manipulating sexual situations. The final rendering of 'Falling in Love Again' in *The Blue Angel*, the Scarlet Empress's youthful fantasies of destruction epitomised by a vast Russian bell whose clapper is a man's body, are unsurpassed images of sexual perversity. The sadism of the Empress Catherine is chilling because it is a by-product of her narcissism. John Baxter's comment is perceptive:

'Like another black-plumed lady thirty years later in *Last Year in Marienbad*, she might be part of another world, a world with only one inhabitant – herself.' [2]

Dream of a different kind was evident in the spate of horror movies, mostly made for Universal Studios by European directors (such as Karl Freund) drawing on the Gothic tradition. Tod Browning, a native American and former assistant to Griffith, adapted a Transylvanian theme in *Dracula* (1931), whose studio sets no longer chill as much as the location horror of Murnau, before *Freaks* (1932), a circus melodrama in which all but two of the characters are stunted or deformed in some way, and those two (acrobat lovers) become so by the end; the man is castrated, the woman reduced to a hybrid of chicken and human. The popularity of these films, as well as of obviously more appealing genres such as the Western or the epic, in the post-Depression years gives the lie to the notion that escapism is a simple matter of shrewdly-commercialised euphoria. Forty years later, Sydney Pollack was to remind audiences in *They Shoot Horses, Don't They?* (1969) – about marathon dancing-contests in which financially desperate young people flogged themselves till they literally dropped – that the historical reality of the Depression produced its own grotesquerie and its own horror-stories.

One of the most famous of horror-films was a chance collaboration between two Englishmen. Boris Karloff had been playing bit-parts for years, James Whale had worked as a director of melodrama, before they came together on *Frankenstein* in 1931. Karloff's blundering, would-be pastoral innocence is most moving in the scene where he watches the little girl playing with flowers on the surface of a pond. The anti-hero of the gangster film is complemented here by the sympathetic monster.

Whale's other films, combining black comedy and ingenious special effects, culminate in *The Bride of Frankenstein* (1935). Elsa Lanchester plays both Mary Wollstonecraft, the author, and the central character of the story, the monster's hideously-crafted 'bride', thus appearing as her own spectral double.

Better-known than all the rest, though, even before the retrospective publicity accorded by the 1977 remake, is the 'King' of trick films. The *King Kong* that Willis H. O'Brien constructed for Ernest Schoedsack and Merian Cooper in 1933 was a tiny felt-covered dummy with a larger animated model 'doubling' in certain sequences, and the special effects pioneered opened up a whole new spectacular field to Hollywood. Kong tenderly undressing his captive Fay Wray, humiliated in chains for a city audience, or roaring defiance at the technological and military battery unleashed against him as he sits astride the Empire State Building makes this a film where even more than in *Frankenstein* the audience have an overwhelming tendency to sympathise with the monster. Unease about the repressiveness of the city meshes with unease about its insecurity (neither buildings nor aeroplanes are immune from Kong's onslaught). The film is often very funny; it is also prophetic, of trends in the cinema (the 'disaster' movies of the late seventies) as well as of city life.

Comedy

Comedy underwent a far more rapid and less piecemeal transformation as a result of sound than almost any other type of film. Many leading silent comedians simply failed to adapt, and the most famous of all remained bitterly hostile for many years. Chaplin made only two films in the decade, one of which, *City Lights* (1931), was silent except for music. The tramp character indulges his flair for slapstick in a series of meetings with a millionaire, who showers largesse on him when drunk but fails to recognise him when sober, and his devotion to women in a quixotic relationship with a blind flower-seller, for whose cure he pays. The realities of poverty, like those of sexuality, are sentimentalised; but much can be forgiven Chaplin for the moment at the end when the girl, her sight restored, identifies her shabby benefactor (the title is an incredulous 'You?') Chaplin and she gaze quiveringly at each other – and there the film ends, leaving us to provide our own resolution, or accept none at all.

Chaplin's sound début came in 1936 with *Modern Times*, a satire on industrial society which begins with a neat comic example of early Eisensteinian montage – a flock of sheep juxtaposed with commuters rushing into the subway – and incurred censorship trouble in some countries because of the scene where Chaplin picks up a red 'danger' flag that has fallen from a truck and becomes the unwitting leader of a strike procession. His reluctance for so long to concede the victory of sound may well have been due to the bland, piping voice which he was not to put to effective use until *Monsieur Verdoux* in 1947. *Modern Times* is a great screen comedy, but from the thirties onwards Chaplin was to preserve his impact only at the cost of ever fewer appearances.

Paramount immediately appreciated the comic potential of sound, signing up the Marx Brothers in 1929 after their success on Broadway with *The Coconuts* and *Animal Crackers*. *Monkey Business* (1931), *Horse Feathers* (1932), and *Duck Soup* (1933) followed; it is ironic that it was the lack of success of the last-named, one of their very best films and in its satire on nationalism the one most relevant to the time of its making, that led to their departure for MGM (Metro-Goldwyn-Mayer) in 1934. Irving Thalberg, who looked after their films there, insured against further flops by padding out the slapstick and wisecracks with romantic intrigues and musical numbers the mention of which still makes afficionados groan. Even so, these films contain some of the greatest Marx Brothers moments; few sequences have ever been better choreographed than the destruction of the performance of *Il Trovatore* at the end of *A Night at the Opera* (1935), in which the music is made to work along with the comedy instead of serving as a tedious entr'acte.

The Marx Brothers' work could justly be described as being for children of all ages. Harpo's refusal to speak (a rejection of the 'grown-up' lingual world where reality never conforms to desire) is complemented by Groucho's manic, wisecracking proliferation of language, a lunatic spate of insult (whose butt was normally the monumentally stoical Margaret Dumont) and sexual procrastination (from *Duck Soup*: 'I could dance with you until the cows came home. On second thoughts, I'd rather dance with the cows until you came home'). Chico is the only one who uses language with something approaching normal frequency (albeit with a thick Italian accent), which may be why he is the least interesting. The films continue to make us laugh, not only because of Groucho's property moustache and loping gait (the original 'silly walk'), but because their world is one where language does not have to conform to the adult order, where the mute and the compulsive talker are joint kings.

All the Marx Brothers' films involve some relatively stable world which the brothers make it their business systematically to disrupt. Laurel and Hardy operate in exactly the reverse way; both (particularly Hardy) are compulsive ingratiators, desperate to achieve petty-bourgeois acceptance as piano-movers or Christmas-tree salesmen, but perennially ending in trouble. They had perfected the style in silent films for Leo McCarey (director of *Duck Soup*), before moving into sound shorts and then into features, best-remembered among which is probably *Sons of the Desert* (1933), released in Britain as *Fraternally Yours*. Here they receive invitations to their old reunion, and insist that whatever their wives say they are going (Hardy: 'I'm the horse in this house!')

Their wives, of course, object; Laurel and Hardy, of course, dare not brazen it out, but resort to subterfuge; their eagerness to be two of the boys leads to their being found out, and the result, of course, is 'another fine mess'.

Stan Laurel, a Lancastrian by birth, and former colleague of Chaplin's with Fred Karno, was the innovator of the pair, while in David Thomson's memorable phrase '. . . on a day-to-day basis, Hardy was content to turn up and fall in the whitewash'[3]. Few comics have fallen in the whitewash better or more often, until problems with Hal Roach (their producer at MGM) led to a split in 1940; their subsequent films are not of the same standard.

The most startling *volte-face* between silents and sound turned W. C. Fields from a leading comedy-juggler into the greatest sound comedian of them all. This was originally because David O. Selznick (director of production at RKO and MGM) would not have any juggling in Fields's sound films, for which he deserves eternal gratitude. Initially in a series of Mack Sennett-produced shorts (1932/3), then in features for various directors, Fields expanded his own personality into a unique screen persona – bibulous, shifty, and grasping. The plots of his films (often written by Fields himself, under such aliases as 'Mahatma Kane Jeeves') are episodic and preposterous, but we have seen that the greatest of Hollywood cinema depends on other things than ingeniously-crafted plot. The other actors (especially women and above all children) are remorselessly upstaged in a savage pushing of the star-system to its limits. The great lines are often *non sequiturs*, or pointless asides, relying on nasal, gravelly delivery (from *The Fatal Glass of Beer*, 1933, with a snowstorm outside Fields's Klondike shack: 'Guess I'll go outside and milk the elk'; from *The Bank Dick*, 1940, in which Fields has plied with drink the investigator sent to look into 'irregularities' in his branch: 'Ya look kind of ill – let me get you a nice breaded veal cutlet with tomato sauce'). The comedy has been denounced as misogynistic, but that is only part of the picture; Fields distrusts women because they make up something like 50 per cent of the human race. No comedian has ever made less attempt to win the affection of his audience, nor taken the stance of the 'man alone' to such ferocious limits. Where Groucho is a whoopee cushion, Fields is dynamite.

It is impossible to identify his best film. It ought to have been *My Little Chickadee* (1940), in which he was joined by Mae West, but the two abrasive talents tended to detract from each other. The Sennett-produced shorts (particularly *The Pharmacist*, in which Fields's 'daughter' eats a pet cage-bird) have a surrealistic cruelty to them that became modified at feature-length. *The Man on the Flying Trapeze* (1935) is Hollywood's most vicious onslaught on the American family up to – and possibly including – Mike Nichols's *Who's Afraid of Virginia Woolf?* of 1966. *Mrs Wiggs of the Cabbage Patch* (1934) clearly wins on title, *Never Give a Sucker an Even Break* (1941) on preposterousness (Fields's whisky bottle falls out of an aeroplane window, so he unhesitatingly jumps out after it). Fields's greatest performance was undoubtedly his last; on-screen and off-screen personality fused in one glorious misanthropic *coup* when he died in 1946 . . . on Christmas Day.

Comedy films are usually attributed to stars rather than directors; even where the two coincide this remains true, for mention *A Woman of Paris* (1923) and people immediately think of 'the "Chaplin" film without Chaplin in it'. Partly this is a logical consequence of the big-studio system, with its tendency to give prominence to the star and to relegate the director to journeyman preparer of competent vehicles; partly it springs from the anarchistic streak that runs through the bulk of thirties comedy (even the Marx Brothers, superbly though they interweave, were recalcitrant individualists, and by all accounts intensely unnerving to directors as a result). Partly it has to do with the fact that the main comedy performers never appeared in other types of movie, lacking even the minimal mobility that took John Wayne from Western to war-film and back, and thus tended to appropriate their films to themselves.

The major exception to all this was the so-called 'screwball' comedy, a genre which reached its peak in wartime but was presaged by two Hawks comedies of the thirties. Hawks's *Twentieth Century* (1934) parodies Hollywood as many later 'screwballs' were to do in a superb comic duologue between 'producer' John Barrymore and 'star' Carole Lombard. This was followed four years later by *Bringing Up Baby*, whose plot involves a dinosaur bone of crucial scientific importance, mistaken identity between a missing pet leopard and a dangerous escaped one, a whimsical pet dog, and a myopic zoologist. Fields could hardly have done better in the realm of the implausible, but Hawks, drawing superb performances from Cary Grant (alternately tender and incensed as the 'absent-minded professor') and Katharine Hepburn (revealing ever more intelligence beneath the scatty rich-girl façade as the film goes on) makes of it a good deal more than another crazy comedy. It confronted the socialite and the academic scale of values, and unmaliciously revealed neither to be adequate (the academic scale literally falls apart with the collapse of Grant's dinosaur at the end), and the scene in which circumstances force Grant to don women's clothing and he blurts out by way of explanation: 'Well, I . . . I just went gay all of a sudden!' is one of the most perceptive as well as one of the funniest examples of sexual ambiguity. *Bringing Up Baby* shows that great screen comedy does not need to be the purely individualistic matter as which it is often regarded.

The stars – Grant, Hepburn, Wayne, Gable, Davis, Dietrich, Bogart, Tracy – came more numerous and more brightly into the foreground of thirties Hollywood; the directors have to some extent been rescued from relative obscurity by the *auteur* theory and developments from it. But power remained overwhelmingly with the studios and their producers. Irving Thalberg, who never appeared in or directed a film, and refused even to have his name on the credits, was more influential on the Hollywood institution, on the financial and administrative machinery of thirties American cinema and its repercussions on the films made, than any of the stars or directors whose work we have looked at. (A producer puts up the money for a film and has overall control in the last resort. A director is in charge of the actual shooting and today, with certain exceptions such as Val Lewton, is regarded as the 'maker' of the movie.) It was Thalberg who intensified company control over products by instituting the producer as middleman between MGM and the director, a move whose effects on Hollywood were decisive. Samuel Goldwyn, of 'A verbal contract isn't worth the paper it's written on' fame, who after selling out his own company moved to United Artists, David O. Selznick who moved from RKO to MGM to Selznick International Pictures, Louis B. Mayer whose commercial flair worked in tandem with his execrable taste to keep MGM's bank-balance high even when the quality of its product was low – these men exercised equivalent power, but it would be as dangerous to fetishise their importance as individuals as to forget their existence in star- and director-struck absorption. They were the most powerful cogs in a machine not they, but the market, operated. Who 'made' (as movie or as success) *Gone with the Wind* (1939)? – Vivien Leigh as Scarlett O'Hara? George Cukor, Sam Wood, or Victor Fleming, the three directors who at various stages worked on it? Clark Gable as Rhett Butler? The scriptwriters, too numerous to mention? Selznick himself, who personally took control of the whole film and ruthlessly engineered its flamboyance, then watched $70 000 000-worth of profits (USA and Canada alone) go to MGM, to whom he was heavily mortgaged? Selznick, clearly, has a stronger claim than any of the others; but all were interdependent, and in their turn dependent on the vagaries of the market.

6 The War Years

The Second World War did more to European cinema than transform the industry into a vast propaganda machine. Blackouts, requisitioning of premises, calling-up of performers and technicians, and general economic scarcity obviously had an immense effect on the industry, but even during the height of the Blitz London cinemas were constantly packed, and actually became places of refuge as well as entertainment. And the development of the documentary was of great importance to the propaganda machine.

The GPO Film Unit, taken over by the newly-created Ministry of Information in 1940, developed into a versatile and flexible mechanism for disseminating information. Harry Watt's *Target for Tonight* (1941), describing the preparation and execution of a bombing-raid over Germany, had considerable morale-boosting value; his pilots and navigators go quietly about their business with no suggestion of any qualms about, or even awareness of, their purpose, and the Englishman remains classically unruffled under stress. The follow-up, *Nine Men* (1943), was in fact a fiction film, mocking up a drama of nine soldiers stranded in Libya, but it scrupulously adhered to the conventions and appearances of documentary.

Humphrey Jennings came to the Documentary Unit from surrealist painting, the study of anthropology and psychoanalysis, history, and literary criticism – an intellectual versatility atypically English, but bound together by his desire in Kathleen Raine's phrase 'to discover and reactivate the collective symbols of Engand' [1], to understand and add to the emblems of national self-consciousness. This desire rested upon the view of culture and society as organic wholes that has characterised much twentieth-century English intellectual life (the work of F. R. Leavis in literary criticism is perhaps the most striking example). This may go some way towards explaining why he was the outstanding English documentary director, at least of the war years. *Listen to Britain* (1941) ranged across a country threatened with imminent invasion; *Fires Were Started* (1943) deals with the Auxiliary Fire Service in the Blitz, a documentary reconstruction that was to win admiration from Italian neo-realist directors. *Diary for Timothy* (1945), with commentary by E. M. Forster, weaves around the day-to-day life of a baby towards the end of the war a panorama of other lives (including an air-pilot and a coal-miner, both badly injured). Documentary-realist conventions (absence of a script, use of 'real-life' actors) mingle with a slightly academic but still striking use of montage (a conversation about V-bombing linked to the graveyard scene from *Hamlet* via the sound of a bomb exploding). Such moments reinforce Jennings's claim to be the outstanding British 'war-poet' of the Second World War.

The documentary movement in these years retained what we have seen to be its distinctive characteristics – use of prominent artists from other media, a radicalism implicit in its treatment of the lives of working people, but lacking in real political bite, a very 'English' liberal sensitivity of which the involvement of Forster with *A Diary for Timothy* may serve as an indication – and, doubtless emboldened by its now centrally important position, developed these qualities more freely and poetically than before. It even came up with one of the great British screen comedians, Richard Massingham, in the unlikely medium of short Ministry of Information films warning against extravagant use of water in the bath, or the coughs and sneezes that spread diseases (in this film Massingham is seen coerced into using his handkerchief by being doused in pepper). Massingham – in this respect a precursor of the Goon Show/Monty Python tradition of British humour – pushes English whimsy towards genuine surrealism by his exaggeration (he has breakfast in bed on a pedestrian crossing in a film exhorting us not to dawdle when crossing the road), and his interest in the physical surface properties of things. In *Another Case of Poisoning* (1949), the flies crawling over pork-pies in a shop-window do go some way towards justifying the French critic Henri Langlois's otherwise rather grandiloquent comparison with Buñuel.

Balcon's Ealing Studios were fully involved in the war effort, via low-budget features as well as documentaries; Balcon's economical style of production stood him in good stead. By contrast, the Rank Organisation – object of a Monopoly Commission investigation in 1943 – went in for lavish studio-bound films at a time when they were financially and socially inappropriate, for which it earned much opprobrium. Certainly it is difficult to see how James Mason chastising Margaret Lockwood's treacherous actress with a riding-whip in Leslie Arliss's *The Man in Grey* (1943) could have helped in the struggle against Nazism. Rank did produce Noel Coward's *In Which We Serve* (1942), whose romanticised portrayal of service life earned him a special Academy Award despite his racist sneering at 'macaronis', and acted as distributor for the films made by Michael Powell and Emeric Pressburger (nicknamed 'the Archers'), which included *One of Our Aircraft is Missing* (1942), and the extraordinary *A Canterbury Tale* (1944), in which a zealous magistrate pours glue into the hair of Kent girls for fear that they may seduce the local troops. But by and large Rank's effect was a pernicious one, economically as well as in other directions.

The other side

Before going on to examine developments in the other major cinema industries on the Allied side, we shall glance at the German industry, predictably subservient to the Nazi machine throughout this period.

It may appear at first surprising that 1000 of the 1097 feature films made in Germany under the Nazi régime were *not* commissioned by the Ministry of Propaganda; but this betokens, not any independence from government control, but rather a shrewd sense of the market and a control so pervasive and omnipresent as to make overt ministerial intervention largely unnecessary. Propaganda features from the outset lost money, so Goebbels ('Mickey Mouse' to the industry) relied heavily on newsreels, which ran for up to forty-five minutes. The feature films shown with these continued the original Nazi practice of using standard genre formats with a gross pro-Nazi bias.

Biographical pictures distorted their subjects beyond recognition; Veit Harlan's *Der Grösse König* (*The Great King*, 1942) relates the story of Frederick the Great in a way that deliberately invites comparison with Hitler, and even Emil Jannings's fictional steel magnate in Harlan's *Der Herrscher* (*The Ruler*, 1937) makes a demagogic speech about the virtues of leadership and insists that his employees call him 'Führer' . . . *Ich Klage An* (*I Accuse* – Wolfgang Libeneiner, 1941) incorporates a plea for the policy of euthanasia through its tear-jerking tale of a doctor's mercy-killing of his suffering wife. War films, in whose titles the word 'Kameraden' appears with grotesque frequency, unsubtly exalted national pride and a virile brotherhood bordering on the pederastic, in which they followed such early Ministry-commissioned features as *Hitlerjunge Quex* (1933). Quex (played by an unnamed Hitler Youth militant) renounces the slatternly, debauched Young Communists in favour of the Hitler Youth's golden locks and pristine kneecaps, for whose cause he dies a martyr.

The greatest asset of these films is their mind-numbing tedium, particularly when shown in tandem with Goebbels's newsreels; comradeship, obedience, nationalism, and leadership were unceasingly projected through the twin (and in a Fascist context equally meaningless) spectra of 'fiction' and 'fact'. As cinema, as one might expect, they are rubbish, but the Nazi industry does have the unwanted distinction of having inaugurated a new 'sub-genre': the racist film. The Jews, needless to say, were the principal target, notably in Harlan's *Jud Süss* (1940). This 'historical' melodrama recounts how the province of Wurtemberg comes under the thrall of the Jews (vanquished and expelled at the end), after its Grand Duke has enlisted the moneylender Süss Oppenheimer as his Finance Minister. The Jews, predictably, are presented as unkempt and lecherous parasites, but this is carried out with considerable skill, and Ferdinand Marian and Werner Krauss give extraordinary performances as Süss and his secretary. Harlan burnt all available copies of the film after the war in an attempt to rehabilitate himself, though a few still survive.

The British came in for much the same treatment in *Ohm Krüger* (1941), a pro-Boer account of the war in South Africa, in which Ferdinand Marian again does his greasy, insinuating number, this time (with considerable historical justification) as Cecil Rhodes. But perhaps the apogee of Third Reich cinema is Harlan's *Kolberg* (1945), not least because of the conditions of its production. While the Reich crumbled, Goebbels devoted a fortune to the making of this spectacular film about the resistance of the city of Kolberg to the Napoleonic troops. (In real life, the city fell, but in the film, of course, it holds triumphantly out.) A hundred railcars of salt were diverted to the film-set for use as property snow while the population starved; blank bullets for the film were manufactured in preference to real ones, although there was no more ammunition for the Eastern Front. The film was completed in 1945, by which time hardly any cinemas were open and the 'première' took the form of a copy parachuted in to the beleaguered garrison at La Rochelle. No more spectacularly grisly farce can have been enacted in the history of art.

France

The French cinema suffered badly during the Occupation (not least with the departure of Clair and Renoir to the United States), but was still able to function as an industry, largely because the imported German films were so bad that nobody went to see them. Censorship was heavy, and funds and manpower in short supply, but Marcel Carné was able to circumvent both problems in *Les Visiteurs du Soir* (*Evening Visitors*, 1942) and *Les Enfants du Paradis* (*Children of the Gods*, 1945). The former film is a startling mirror-image of what the critic André Bazin called the 'poetic realism' of his pre-war films. The setting is a lavish medieval castle, visited by the Devil (Jules Berry at his most malevolent) and his assistant (Arletty at her most wearily worldly-wise); they turn the recalcitrant pair of lovers to stone at the end, but their hearts persist in beating no matter how hard the hysterical Berry whips them. Fatalism in a modern setting is replaced by a somewhat precious medieval allegory of hope, seen by many – rather tendentiously – as an oblique allusion to the invincibility of the Resistance.

Les Enfants du Paradis plays for three-and-a-quarter hours and was three years in the making. Part of the reason for this is that for as long as the actors and crew were in the studio they were exempt from conscription – a great cinematic instance of a virtue made out of necessity. The film is set in the Boulevard du Temple, the main theatre street of Paris in the 1840s, and theatricality is its visual and thematic mainspring. It has survived primarily for its superb performances – Arletty (Garance) loved and lost, Louis Salou haughty as the rich Count who protects her, and above all Jean-Louis Barrault as the mime Debureau (an innocent reminiscent in his deeper wisdom of Dostoevsky's 'idiot' Prince Myshkin) and Marcel Herrand as the nihilistic Lacenaire, poet and criminal, whose real-life original inspired Dostoevsky. Its dialogue (by Prévert) has the barbed elegance of the best nineteenth-century comedy, and its settings are invariably theatrical, whether on a stage (Pierre Brasseur mercilessly burlesquing a bad melodrama in which he is constrained to act), outside in the street (the final sequence in which Barrault vainly pursues Arletty through the throng of masked carnival revellers), or in between (Barrault denouncing a pickpocket by mime on the small stage outside his theatre at the beginning). Never for a moment does this become tedious – partly because of the sheer variety of sets and actors, partly because of the contrast between Debureau and Lacenaire, between the sensitivity powerless to act effectively and that powerless to act other than destructively. Lacenaire sated by his final 'performance' as he waits calmly in the Turkish bath where he has just murdered the Count looks forward to the violent universe of the post-war years, the ethical and existential ambiguities of writers such as Camus and Sartre and of film-directors such as Godard whose work we shall discuss in Chaps. 10 and 12.

Prévert also scripted Jean Grémillon's *Lumière d'Été* (*Summer Light*, 1942), a doleful allegory set in an aristocratic castle, far more typical than *Les Enfants du Paradis* of the wartime French cinema. Cocteau's baroque perversity was in its element with the Serge Poligny-directed *Le Baron Fantôme* (1943), again revolving around a château in which a nobleman disappears and a gamekeeper pretends to be the Dauphin. Jean Delannoy directed *L'Éternel Retour* (*The Eternal Return*, 1943), though one needs constantly to remind oneself of the fact, so pervasive is the Cocteau imprint. It was this film that Richard Winnington inveighed against as a 'dolorous bag of tricks . . . often superbly beautiful in its execution, but rotted'[2], influenced no doubt by the choice of the Tristan and Isolde legend which he saw as tacit evidence of collaboration. Even so, one cannot but sympathise with his reaction; the musty mystery brew distilled by Cocteau, Poligny, Jacques Becker *et al* palls very rapidly.

The dangers of contemporary subject-matter were graphically illustrated by Henri-Georges Clouzot's *Le Corbeau* (= 'crow'; also French slang for 'poison-pen'), of 1943, about malicious letters in a small provincial town – the kind of material Claude Chabrol was later to make his own. The malice distilled by the film was eagerly taken up by the Nazis as proof of French decadence, and after the Liberation Clouzot had immense difficulty in resuming his career.

Robert Bresson made his first major film in 1945, *Les Dames du Bois de Boulogne*, based on an episode from a Diderot novel, with dialogue by the omnipresent Cocteau. This clearly marked a major new development in French cinema – in the importance attached to fidelity to and presentation of verbal text, in the starkness of the décor – neither evocative nor 'realistic' – and above all in the austere photography of faces, with its concentration on the soul rather than the psyche. Bresson was to be a leading figure in the French revival of the next two decades.

Russia

The Soviet industry was monolithically mobilised behind the war effort after the German invasion of 1941. Studios were evacuated to the East, where feature production went on apace. Newsreels were also prominent, and some of them, such as *The Defeat of the German Armies near Moscow* of 1942, were sold to America (where English commentaries were of course dubbed). Few wartime features have survived (few were probably intended to), apart from the final part of the Gorky trilogy, *My Universities* (1940), which Donskoi followed with *The Rainbow* (1944), about Ukrainian partisans, and Eisenstein's swan-song, *Ivan the Terrible* (1944–1946).

Of all Eisenstein's films, this is the one from which collision of images, which formed the backbone of the 'montage' in his earlier theoretical writings, is most largely absent, in which the single image as icon (literally so in the cathedral scenes) assumes the greatest importance. The story of the sixteenth-century Emperor is told in images of such barbarous ecstasy that the colour scenes in Part Two (filmed thus simply because some colour footage suddenly happened to become available) appear superfluous, a gilding of a bizarre and exotic lily. Nikolai Cherkassov as Ivan was clad in costumes so heavy and elaborate that he collapsed from exhaustion, and the brooding contrasts of light and shade intensify the Gothic visual power of the film. *Ivan* now seems to have more to do with the Sternberg/Dietrich films than with an aesthetic based on Marxist dialectic, with the ecstasy of the single image than with the conceptual framework elaborated in its director's theoretical writings.

Stalin's paranoia was such that by 1946 he suppressed the second part of what was to have been a trilogy (no doubt suspecting allusions to his own tyranny). Eisenstein, desperately ill after a heart attack, was forced to sign a humiliating disclaimer, and, mentally and physically exhausted, died in 1948, his project uncompleted.

Critics have found it difficult to deal satisfactorily with Eisenstein. No other cinematic figure could unquestionably rank among both the greatest theorists and the greatest directors in the history of the medium; yet the passages in his films which best illustrate his theories (e.g., the matching of image and music in *Alexander Nevsky*) are often those that seem the most laboured, while his theories often rely on rather mechanistic ideas of audience response and of film-as-language. But nobody in pre-1960s film history produced propaganda works that were such exciting works of art, nor has anybody until very recently made so serious and sustained an effort to ascertain how the cinema relates to other, not merely aesthetic, disciplines. He remains one of the greatest figures in the history of revolutionary aesthetics as well as in that of the cinema.

Wartime Hollywood

The war affected Hollywood less than it did European industries. Leading directors such as Ford, Capra, and the young John Huston made documentaries about it, many others incorporated it into their subject-matter, but it made very little difference to the basic structure and functioning of the industry, nor to the established genres, whose 'goodie/baddie' conflicts could often be transferred intact to war-films.

This does not mean that there were not individual directors who reached their peak in the war years, many of them European ex-patriates. William Wyler in *The Little Foxes* (1941) filmed a Lillian Hellman play about an avaricious Southern family, and against a quaintly idealised British background in *Mrs Miniver* (1942) achieved considerable tension as well as tenderness, notably in the scene between the Nazi pilot and Mrs Miniver.

Wyler's career was to reach its peak in 1946 with *The Best Years of our Lives*, which relates the readaptation to civilian life of a soldier, a sailor, and an airman with a developed use of deep-focus and a flexible yet unobtrusive use of camera-movements that mark his major contribution to cinematic language and art.

Michael Curtiz also made creative use of his 'exile' with *Mission to Moscow* (1943), a rather disingenuous contrast of Nazism and Stalinism and one of the few American films to endorse the latter, and, above all, *Casablanca* (also 1943). Alan G. Barbour's description of this as '*the* representative film of the forties'[3] has sound justification. It orchestrates around a melodramatic wartime plot some of the finest actors of the period (Peter Lorre, Paul Henreid, Claude Rains, Sidney Greenstreet, Ingrid Bergman, and Humphrey Bogart); its dialogue plays romantic sentimentality and taut cynicism off in the best Hollywood tradition; it gets maximum mileage out of a popular song ('As Time Goes By') whose long-term success it ensured; and Rick's Café, a cosmopolitan enclave whose habitués come and go in accordance with the rules they have prescribed for themselves, cannot implausibly be seen as a microcosm of wartime Hollywood, likewise international and nihilistic but for the profit motive and conventions of genre.

The film elevated Bogart from star to superstar, simply by bringing out the vulnerability and tenderness that had always been the unavowed other side of his hard-bitten cynicism. After thirty-three years, audiences still choke back a tear (the approved Bogartian reaction) when he bids Ingrid Bergman farewell at the airport with: 'Here's looking at you, kid.'

Bogart had made a major impact two years before, in John Huston's feature début *The Maltese Falcon*. The performances are as memorable as those in *Casablanca*, from Bogart as the cynical-but-loyal private eye Sam Spade, the sinisterly bloated Sydney Greenstreet leading the search for the bejewelled falcon of the title, and Peter Lorre camping it up as his accomplice. The plot is so complicated as to become virtually irrelevant, a common feature of gangster films of this period (the makers of *The Big Sleep* had to telephone the author, Raymond Chandler, to clarify who committed one of the film's many murders).

Bogie acted again for Huston in *Across the Pacific* (1942), whose patriotic ending prefigured Huston's involvement with the documentary during the rest of the war, and for Curtiz in *Passage to Marseilles* (1944), a 'Chinese box' of flashbacks that transposes gangster-film incomprehensibility to the war-movie, before the first of his master-pieces for Howard Hawks, *To Have and Have Not* (1945). As so often in Hollywood, on- and off-screen reality interwove as Bogart and his co-star Lauren Bacall (twenty-seven years younger) fell in love, which contributed both to the myth of the movie and to the electricity of the scenes between them (Bacall to Bogart as she leaves his room: 'If you want me, just whistle. You know how to whistle, don't you? You just put your lips together – and blow.'). The film remains a triumph for Hawks as well as Bogart, in its handling of the relationship between Bogie and his devoted alcoholic shipmate Walter Brennan, and in its impeccable walking of the tightrope between straight thriller and comic melodrama. If forties Hollywood had given us only this and *Casablanca*, it would deserve to be remembered.

Hawks alone gave us much more during the war, notably the flying-dramas *Only Angels Have Wings* (1939) and *Air Force* (1943), the first of which features a superbly ambivalent performance from Cary Grant. Grant had been a star-name since the mid-thirties, and displayed astonishing versatility and staying-power until his retirement in 1966. Intelligent urbanity and a superb sense of timing largely account for this, but David Thomson's comment goes to the heart of it:

'The essence of his quality can be put quite simply: he can be attractive and unattractive simultaneously; there is a light and dark side to him but, whichever is dominant, the other one creeps into view.'[4]

This is true of the Hawks film, where he oscillated between the *macho* and the debonair, but the best illustration of it is in the problems posed for RKO by Hitchcock's *Suspicion* (1941). The original intention was that he should have been plotting to murder his wife (Joan Fontaine); but RKO vetoed the idea that he should play a murderer, so the ending was altered accordingly. It is a remarkable tribute to Grant's ambiguity that the altered ending should blend in so well with the rest of the film.

Hitchcock began the decade with two adaptations of Daphne du Maurier. *Jamaica Inn* (1939) and, particularly, *Rebecca* (1940), are both considerable improvements on their meretricious originals, thanks to Hitchcock's visual flair (as in the final conflagration in *Rebecca*) and taste for discreet self-parody. His other wartime work is erratic: *Lifeboat* (1944) takes place within the smallest space of any film ever (a boat adrift at sea), but its lacklustre studio reconstruction breaks no other records, and not until *Notorious* (released in 1946, two years after its making), a convoluted drama of spying and jealousy bringing together Grant and Bergman, did he return to what is generally regarded as his best form.

Grant was reunited with his *Bringing Up Baby* sparring-partner Katharine Hepburn in Cukor's *The Philadelphia Story* (1940), in which her acerbic intelligence once again complemented his perfectly. James Stewart won an Academy Award for his role as Hepburn's would-be husband, and the film was probably the best of Cukor's wartime output.

John Ford too devoted much of his energy in this period to documentary-making, the major exception being *They Were Expendable* (1945), about the 1941 American retreat from the Philippines. Much about this film is embarrassingly chauvinistic, not least its deification of General Macarthur; but the chauvinism is muted by comradeship in the face of defeat, in accordance with the mingled stoicism and sadness implied in the title.

It was at the instigation of documentary-maker Robert Flaherty that Renoir came to the USA in 1940, to make his début in the following year with *Swamp Water*. This melodrama of jealousy, shot entirely on location in Georgia, was followed by *This Land is Mine* (1943) and *The Southerner* (1945). Renoir's American films, many of which were quite successful commercially, at first sight provide striking confirmation of the *auteur* theory; the importance of water, of nature (plants and animals), of the melodramatic in the everyday, are as vividly in evidence in *Swamp Water* as they had been in *Toni*. But Eric Rohmer detected in *The Southerner* 'the shadow of a great moral or metaphysical idea . . . of a *God* with whom Renoir's work up to this period has hardly been concerned at all'[5]. The full relevance of this development (not necessarily a felicitous one) will become plain when we discuss *The River* of 1950; for the moment it is enough to note how the impact of working in a country where (to quote Rohmer again) 'the grandeur of man resides not in abandoning himself to nature but in defying it, dominating it' comes through in Renoir's work, both in its subject-matter and in its arrangement of images.

Billy Wilder is not usually thought of as an 'emigré', yet he had a long scriptwriting record in the German industry before arriving in America in 1938. He has invariably scripted his own movies, which is exceedingly rare in Hollywood; they have both gained (he is a master of memorable dialogue) and lost (he is too complaisant towards his own inventions, too prone to include a brilliant exchange for its own sake at the expense of the scene as a whole) as a result. *Double Indemnity* (1944) is a taut and cynical thriller, *The Lost Weekend* (1945) was the first major Hollywood film to treat alcoholism as tragedy and pathology rather than as a source of embarrassment issuing indifferently in laughter or moralising. Ray Milland's performance deserved its Oscar, and a tabooed subject became accessible to serious treatment; but Paramount insisted on tacking on a quite inapposite happy ending. The bleak power of Milland's performance far outweighs this in retrospect.

The horror movie and the musical retained their thirties popularity as complementary escape-valves in times of stress. The outstanding horror name was not a director, but a producer – Val Lewton. Lewton tends to be regarded as the real *auteur* of the low-budget B-features he produced, often in under a month, for RKO with such directors as Jacques Tourneur (*Cat People*, 1943) and Robert Wise (*The Body Snatcher*, 1945). These films well distil one of Hollywood's greatest strengths – the capacity to produce atmosphere, notwithstanding preposterous plots and often cut-price acting, through what James Agee described in another context as 'a general quality of tension and pleasure in good craftmanship'[6]. Alongside the Hollywood myth of lavish spectaculars and highly-paid superstars, there grew up – in no small measure thanks to films like Lewton's – a complementary myth, that of the low-budget 'B' picture, whose influence on French directors in particular was to be immense.

The musical and MGM went together during the forties, through the interaction of two men – the producer Arthur Freed and the director Vincente Minnelli – and one woman – Minnelli's then-wife Judy Garland, who made her début for him in *Meet Me in St Louis* (1944), and graduated from teenage to adult star with her rendering of 'The Trolley Song'. Minnelli had preceded this with *Cabin in the Sky* (1943), in which Lena Horne led an all-Negro cast. Busby Berkeley, Norman Taurog, and even Norman Z. McLeod (of early Marx Brothers fame) also became associated with the 'MGM sound' thanks to Freed's lyric-writing enterprise, and his skill as a talent-spotter, which caused his musicals to stand out from the rather bland MGM run. We shall see how they continued to exert influence until the virtual demise of the genre in the fifties.

Screwball comedies

After ten years as a Paramount screenwriter, Preston Sturges in 1940 offered them a free screenplay if he could direct it himself. *The Great McGinty* was the first of the 'screwball' comedies that dominated wartime Hollywood humour. Their characters are often rich, treated like those in Scott Fitzgerald's novels with an uneasy blend of fascination and mockery; the hedonistic antics of the 'Ale and Quail Club' in *Palm Beach Story* (1942) serve as a good example. The chaotic speed of the largely episodic plots is intensified by the prodigious speed of the camera-movements, but Sturges avoids the pointless zaniness that bedevilled his imitators by constant mocking reference to American institutions. Puritanism and the fertility-cult are adroitly played off in *The Miracle of Morgan's Creek* (1944), about a girl by the name of Kockenlocker who when drunk at a party gets pregnant, but is saved from disaster when she gives birth to sextuplets and becomes a national hero. The paranoia of the wealthy feeds on itself in *The Lady Eve* (1941), in which the heir played by Henry Fonda so determinedly isolates himself from the other passengers on a liner that he attracts the special attentions of a confidence-trickster, and then of his daughter, whence the happy romantic resolution.

But the most interesting Sturges comedy to a modern audience is *Sullivan's Travels* (1942), for its mockery of the Hollywood institution. The film director Sullivan, deciding to abandon the frivolous musicals he has been making for a cinema of social conscience, has great difficulty maintaining his incognito in the world of the poor until a misunderstanding sends him to jail. Watching prisoners laughing at a Mickey Mouse cartoon, he concludes that audiences are simply not interested in social justice, and that his studio colleagues have been right in their assertions that the cinema is essentially for escape and entertainment. The irony is difficult to localise – it may be at the expense of Sullivan's ingenuousness, or based on the folly of those companies (such as Warner Brothers) who imagined that films about the poor could ever interest anybody, or aimed at Hollywood's heartlessness. The ambiguity of the film probably accounts for its continued interest, as well as the quality of the shooting and acting (Joel McCrea, Veronica Lake, and a repertory supporting cast who figure in most of Sturges's films.

Welles/Kane: a legend in his lifetime

The greatest new director of the war years also relied upon his own company of actors. Orson Welles built the company up around him at New York's Mercury Theatre and also for the radio, where he became notorious for an adaptation of *The War of the Worlds* so realistically presented that it caused nationwide panic.

In 1941, RKO gave him complete freedom to direct *Citizen Kane* from a magnificent screenplay by Herman J. Mankiewicz. The film was very nearly never seen; William Randolph Hearst took Welles's tale of the (intermittent) public triumphs and private anguish of a newspaper tycoon who branches out into politics and culture as a reference to himself, and the abject Louis B. Mayer offered to buy out the producers and destroy the negative. They had the good sense to refuse.

The legendary power of the film has nowhere been better illustrated than in the flashback scene from Truffaut's *La Nuit Américaine* in which the boy (later to become a director) sneaks up to a cinema at night to steal a *Citizen Kane* publicity poster; no other film would have had the requisite mythical resonance. Welles (like Kane) is/was a consummate egoist, and every second of the film bears his authorial stamp; at the same time, the interplay of scriptwriter, cameraman (Gregg Toland who had worked with William Wyler), composer (Bernard Herrmann), co-producer (John Houseman), and cast (including Everett Sloane and Joseph Cotten) – almost all new cinema names – is integral to the work's success. Welles and Toland between them evolved a camera-style that Americanises German Expressionism, in its heavy chiaroscuro (contrast of light and dark), use of décor as a frame within the frame on the screen (as when the ceiling is visible in many of the fraught Kane *ménage* scenes), distortion via camera-angle, and above all use of deep-focus to develop the action spatially as well as temporally. Kane's rampage through the corridors of his castle Xanadu when his second wife has left him is among the most memorable examples of this; we see him suddenly become calm, mutter the word 'Rosebud', and walk forward, apparently endlessly, through a corridor of bemused attendants. Expressionism here nurtures the romantic side of the American individualist myth; the man alone is revealed, through lighting and the composition of the set as well as the acting, as a tragic figure, albeit a self-willed and self-dramatised one. Robert G. Porfirio sees both the film's visual style and its 'morally ambiguous hero'[7] as an early example of the *film noir* – the convoluted, gloomy blend of German Expressionism with Hollywood conventions that became a dominant sub-genre in the late forties.

The development of the narrative on two or more simultaneous levels by the use of deep-focus is complemented by rapid cuts denoting progress in time, as in the succession of tableaux depicting the break-up of Kane's first marriage, each at a different time but the same breakfast-table. The use of flashback, particularly subjective flashback (the same event seen through different people's eyes), remains almost unprecedentedly extensive. The whole film can indeed be seen as a gigantically wilful effort by Kane to impose his own view of (and on) the personal and political events it narrates, most strikingly in the sequence where his second wife, Susan, makes her début in opera – at Kane's insistence and with his backing – and we hear her frail tones die away in an embarrassed silence broken only by Kane's wild applause, but also in the account of his political ambitions and refusal to admit their thwarting when he is sexually compromised, until the ballot-box leaves him no choice.

Flashbacks within flashbacks, unexampled skill in the development of narrative, across time and within the space of the image, varied use of frames-within-frames (particularly in the theatre and library scenes); the film remains thrilling and stimulating to watch, at the same time as its romanticisation of the individualist hero constitutes a piquantly ambiguous comment on twenties and thirties America. The two aspects fuse in the final shot, half-dimissed by Welles himself as 'dollar-book Freud' but a key moment in cinematic narrative. The journalist who has spent the film in an attempt to discover the sense of Kane's dying word, 'Rosebud' – it is through his investigations and questioning of Kane's associates that the story is unrolled – renounces his fruitless quest and goes home. The lumber from Xanadu is piled up to be burnt. As the flames lick higher, the camera homes in on Kane's childhood sled, taken away from him by force in the earliest of the flashback scenes we see, when his guardian comes with the news of his parents' unexpected wealth and takes the young Kane, against his will, to New York so that he shall make the best use of the opportunity thus offered. Kane lashes out at Thatcher with the sled, but we do not see the name on it until the very end of the film, when 'Rosebud' fills the screen just before it is consumed by the flames. . . . Fuel, obviously, for the myth of the ruthless but ultimately soft-hearted individualist (a comparison with the Bogart persona is interesting), but also a moment that turns us from apparently passive consumers 'outside' the film into the only repositories of its secret. The camera here tells us what the film hitherto has failed to discover – the *secret* of the ending's extraordinary power.

Citizen Kane received immense critical acclaim, but did not do particularly well at the box-office, setting the tone for the rest of Welles's career, which has become legendary for its record of maimed, abortive, and uncompleted projects. His second film, *The Magnificent Ambersons* (1942), was cut by RKO from 148 to 88 minutes. Based on a novel by Booth Tarkington, it relates the decline of an old-school middle-American bourgeois family during industrialisation, following notably the fortunes of the scapegrace heir George. Decline and failure, already strongly marked themes in *Kane*, become more plainly so here, thrown into ominous relief by Welles's own problems with the studio system of which he was yet one of the most remarkable products. *Casablanca* may be the decade's most typical film, but Welles/Kane was in many ways its, and Hollywood's, most strikingly typical product.

7 Hollywood, 1945 to 1955:
Paranoia and Decline

To have predicted to anybody involved with Hollywood in 1946 that the industry was about to go into a severe financial and artistic decline would have appeared the height of folly. The American cinema had emerged from the war as the most rapidly and arrogantly successful mass-entertainment institution of all time. Within ten years – the period to be analysed in this chapter – audiences had halved, the vast production and distribution concerns were in the process of decomposition, and much of the industry's best talent was either blacklisted or in exile.

The reasons for this now seem all too obvious. Hollywood was clearly riding for a fall. Anti-trust actions, started against MGM and Paramount after the war, forced the major studios to separate production and distribution, and brought to birth a new species of entrepreneur, the independent producer, who financed films through advances from the distribution chains. This meant that performers could no longer rest snugly in big-studio security; the realities of the market economy, ever-present, were more obviously so now.

A bigger threat was television, the prime reason for the halving of audiences between 1946 and 1956. Hollywood's reaction was predictable: initial derison, followed by a frantic casting around for technological counter-attractions. The drive-in cinema, launched at the end of the forties, was not to reach its full mythical glory until the greater teenage independence of the fifties, but it did play its part in reaching a younger clientele. The big year was 1952, which saw the advent of 'three-dimensional' cinema. Most 3-D films, as they came to be known, were artistically meretricious and about as plausible as the figurines in children's cardboard cut-out theatres. To get the full effect, audiences had to wear special glasses, pair after pair of which left cinemas never to return. It is not surprising that this turned out to be the original cinematic nine-days' wonder.

Much more prophetic was Cinerama, introduced in the same year – the first of the 'big-screen' systems designed as a deliberate (and partially successful) counterweight to the dominance of the small screen at home. Cinerama relied on three screens, each twice the size of the traditional one, and now appears as cumbersome and irrelevant as the Brabazon aircraft and other roughly contemporary products of the drive towards immensity. Ten years passed before it was used for a feature film, ten years in which a diet of avalanches, battles, and roller-coaster trips began to pall with audiences.

But it had pointed one obvious way for the movies to follow, taken up by Twentieth-Century Fox with *The Robe* in 1953 – the first CinemaScope production. The 2·5 : 1 oblong of the CinemaScope screen required circuits to invest in special lenses and stereophonic sound, and producers to be prepared to stake enormous sums on the kind of lavish spectacle that would fill it. Through the fifties at least, it succeeded in these objectives. De Mille rode again, but the wide-screen soon proved itself adaptable to more than blockbusting crudity.

None of these developments could help the cinema win its war against television, nor could they have been expected to do so; the laws of mass-entertainment obsolescence are severe. But the two media did achieve a kind of symbiosis in the fifties, with the sale of old films to television companies and, in 1955, Delbert Mann's filming of *Marty* from a Paddy Chayefsky television script, which won Ernest Borgnine an Oscar nomination and was widely hailed as television's first major contribution to the cinema.

Democracy, patriotism, and shattered lives

Hollywood, as the most successful entertainment institution of American society, had always been extremely vulnerable to pressure from it, as had been obvious from NASCAP'S protests at *Birth of a Nation* right through to the Hays Code and the Legion of Decency. But previous pressures had been neither so well-orchestrated nor so ruthless as that which began on 18 October 1947, when the McCarthy-inspired House Committee on Un-American Activities gathered in Washington to begin its 'investigation of communism in motion pictures', and cast a shadow over the entire decade which neither the wide-screen nor cooperation with television could efface.

Within a fortnight of the Commission's first meeting, ten prominent Hollywood figures, including director Edward Dmytryk and scriptwriter Dalton Trumbo, had been called to comment on allegations ('evidence') that they were Communist Party members, pleaded the Fifth Amendment, refused to answer, and been sent to prison for contempt of Congress. The response of the Association of Motion Picture Producers was to condemn the 'Hollywood Ten' and officially blacklist them until they had purged their contempt and sworn that they were not Communists. Within four years, two hundred writers, actors, and directors were likewise blacklisted, and many of the most promising talents went into exile. Joseph Losey, whose tense remake of Lang's *M* (1951) had put him in the forefront of American directors, left for England two years later, as did the scriptwriter Carl Foreman.

Hollywood did not of one accord take this lying down. Humphrey Bogart led a protest march through Washington against the investigations in 1947; the Jewish comedian Zero Mostel clowned his way through the interrogation and finished by thanking the Committee, whose proceedings were broadcast, for giving him his first television exposure in years; Chaplin, Katharine Hepburn, and John Huston were also in the ranks of the opposition. Nor should it be concluded that all the proscribed performers starved; with impeccable self-regulating logic, the studios came up with a black market as partial counterweight to the blacklist. In 1956, 'Robert Rich' failed to turn up to collect his Oscar as scriptwriter for *The Brave One*, for the very good reason that, as embarrassed investigation revealed, he was none other than the blacklisted, and sometime jailed, Dalton Trumbo.

But the investigations, as severe a governmental surveillance of artistic expression as that practised by the Stalinism they condemned, left behind a trail of suicides, illness, shattered homes, and wrecked careers. There is no doubt that the haemorrhage of talent and the stifling of controversial subject-matter which McCarthyism entailed enfeebled the industry's challenge to television, and caused the name of Hollywood to stink in nostrils round the world for a long time afterwards. Commercial and political pressures combined to push the industry inexorably towards 'safe' material which spectacular innovations could not for long offset. William Wellman's *Iron Curtain* (1948) was symptomatic of the type of Cold War offering that Hollywood encouraged until forced to bow before the iron free-market law and admit that such films were not box-office. Thereafter, on the whole, it was the reign of the non-controversial.

Live filming: location shooting and method

One major development of these years can largely be described as a reaction against escapism, evident in the decline of the musical, but even more so in the dual movement away from stylised to more 'natural' acting and from studio to location shooting. The costly creation of illusion was no longer such a major preoccupation. This was partly due to the need to cut costs, but may also have been a by-product of the improvement in the American economy consequent upon victory in the war; escapist entertainment, we have seen, thrives on economic decline.

The change in acting style had much to do with the work of Lee Strasberg in his New York Actors' Studio. Strasberg's approach – influenced by the Russian Konstantin Stanislavsky – was founded on an intense rapport between director and actor, and even more between actor and character. Empathy was the key; polished articulation à la Cary Grant gave place to an often exaggerated naturalism in which grunts, mumblings, and pauses assumed equal importance with the written script. The actor and director most closely associated with this style, Marlon Brando and Elia Kazan, came together in the Tennessee Williams adaptation *A Streetcar Named Desire* (1951). Much of the film's force rests on the conflict of style between Vivien Leigh's overwrought escapist Blanche Dubois and the morose, muttering Kowalski who rapes her.

The Brando/Kazan pairing was repeated the following year for the Mexican Western *Viva Zapata!*, remembered principally for giving its name to a style of moustache, and in 1954 in *On the Waterfront*, winner of seven Oscars though undoubtedly overrated at the time. Critical reaction has put in their place comparisons between Brando's bloodstained stagger at the end, when he defies intimidation to return to work, and Christ's journey to Calvary; and the film's ostensibly radical stance rests on the assumption that dockland trade unions are almost entirely crooked. Given Kazan's cooperation with the McCarthy investigations, one must agree with David Thomson when he says that 'the possible comparison between the Brando who informs on the mob and Kazan's own willingness to talk is embarrassing'[1]. Still, it remains important as one of the first major manifestations of the youth cult of the fifties and sixties.

This cult found its first martyr in James Dean, who starred for the first time (in Kazan's *East of Eden*) in 1955, the year he was killed in a car-crash. Brando (as in *Streetcar*) could brim over with meanness; Dean never did, but rather exuded a prematurely sullen idealism, which in *East of Eden* leads him first to track down his errant mother (found running a brothel), then to bring her together with his brother in a hoped-for reconciliation that results in tragedy. Like Valentino, Fields, or Bogart, Dean was a superstar rather than just a star because of the (studio-nurtured) convergence between on- and off-screen persona. In *East of Eden* and even more in *Rebel Without a Cause* (1955), made for Nicholas Ray, he appeared already cut out for a gratuitous fifties style of martyrdom.

Ray had established himself as a major post-war figure with his first film, *They Live by Night* (1948), echoing *You Only Live Once* in its fatalistic tale of love-on-the-run, but of an undeniable originality in the tenseness and vividity of its camera-style. The concern with mis-understanding and the violence that emanates from it informs all his work, however disparate the genre. *In a Lonely Place* (1950) – in title and theme an archetypal *film noir* – drew from Bogart his most sombrely violent performance as a psychopathic scriptwriter, and *Rebel Without a Cause* owes as much to Ray's direction as to either the acting or the legend of Dean. The title is misleading; Dean rebels, not through nihilistic bloody-mindedness, but because in the words of his lacklustre British contemporary Jimmy Porter 'there aren't any good brave causes left'[2].

Plenty of people in the American cinema, just after the war, had thought there were. These were the years of the 'problem picture' – Gregory Peck posing as a Jew in Kazan's *Gentleman's Agreement* (1947) to write a series of magazine articles exposing racial prejudice; Jeanne Crain in Kazan's *Pinky* (1949) as an exceptionally pale-skinned Negress (supposedly to show the two-way nature of prejudice, but obviously to play safe in the love-scenes with a white man); Edward Dmytryk also tackling anti-Semitism in *Crossfire* (1947) – his last Hollywood picture before imprisonment. The sensitivity with which such subjects constantly needed to be handled is illustrated by the fact that the last-named film was adapted (shades of *The Children's Hour*) from a novel in which the psychopath's target was not a Jew, but a homosexual. Tolerance went only so far, and sometimes (witness Dmytryk's blacking) not even so far as that.

But the problem picture was important as a manifestation of the urge – albeit often emasculated – towards greater authenticity in subject-matter and setting. Thrillers moved out of the studio, beginning with Jules Dassin's *The Naked City* of 1948, whose pursuit sequences owe much of their power to the use of real New York locations. The location thriller quickly generated its own conventions (detectives in snap-brim trilbies, third-degree interrogation sequences, documentary-style presentation), which were promptly cannibalised by television detective series, and had an important effect on much fifties film-making.

The major figures in the low-budget location film were the producer Stanley Kramer and the scriptwriter Carl Foreman. Kramer churned out a series of dramas which turned social pseudo-realism into big box-office successes. Robert Rossen's *Body and Soul* (1947), about a Jewish boxer, Laszlo Benedek's motorcycle drama *The Wild One* (1953), and the Fred Zinnemann Western *High Noon* (1952), with Gary Cooper racing the clock for support against a gang of outlaws bent on revenge and Grace Kelly overcoming her pacifist scruples as his newly-wed Quaker bride, will serve as examples of the house-style. *High Noon* was actually interpreted as an allegory of McCarthyism (largely on the strength of scriptwriter Foreman's blacklisting), which appears even more ludicrous than it would otherwise do when we remember that Gary Cooper was a 'friendly' witness for the Commission. The film derives much tension from its tight boundaries in time and space (the action takes place in one small town, and lasts no longer than the eighty-five minutes of the film); but the high-cultural claims made for it (comparison has been made with the starkness and economy of classical tragedy) are interesting more as an index of Hollywood's craving for respectability than for any light they cast on the film, and *High Noon*'s most revealing moment in many ways remains Grace Kelly's firing of the shot that helps to save her husband, and then her collapse on his shoulder. A man alone is here shown to be inadequate without a woman beside him; and her principles, with his broad shoulder to cry on, can easily be seen as mere scruples. The fusion of traditionally 'male' and 'female' qualities into a solid couple had rarely been more persuasively advocated.

Kramer, financially highly successful as an independent, was much less so for Columbia, who in 1954 bought him out of the remaining two years of his contract for them. He thereupon turned to independent production and direction, with as we shall see still more grandiloquent results.

Much more authentically redolent of American problems and experience are the films of Samuel Fuller, succinctly described by their director in his brief cameo appearance in Godard's *Pierrot le Fou*:

'The film is like a battleground. Love. Hate. Action. Violence. Death. In one word . . . emotion.'

The laconic, amoral brutality of Fuller's work has led to charges of neo-Fascism; yet his pessimistic presentation of the plight of the Red Indian in *Run of the Arrow* (1957), or his cynical view of the police in *Pickup on South Street* (1953) are arguably far more durable, and far more thought-provoking, than Kramer's glossier liberalism.

The leading auteurs

The major thriller figures of the war years remained active in the following decade. Hitchcock continued to experiment, sometimes clumsily, as in *Rope* (1948), shot in one continuous take, sometimes brilliantly, as in *Rear Window* (1954), in which all the action takes place in one room and the murder is detected, in a microcosm of the film-viewing process, by the peeping-tom in the flat opposite. *Strangers on a Train* (1951) turned the boyishly debonair Farley Granger into a tennis-playing murderer-by-default, demonstrating that, while Hitchcock may have described actors as 'cattle', and while his films certainly depend upon acting performance less than the bulk of Hollywood cinema, he was still capable of metamorphosing an actor's screen persona.

John Huston branched out from the thriller to adapt the Stephen Crane Civil War tale *The Red Badge of Courage* (1951), but his most notable work continued to be with Bogart. *Key Largo* (1948) played his burnt-out war hero off against Edward G. Robinson's gang-leader terrified of the approaching hurricane, and it was with Huston that Bogart won his only Oscar in 1951, as the boozy boat-captain Charlie Allnutt teamed with prim Katharine Hepburn in *The African Queen*. It is ironic that this comedy-melodrama, with its preposterous plot turning the Bogart and Hepburn characters into war-heroes, should have earned a place in Hollywood legend for a certain 'realism' in its making. It was shot on location in the Congo, where illness, attacks from marauding ants, and the sinking of the boat held up filming. Huston is supposed to have said to Bogart after he had received his Oscar: 'It's like I said, kid. Real leeches pay off in the long run!'

But Bogie's greatest performance of the post-war years was his first, as Philip Marlowe in Hawks's *The Big Sleep* (1946). The plot is quite incomprehensible, but that matters not at all. The dialogue (by William Faulkner after Raymond Chandler) is laconic and charged – the Hollywood screenplay at its greatest. The atmosphere of sweaty decay distilled by the hothouse in which detective Philip Marlowe is briefed, and by the General's degenerate daughter, is unrivalled; the poisonings and shoot-outs are directed with masterly timing. Bogart did undoubtedly deserve an Oscar, but it was surely for this or *Casablanca* rather than *The African Queen*.

Hawks's other films of the period maintained his previous level. *Red River* (1948), with a superbly tyrannical performance from John Wayne and magnificent filming of cattle-drives, is one of the great Westerns; *I Was A Male War Bride* (1949) again plunged Cary Grant into the sexual ambiguities of *Bringing Up Baby*; and *Gentlemen Prefer Blondes* (1953) came closer to realising Marilyn Monroe's comic potential than any other film, via her majestic rendering of 'Diamonds Are A Girl's Best Friend'.

The Western thrives but the musical declines

Blondes was one of the last great Hollywood musicals, as well as one of the funniest. The wide-screen largely accounts for this, promoting as it did lavishness of décor and scale as against poise and performance; the general anti-escapist reaction and (from the late fifties) the upsurge of rock'n'roll further undercut the genre's position. MGM's Vincente Minnelli dominated the field throughout our period, from *Ziegfeld Follies*, with Fred Astaire, in 1946, through Gene Kelly's almost baroque choreography in *An American in Paris* (1951), to 1954 and *Brigadoon*, whose tale of a ghost village that returns to life once a century, and in which Gene Kelly chooses to stay for love of one of its inhabitants, can appear in retrospect as a swansong for the genre. Stanley Donen, a choreographer for MGM since the early forties, co-directed *On The Town* with Gene Kelly in 1949, and with *Singin' in the Rain* (1952), and the Southern-States *macho* of *Seven Brides for Seven Brothers* (1954) pointed a potentially fruitful line of development with his use of outdoor locations, unfortunately too often framing this with Hollywood-sexist treatment of plot and character.

The Western, more obviously adaptable to the wide-screen, thrived meanwhile, despite being taken up wholesale by television and a recrudescence of the 'singing cowboy'. Gene Autry, founding-father of the species, had been around since the thirties; Roy Rogers, its most notorious exponent, arrived on the scene in 1937 for a fourteen-year Republic career.

Ford, with *My Darling Clementine* (1946) and *Rio Grande* (1950), maintained his earlier *Stagecoach* form, though outside the genre he tended to lose his touch (as in his adaptation of Graham Greene's *The Power and the Glory*, *The Fugitive* of 1947, which ruined the quiet tension of its original). Raoul Walsh, whose sombre *High Sierra* (1941) transplanted to the Western the *film noir* atmosphere more often associated with the gangster movie, worked across a variety of adventure genres: war films (*Objective Burma*, with Errol Flynn, in 1945) and gangster movies (a great performance from James Cagney in *White Heat* of 1949), as well as the Western. Anthony Mann established himself during these years as a major Western director, especially through his work with James Stewart. *Winchester '73* (1950) brought out a power and violence in Stewart's playing difficult to foresee on earlier evidence, and the collaboration continued through to 1955 and *The Man from Laramie*, which filled British cinemas largely on the strength of its highly successful theme-song. The musical might have been on the way out, but popular music and Hollywood were to maintain as close and supportive a relationship as ever.

Comedy

Comic films of this period showed a depressing tendency to mark time. The Marx Brothers' United Artists swansong, *Love Happy* (1950), is embarrassing to watch, though the scene in which Groucho waltzes with a youthful Marilyn Monroe must rank among the cinema's most bizarre and anachronistic rendezvous. Laurel and Hardy were in virtual retirement, Keaton made only a series of drink-ravaged cameo appearances, and among the great names of screen comedy only Chaplin remained active. After *The Great Dictator* (1940), with its Mussolini and Hitler parodies, came *Monsieur Verdoux* (1947), his least overtly comic film, which aroused fury in the USA for the untroubled polish of Chaplin's performance as Bluebeard the wife-murderer. Verdoux is ever-ready with a justification for his behaviour, even daring to adduce the Depression as an extenuating circumstance, and ever-prepared to turn his justifications back on themselves, so that we never know where we stand or how seriously to take them – it is the film's slipperiness rather than its surface cynicism that remains disturbing today. Suspected of Communist sympathies, Chaplin exiled himself to Switzerland in 1952, the year in which the dreadfully sentimental *Limelight* was released. He has made films since, but they are best forgotten.

The Sturges screwball comedies continued, with somewhat blunted impact, until 1949, after which he left for France and made only one more picture. The pace of verbal comedy in this period, although still rapid, became slightly less frenetic, as is evident in the work of its exponents, Katharine Hepburn and Spencer Tracy. They had first come together in 1942 (George Stevens's *Woman of the Year*), and, despite Hepburn's alleged box-office jinx, were to make eight more films together. Tracy's gruff bonhomie (muted from his more violent thirties persona) acted as the ideal foil for Hepburn's supremely intelligent sensitivity. *Pat and Mike* (1952), about a sports coach, is one of their best joint attempts (for George Cukor), but arguably even better is *Adam's Rib* (Cukor, 1949). This features Hepburn, majestically logical in cross-examination – the reverse of the 'scatty' Hollywood feminine stereotype – and Tracy, fighting a losing battle against his own sexism, as married lawyers on opposite sides of the same case. Forties and fifties Hollywood may have extended the cumbersome hand of benevolence to Negroes and Jews via the 'problem picture', but nowhere did it treat women so intelligently or unchauvinistically as here.

Cukor's other major work of the period was *A Star is Born* (1954), with Judy Garland. This remake of a 1937 William Wellman original was itself remade by Frank Pearson, with Barbara Streisand, in 1976. The intensity of Judy Garland's singing of 'Born in a Trunk' remains unequalled, and James Mason's suicide by drowing off Malibu Beach is a great moment of screen melodrama. Hollywood's obsession with itself (of which the three versions of the film are proof enough) has never been so superbly demonstrated.

Hollywood and the theatrical

A Star is Born is evidence that, for all the popularity of location features and problem pictures, theatricality was as prominent an element of Hollywood cinema as it had always been. It loomed large in Orson Welles's work of the period, notably the Shakespeare adaptations *Macbeth* (1948), shot in three weeks, and *Othello* (1952), but also in the thrillers *The Lady from Shanghai* (1948) and *Confidential Report* (1955). *The Lady from Shanghai* echoes Sternberg in its masochistic exoticism, but only Welles could have thought of the final shoot-out in a hall of mirrors, the logical conclusion of this highly-charged, self-obsessed sub-genre; there again, probably only Welles would have left so many loose ends for the studio to sort out before release. . . . Mr Arkadin in *Confidential Report* is a malevolent alter ego for Kane, frustrated into suicide by the failure of his homicidal plans to prevent his daughter from learning about his criminal past. In these films as surely as in the Shakespeare adaptations, Welles's aptitude at generating (melo)drama, via deep-focus, chiaroscuro, and his own resonant voice comes through; but problems with studios and sometimes appalling carelessness in detail had begun to blight his *oeuvre*.

The European theatrical influence remained strong, notably in the work of Joseph L. Mankiewicz, producer of *Fury*, who moved into direction after the war. Mankiewicz's films are prone to complex plots, sardonic dialogue, and a preoccupation with the *femme fatale* (right through to *Cleopatra* of 1963), all very much in the nineteenth-century tradition of dramatic comedy, as evidenced by *All About Eve* (1950), which won Mankiewicz Oscars for both screenplay and direction, and showed Anne Baxter making her way to the top of the acting profession at the expense of Bette Davis. Only in the Hollywood studio system could a director have filmed successively Shakespeare and Damon Runyon, making commerical hits of both, as Mankiewicz did with *Julius Caesar* (1953) and *Guys and Dolls* (1955).

Max Ophuls's Hollywood career was brief, compared to his pre-war experience in Germany, Italy, and France and his five years work in France again from 1950. Why, then, choose to discuss his *oeuvre* here? Partly because his Hollywood films are the greatest products of the European theatrical tradition also exemplified by the work of Mankiewicz; partly also because *The Reckless Moment* (1949) is unequalled outside the work of Renoir in its treatment of passion and desire broken by a rigid and stultifying framework. Joan Bennett inadvertently kills her daughter's unsavoury lover; James Mason, sent by his 'business' partner to blackmail her, falls in love with her, and sacrifices his life to protect her. At the end, on Christmas Day, her husband, a serviceman away on duty, rings up to ask how everybody is, and Joan Bennett reassures him that everything is fine before putting the phone down and bursting into tears. . . . The tragedy breaking through the blithe façade of the great American family celebration is stunning in its impact, not least because of the way in which it rhymes with the beginning of the film; two attempts to curb desire in the name of social stability lead to violent death and suffering, and we are not even shown the established order imperturbably closing ranks as in *La Règle du Jeu* in a final reassertion of itself. Ophuls's handling of the scenes between James Mason and Joan Bennett, with their slow build-up of sexual tension, would alone confirm him as a great director.

Such a claim may read rather oddly, given that Ophuls is widely regarded as an exhibitionistic exponent of the tracking-shot to embellish glossy and frivolous intrigues. But this view masks the genuinely tragic component, nowhere more in evidence than in the first episode of his French film *Le Plaisir* (*Pleasure*, 1952, based on Maupassant short stories), in which a debonair man collapses on a Paris dance-hall floor across which the camera has tracked relentlessly. The man is taken home, where we discover that he collapsed from asphyxiation as well as exhaustion; his youthful countenance is quite literally a mask, peeled off by his wife to reveal the raddled features of an old man. Again, the tragic constraints lie within social institutions and conventions (here, the need to prove oneself attractive on the dance-floor), in their meshing with and determining of individual emotions.

The same could be said of *Letter from an Unknown Woman* (1948), whose chocolate-box European studio exteriors blinded many to its tart and poignant irony, or of *Madame de . . .* (1953), where the passage of a pair of earrings between husband, wife, and lovers becomes a touchstone for infidelity at the same time as a sardonic reflection on the importance of money and material possessions in upper-class marriage. Ophuls's European and American films have been discussed together, in what might appear a flagrant flourish of auteurism, because their social and emotional preoccupations are remarkably homologous. The endless camera movement is a flight from the pain and tension caused by the struggle of transience or sexuality (the 'reckless moment') against convention.

Another leading practitioner of what could loosely be characterised as social melodrama was Douglas Sirk, a Dane born in Germany. Low-budget work for Columbia and Universal produced *Written on the Wind* (1956) and *Magnificent Obsession* (1954) among others, unashamedly tear-jerking in their handling of such performers as Rock Hudson and Dorothy Malone, but firmly anchored in social realities. In Sirk's work as in that of Ophuls, the ever-present Hollywood tendency towards theatricality fuses with that towards treatment (often perforce implicit) of social problems.

Conclusion

The decade was a turbulent one, and only rarely did this turbulence have a productive effect on the films made in Hollywood; it is with good cause that Penelope Houston speaks of this period as 'the nervous years'[3]. The tendency towards grandiloquence and the increase in screen size fuelled each other, so that many of the era's most successful films now look ludicrously pompous, and the work of a Hawks or an

Ophuls, in which what is unsaid is often as important as what is explicitly stated, is very much an exception.

Gloria Swanson says it all in Billy Wilder's *Sunset Boulevard* (1950), as the downfallen silent star living in decayed splendour, attended by her former director and husband, now her butler (Erich von Stroheim), and a clutch of old Hollywood contemporaries, including Buster Keaton and the gossip columnist Louella Parsons, both playing themselves. When this morgue is unwittingly invaded by aspirant writer Joe Gillis (William Holden), who thereby precipitates his own death, he mentions to Gloria Swanson that she used to be a big star. The reply, in its vicious accuracy, is one of the great Hollywood lines: 'I *am* big. It's the pictures that have got small.'

8 The 'Neo-Realist' Years: European Cinema, 1945 to 1955

I shall here survey European cinema country by country, very much as has been done hitherto, stressing the developments in the area of theory that have tended to accompany film practice in Europe, particularly since the Second World War.

Italy and neo-realism

The relatively little space allocated to the Italian industry thus far indicates how unimportant its pre-1945 production, dominated by costume melodrama and tales of upper-class intrigue, had been. What is most surprising about the burgeoning of Italian cinema in the forties and fifties – an era in which it emerged from total obscurity to become the most influential in Europe, if not the world – is that much of the impetus for it came under the Mussolini régime, which founded the Centro Sperimentale film-school in Rome and harnessed its products to its propaganda machine. To an audience watching the fiercely anti-Fascist *Paisa*, or *Bicycle Thieves*, whose political stance is overtly one of left-wing humanism, it may well seem inconceivable that a totalitarian régime provided some of the conditions which made this new development possible. But it is gratifying to reflect that Mussolini's injection of resources into Italian industry was inevitably to have results contrary to those he would have wished.

It was in a 1942 article by Umberto Barbaro of the Centro Sperimentale that the expression 'neo-realism' was first used; thereafter it rapidly became a battle-cry used with more vigour than precision. The general characteristics of the 'neo-realist' cinema can perhaps best be defined by contrast with what had gone before, like those of the Hollywood location thriller with which it had certain points in common. Lack of funds meant low budgets; low budgets meant little-known or non-professional actors, almost exclusively location shooting, and no reliance on elaborate, and probably expensive, scripts. It was to become fashionable in sixties and seventies American experimental cinema to speak of 'minimalist' film-making; the concept has a utility beyond the specific context in which it came into being, for the post-war European cinemas too were discovering (usually under the pressure of economic necessity, later too under that of ideological considerations) how many of the component parts of the cinematic institution can productively be dispensed with. The French critic André Bazin was to say of Vitterio de Sica's *Bicycle Thieves*:

> '*Bicycle Thieves* is one of the finest examples of pure cinema. No more actors, no more story, no more sets, which is to say that in the perfect aesthetic illusion of reality there is no more cinema.'[1]

'No more cinema' is here to be understood in a duel sense; no more reminders of the camera's presence or of the editor's importance (a position on which issue can certainly be taken with Bazin), but also no more old-style bourgeois cinema, no more star-system, no more lavish budgets to be cajoled out of cautious backers (*Bicycle Thieves* cost only £18 000 to make), no more studio sets that were merely wasteful and expensive reproductions of what was everywhere to be found in the streets. When the scriptwriter Cesare Zavattini said in a now famous interview: 'Here was a tree; here an old man; here a house; here a man eating, a man sleeping, a man crying', he understood quite literally that these were what one saw, what the camera saw, when wandering out into the streets in search of material. Neo-realism is among other things an important part of the 'Lumière tradition' of *ciné-vérité*.

Such views now appear simplistic, not to say naïve. They rest on that notion of the camera as transparent 'window-on-the-world' which we have examined in Bazin's discussion of Renoir, and which subsequent film production was to discredit; their populist implication that anything observed actually going on was *ipso facto* cinematic, while it undercuts traditional élitist views of culture, smooths over the complex social determinants of action and behaviour (behind the camera as well as in front of it), and takes little account of the differing reactions of different audiences. And it was a vulgarised version of these views that lay behind the tedious 'slice-of-life' ethos which had a great effect on the British cinema, and an often quite overwhelming one of British television, in the fifties and early sixties. But, situated in their context as a massive reaction against the imperialistic domination of Hollywood and tendencies to equate quality of product with size of budget, their views can be seen as revolutionary; and the effect of the best neo-realist films remains immense.

Roberto Rossellini gained his first experience in the industry helping with pro-Mussolini wartime films, but did not make a real impact until the swift *volte-face* of *Rome, Open City* (1945). This film was shot quite literally while the German army was leaving Rome, with materials way below professional quality – handicaps that it turned to spectacular advantage. The incidents the film relates (child saboteurs in the Resistance and the execution of a priest by the Germans) were based on historical reality, and filmed precisely as though they were historical reality, in a grainy black-and-white whose very immediacy and rawness served as immediate touchstones of its 'authenticity'. The professional actors – Aldo Fabrizi as the priest and Anna Magnani as the housewife Pina, gunned down in the street as the camera retreats – in no way stand out from the amateurs, and the sharpness of the film's impact blinded many critics to its shortcomings.

For *Rome, Open City* is a flawed film, though undoubtedly a great one. The split in Italy between Catholicism and Communism has long been a major political and intellectual issue, and few of the Italian directors we shall discuss were unmarked by it. The pity of *Rome, Open City* is that it attempts to heal the split on the supposedly intermediate terrain of liberal humanism, presenting Don Pietro's courage and resistance under torture as but the obverse of the Communist Francesco's 'idealistic' hopes for the future. Both men lay their lives on the line for the greater good of 'humanity', but nowhere is there a hint that very different ideologies motivate them, or that in peacetime these ideologies and the contradictions between them would be likely to complicate and confuse their relationship and by extension the whole of Italian society. Rigorous analysis of what each character stands for is replaced by an undialectical Popular Frontism of men of good will, and the film is the poorer for it.

Paisa (1946) was funded by the profits its predecessor made in America. Episodic, not to say anecdotal, and filmed with each character speaking his own language, its tales of partisans and American troops have a similar immediacy to *Rome, Open City*, particularly the last episode, in which British, American, and Italian resisters are executed *en masse* by drowning in the Northern swamps. Again, however, Rossellini exposes himself to the reproach of ignoring the different ideologies by which his characters live and die. Robert Warshow makes the point (about a scene in which Fascist snipers are captured in the street) that 'the scene derives its power precisely from the fact that it is not cushioned in ideas; events seem to develop according to their own laws and take no account of how one might – or should – feel about them'[2]. This is precisely the kind of criticism Brecht levelled at the 'naturalistic' theatre and – by implication – Eisenstein at non-montage-based cinema. Our critical awareness of why things happen as they do, and how they might possibly be brought to happen otherwise, is bound to be blunted by a vision that presents them inexorably just as they are. *Paisa*'s realism is closer than it seems to the poetic pessimism of the pre-war years.

Germany Year Zero (1947), like numerous films of this period, takes as its central character a child, here going to the bad in ruined Berlin, poisoning his starving father and then committing suicide. Rossellini's other work of the period was not to plunge such nihilistic depths; his major fifties films were made with his then wife, Ingrid Bergman. *Viaggio in Italia* (1953) anticipates the work of Antonioni and much other modern cinema in its open, even hesitant account of an English couple (Ingrid Bergman and George Sanders), whose jeopardised marriage is at least temporarily saved by their business trip to Italy together. However much his work is open to criticism, Rossellini may well be seen as this period's most important narrative innovator.

The other neo-realist director to take the film world by storm in the late forties was Vittorio de Sica. *Sciuscia* (*Shoeshine*) of 1946, like *The Children Are Watching Us* of four years earlier, centres on children, here two urchins of Rome whose passion to own their own horse leads them into the black market and eventually to a murderous quarrel. This was followed by *Bicycle Thieves* (1948), arguably the most influential of all the neo-realist films. Its story is of extreme simplicity. A bill-poster, with his young son, searches the city streets in despair because his bicycle, essential to his job, has been stolen from him. Unable to find it, he steals another, and is caught and humiliatingly rebuked. An everyday urban non-event, but a tragedy to those involved; it is these two views that de Sica and Zavattini communicate simultaneously, through extraordinary performances by a non-professional cast and a direct physicality in the location filming (as when it rains, or when the distraught father impatiently slaps his son) which retains great impact. *Bicycle Thieves* is a sentimental masterwork, a fact which it is no use trying to avoid. Unsentimental films about children tend by and large to deal with children alone, or at least severed from their parents (*Les Enfants Terribles*, *Les Quatre Cents Coups*); the parent/son bond is so crucial a nexus of bourgeois sentiment that it would be unrealistic to expect a film of this period to deal unsentimentally with it. What works well in *Bicycle Thieves* is the selection and use of trivial everyday gesture as a vehicle for the sentiment, as in the restaurant where the father, despite looming unemployment, asks his boy: 'Could you go a pizza, son?' and the boy smiles delightedly. . . . What other European sound film – always excepting Renoir's *Toni* – had up until then had such instant (and, as it turned out, durable) appeal to such a wide range of possible audiences?

Miracle in Milan (1951) struck the mood more generally associated with Britain's Ealing comedies in its tale of a shanty-town beneath which oil is found, and in *Umberto D* (1952) de Sica reversed the age-scale of *Bicycle Thieves*; his protagonist here is an old-age pensioner, reduced to begging. By this time, de Sica's sentimental inability to deal with his characters as equals was proving a major drawback, and he fell rapidly from favour when the neo-realist movement started running out of steam.

That last clause might suggest that intellectual and aesthetic movements live spontaneous, organic lives of their own, divorced from the societies in which they take place, and obeying purely internal laws of evolution and dissolution. Nothing could be further from the truth. The decline of neo-realism was in very great measure the result of carefully-organised political, financial, and religious pressures which by the early fifties had made it virtually impossible to get financial backing for a neo-realist movie. For neo-realism was not the most successful Italian cinema of its time, financially speaking. That distinction belonged to the bosom comedies involving Sophia Loren and Gina Lollobrigida, and the Don Camillo films – Franco-Italian co-productions – in which Gino Cervi and Fernandel trivialised the endless Kremlin/Vatican battle. The view of Italy as a good-natured mammary bacchanale promoted by these films was a boost for tourism; not so the grimness of many of the neo-realist features, which actually dared to suggest that it was a country beset by poverty and injustice. (Spain probably avoided a similar problem only by ruthlessly censoring most critical films out of existence.) The result was the effective financial asphyxiation of the movement and the diversifying of its leading members' energies, into acting (de Sica) or television work (Rossellini), as well as into often less uncompromising screen material.

Luchino Visconti is an exception – then again perhaps not a 'neo-realist' at all, or at least the point at which the classification breaks down. The 'realist' style of observation in his work merges with and is sometimes overlain by a flamboyant, exhibitionistic strain, at its best operatic (he is the first of a number of Italian directors, such as Bertolucci and Bellocchio of whom more later, on whom grand opera has been an important influence), at its worst melodramatic and inept. He worked as assistant to Renoir on *Une Partie de Campagne* and *Les Bas-Fonds* before making his first feature, *Ossessione*, in 1942. The plot for this follows closely the James M. Cain thriller *The Postman Always Rings Twice*, with the result that for many years it could not be shown outside Italy. The film transposes the plot to the Po valley, a marshy region of Northern Italy, and its bleak sensuality is still powerful.

Visconti moved into the theatre until 1948, and *La Terra Trema*, about the economic crushing of a family of Sicilian fishermen. The cast were real fishermen, speaking their own dialect and frequently inventing their own lines, but the film – as even its title ('the earth trembles') suggests – is romantic as much as neo-realist. The family's defeat is presented fatalistically, an angle much criticised on the Left, despite – or perhaps because of – Visconti's self-proclaimed Marxist perspective. A good deal of this criticism may well have rested on rather simplistic notions of what revolutionary art should be, but its very existence illuminates Visconti's major contradiction: the realist, the socialist, the anti-establishmentarian, versus the aesthete, the fatalist, the patrician.

His remaining films of the period under discussion, *Bellissima* (1951) and *Senso* (1954), moved a long way from realism, into more theatrical and formalist realms. But for Visconti just as much (in a very different way) for Elia Kazan, the theatrical was never far beneath the surface; for both directors, it formed an essential part of the 'realist' approach to filming.

France

The financial basis of the French industry remained reasonably secure after the war, thanks to extensive co-production, governmental aid, and assiduous promotion of exports. But artistically it languished with few exceptions until the late fifties. Like the Italian industry, its exports relied heavily on the packaged, commoditised sexuality of its leading actresses (Martine Carol, Françoise Arnoul, and the incipient Brigitte

Bardot), working in tandem with a popular mythical view of the country (Christian-Jaque's costume romances with Martine Carol, lacy-pantalooned titillation for an audience reared on the legend of 'naughty Paree', are perhaps the best examples). Unlike the Italians, it produced few films that indicated major new development; this came later, from a rather unexpected quarter.

The major names of pre-war and wartime production remained active. Renoir made only three films in this period, two of which, *The Golden Coach* (a Franco-Italian co-production, 1952) and *French Can-Can* (1955), emphasise even more than hitherto the theme of the theatre. Danglars, the impresario in *French Can-Can*, has often been seen as Renoir's self-portrait. This rather romantic view emphasises Danglars's relentless creativity at the expense of his frequent vulgarity and callousness, but it has a certain justification in the light it throws on the interaction between theatricality and experience. Not only is Danglars, in certain respects, 'like' Renoir, but our view of Renoir is modified by the fact that he produced a character like Danglars. The lived, the 'real', and the theatrical cannot exist in isolation, something no director has realised better than Renoir.

It is perhaps Renoir's forsaking of the theatrical theme that makes *The River* (shot in India in 1951) such an unmitigated disaster. This judgement will crush several critical corns, but, for all its superb colour, the film has worn badly. The performances are inept, Renoir's leitmotif of the river as metaphor for the organic flow of life loses much of its force and becomes bland with the grafting onto it of an Oriental pop-pantheism that prefigures late-sixties rock music. It is far more powerful, because more ambiguous, in *Toni*, where it is contrasted with and acts as a foil to the social-realist tragedy.

René Clair, after wartime work in Hollywood, returned to France, to make films darker and less jovial than before. His 'interest in dream and reality'[3], cited by Roy Armes apropos of *La Beauté du Diable* (*The Devil's Beauty*, 1950), is particularly marked in *Les Belles-de-Nuit* (1952), where Gérard Philipe plays a Walter Mittyesque music teacher whose 'night beauties' are the women he conquers in his compensatory dreams. As his real life becomes more successful, so his dreams degenerate into nightmares. This film, in its use of chase-scenes and the prominence it gives to music, harks back to the early Clair.

There are those who place *Les Grandes Manoeuvres* (1955) among the cinema's greatest love stories. Gérard Philipe and Michèle Morgan certainly give excellent performances in this 'moral tale' – a clear forerunner of Eric Rohmer (ref. pp. 158–9) – about a cavalry officer who sets out to seduce a divorcée for a bet, falls in love with her, but loses her when she discovers his reputation and the news of the bet. But the colour often has the effect of bathing the intrigue in a chocolate-box glow, drawing much of its sting, and the petty-bourgeois hypocrisy of the small garrison-town is rather simplistically presented. A Renoir or an Ophüls would have maintained the essential darkness of the situation somewhat more consistently.

Marcel Carné remained firmly stuck in his pre-war groove. His final collaboration with Prévert, *Les Portes de la Nuit* (*Gates of Night*, 1946), was a spectacular flop, and neither his adaptations of Simenon (*La Marie du Port*, 1950) and Zola (*Thérèse Raquin*, 1953), nor his later attempt to jump on the *nouvelle vague* bandwagon (*Les Tricheurs*, 1958), were enough to offset the decline in his reputation.

The period of transition

Post-Carné, pre-Godard and Truffaut, the French cinema was in a transition period in which its leading directors' work was often marked by a worthy journeyman quality. André Cayatte used his training as a lawyer to produce competent French 'problem pictures'; the title of *Nous Sommes Tous des Assassins* (*We Are All Murderers*, 1952), is sufficient indication of his conscientious liberal humanism. Jacques Becker had worked for a long time as assistant to Renoir, which showed when he came to direct his own films. *Casque d'Or* (1952) is a richly tragic love-story of fin-de-siècle Paris, but for the rest Becker's work tends to plod along some distance behind his mentor. René Clément's first feature, *La Bataille du Rail* (1946), was a mocked-up Resistance 'documentary' that went some way towards anticipating the neo-realists. His best film, *Jeux Interdits* (*Forbidden Games*, 1952), was a commercial failure in France. It begins with a refugee column, crossing a bridge, being strafed by German machine-guns. The little girl orphaned by the attack is taken in by a peasant family, with whose young son she secretly builds a cemetery for dead animals. Their obsession with death is cut short when the girl is taken away by the Red Cross, in a sequence no less harrowing than the beginning with which it rhymes. Among the numerous child-centred films of this period, *Jeux Interdits* remains one of the most impressive and least sentimental.

British audiences at least may well be more interested by *Monsieur Ripois* (UK title *Knave of Hearts*, 1954), with Gérard Philipe as a London-based French Don Juan who cripples himself leaping out of a window to convince his fifth major love of his sincerity. Clément used a British cameraman, Oswald Morris, and his choice paid off handsomely in the superb London location shooting.

Henri-Georges Clouzot's *Le Salaire de la Peur* (*Wages of Fear*, 1953) is another masterpiece of location filming (ostensibly set in South America, but in fact shot in Provence). Four truckers set out to deliver charges of nitroglycerine across bumpy, treacherous roads. The result is one of the great 'journey' movies, also savagely if implicitly critical of imperialistic United States policies in South America. This criticism is particularly effective in the film's first shot, reminiscent of Luis Buñuel; we see two beetles fighting furiously, then the camera pulls back to reveal a small boy manipulating them with strings.

But it is elsewhere that we must look for foreshadowings of the revolutionary new direction the French cinema was later to take. Robert Bresson made only one film in this period, but it is enough to show us what Jean-Luc Godard meant when he said: 'Robert Bresson *is* French cinema.' *Le Journal d'un Curé de Campagne* (*Diary of a Country Priest*, 1950) adds not one word to the text of the Georges Bernanos novel on which it is based. The words are spoken by the largely non-professional cast in an expressionless monotone. The film's efforts at authenticity at times seem to verge on self-parody (a trap Bresson was not always to avoid in the future); Claude Laydu, the priest, deliberately under-ate during filming to give himself the right appearance of ill-health. Yet nothing could be further removed than this film from the naturalism such details might appear to suggest. Raymond Durgnat says in his book on Bresson:

> 'His aim seems to be to attain a conviction without self-awareness (thus Laydu only realised he had been portraying a saint when he saw the complete film).'[4]

'Conviction without self-awareness' could stand as the essence of the kind of sanctity the *Journal* distils; thus in the novel a postscript by the former co-seminarist in whose flat the priest dies is necessary for us to realise that we have been reading about a saint. Bresson's use of faces as windows onto the soul rather than as mirrors/masks of the heart is presaged only, and in a very different way, by Dreyer's *Passion of Joan of Arc*.

Bresson's austere stress on the importance of what the camera does not tell us was one major departure in film language of this period. Another, at the opposite extreme, was Cocteau's *Orphée* (1950). Neither his beguilingly concrete version of *La Belle et la Bête* (*Beauty and the Beast*, 1946), nor the adaptation of his novel *Les Enfants Terribles* (1950) – even more claustrophobic than the original – which Jean-Pierre Melville directed with 'cooperation' (read interference) from Cocteau, suggested that he would be capable of such a crucially influential work as *Orphée*.

The film's basic conception is Romantic in the extreme; Orpheus, attempting to recover his beloved Eurydice, falls in love instead with the Princess of Death who has taken her from him. But its treatment is classical, indeed baroque in its obsessive use of mirrors, which form a dissolving mercury membrane between the kingdom of the living and that of death. This polarisation is one reason why the film works so well; another is Cocteau's linking of his fantasy to the reality of wartime and post-war France. The scenes in the 'zone' (behind the mirror of Death) were filmed in the military academy of Saint-Cyr (bombed by the Germans), and the apparently ridiculous code-messages transmitted to the Princess ('A single glass of water lights the world') would have aroused Resistance memories. In the opening scene, the poet Orpheus (Jean Marais) receives the famous command 'Enfin, étonnez-nous!' (Well, surprise us!), while sitting at a café-terrace in a perfectly ordinary French provincial square – a 'poetic realism' of a rather different kind from Carné's.

Orphée's mirrors and mazes were to have their major influence on the French cinema through the work of a director who made his début as a documentarist in 1948, Alain Resnais. *Van Gogh* traces the painter's career through selection and arrangement of details from his canvases; its point was rather lost on one early viewer who wrote to Resnais to say what a joy it must have been for him to have had the opportunity of visiting and filming the places where Van Gogh had lived and worked. . . . There now appears something prophetic, as well as amusing, in this, touching so nearly as it does the preoccupation with objective and subjective time and place that has dominated Resnais's *oeuvre*. *Nuit et Brouillard* (*Night and Fog*, 1955) is the major documentary example of this. Resnais alternates newsreel footage of Auschwitz with film of the camp as it is today, overgrown with grass and looking for all the world like any disused factory. The commentary, by the novelist Jean Cayrol, makes sure that we do not fall into the trap of forgetfulness, dated though his humanistic high-mindedness now is; beneath the grass and the buildings, 'the old concentration-camp monster' still lurks, just as in Resnais's subsequent films the past will always be a living component of the present from which it cannot be precisely separated.

While there was no documentary movement in France like that in Great Britain, documentary filming flourished in the immediate post-Second World War years, benefiting *inter alia* from lower budgets. Georges Rouqier's *Farrébique* (1946), about a farm in the Massif Central, demystified the 'noble-savage' view of the French peasantry. But the most striking documentary of this period was made by Georges Franju, instrumental in helping Henri Langlois to found the Cinémathèque (ref. p. 43). In *Le Sang des Bêtes (Animals' Blood,* 1949), the workman singing a sentimental ballad as he washes the blood from the abattoir floor is a disjunction of sound and vision far more shockingly surreal, by its very documentary reality and the tendency of the visual image to dominate the verbal, than the little-girl voice of Nicole Ladmiral which delivers the commentary, or the rather obvious irony when the sheep are described as 'following like men' to the slaughter.... Much of the film's strength comes from its refusal to close its audience's perspective with facile conclusions. A Jean Cayrol script might well have called it (after Cayatte) *Nous Sommes Tous des Assassins,* ruining its ambiguity with over-explicitness.

The period also produced France's greatest silent comedian since Max Linder. This is not a misnomer, for although Jacques Tati's films are in sound it is the choreography of the sight-gags that is responsible for most of their humour. His persona in *Jour de Fête* (1949), and even more in *Les Vacances de M. Hulot (M. Hulot's Holiday,* 1953) is in some ways reminiscent of Buster Keaton – abstractly bemused by the workings of the world through which he moves – but presented in a specificially French bourgeois milieu. Like Keaton too, Tati refuses any appealing connivance with his audience à la Chaplin; his holiday romance is a non-starter (with no dreamland compensation), and his feats of disruption are quite unwittingly accomplished, so that at the climax he is likely to be gazing distractedly out of the frame. The perspective of his films gains immeasurably in richness and complexity as a result. It is because he is thus poised on the edge of the order-besotted French bourgeois world – in but not of it – that Tati is so uniquely well-equipped to throw it into chaos.

The foreshadowing of the new wave

Despite the pedestrian quality of much of its output, we can see that the French industry was still accommodating directors concerned with the advance of cinematic language – a concept whose importance in the theoretical and practical development of the medium we have seen as far back as Eisenstein, and which was to receive a vital impetus with the work of directors and critics in France in the late fifties and early sixties.

Bresson used the expression *écriture* (writing) in his critical work, and Alexandre Astruc's article *Le Caméra-Stylo* (*The Camera-Pen*), which appeared in the magazine *Écran Français* in 1948, was of crucial importance:

'. . . the cinema is gradually becoming a means of expression, just as all the other arts have been before it, and in particular painting and the novel. After having been successively a fairground attraction, an amusement analogous to boulevard theatre, or a means of preserving the images of an era, it is gradually becoming a language. . . . That is why I would like to call this new age of the cinema the age of *caméra-stylo*. This metaphor has a very precise sense. By it I mean that the camera will gradually break free from the tyranny of what is visual, from the image for its own sake, to become a means of writing just as flexible and subtle as written language.'[5]

'The tyranny of what is visual' is in some ways a misleading phrase. Astruc was not saying that what was heard would assume equal importance with what was seen (as it does, uniquely, with Bresson), but rather that the dislocation of image and sound-track, so that one did not act as the automatic endorsement of what went on on the other, would open up new narrative horizons. In much the same way, in the development of the novel the dethroning of the omniscient nineteenth-century narrator (notably in the work of Flaubert and Proust) had made possible and necessary far more narrative subtlety and ambiguity. The expression 'the camera-pen' shows that the cinema was beginning to be thought of in France in conjunction with literature as well as with the plastic arts. Cocteau's poetry, Bresson's prose, Resnais's explorations of time were beginning to suggest some of the directions in which such a conjunction was to lead.

Great Britain

Britain's major contribution to the cinema of this decade was, to quote Geoff Brown, 'governed by the same quiet sense of common endeavour conjured up during the war'[6], and precisely for this reason has retained a special place in the affections of the British film-going public. Ealing Studios proclaimed, via Sir Michael Balcon, their intention to show the 'true Briton' in film, and the Britons they showed, though a long way from Balcon's somewhat bombastic early pretentions, have probably done more than any others to mould established views of what the 'true Briton' is. The Ealing comedies were largely the product of two directors, Alexander Mackendrick and Robert Hamer, working with an unrivalled team of character-actors (Alec Guinness, Katie Johnson, Dennis Price, Joan Greenwood . . .). The view of Britain they projected was a perverse and eccentric one, dominated by the triumph of small-scale bloody-mindedness over obstructive authority. Henry Cornelius's *Passport to Pimlico* (1949) relates how that part of London – at the time still a working-class enclave in an upper-middle-class setting – discovers an old deed attesting its right to independence. Mackendrick's *Whisky Galore*, of the same year, deals with Scottish islanders who circumvent whisky rationing when a boatload of the precious spirit is washed up on their shores.

In both films, the sense of organic community which, as Brown suggests, had been rediscovered by many during the Blitz assures a bloodless triumph. What is interesting – quite apart from the high level of photography and ensemble playing – is the way in which this view of British society links with the organic ideas on culture and literature developed by such writers as F. R. Leavis and Raymond Williams in the fifties and sixties. 'Life' – that indefinable organic essence – triumphs over system; small, and in different ways peripheral, communities over centralisation. The quirky anarchy of these films may well be *sui generis* in the cinema, but meshes with phenomena in at first sight far-removed cultural regions.

Most successful among the Ealing comedies are Mackendrick's *The Ladykillers* (1955) and Hamer's *Kind Hearts and Coronets* (1949), probably because both have a black note that pierces their wrapping of waffly English bonhomie (the stiff-upper-lip *film noir*. . . .?). The 'ladykillers' (led by a Dracula-fanged Alec Guinness) visit themselves upon the benign Mrs Wilberforce near King's Cross, to use the upper floor of her house as their base for a robbery. British bourgeois style effortlessly, because to a large extent unwittingly, triumphs; the gang eliminate one another in progressively more grisly fashion and 'Mrs W' is left with the loot (a dénouement read by Charles Barr in his book on Ealing Studios as a metaphor for the Conservative cashing-in on Labour's post-war efforts in the 1951 election).

The Hamer film is in a very different vein – it deals with the family ramifications of the (literally) dying nobility, seen through the eyes of the illegitimate scion Louis Mazzini (a superbly elegant performance from Dennis Price), who determines to do away with the eight members of the D'Ascoyne family standing between him and the peerage. The interlopers are eliminated by a variety of methods; sickest perhaps is the dispatching of the first over the Thames weir, along – regrettably – with his weekend paramour. The film, in its cool verbal and visual style and its total displacement of the moral by the aesthetic, has often been compared to Oscar Wilde, who would certainly not have disowned such lines as 'Revenge is a dish the man of taste prefers to eat cold . . .' The ending is revelatory in its ambiguous irony. Freed from the gallows by a coincidence, Mazzini carelessly leaves his damning diary in his cell. Does he, with characteristic phlegm, rush back to retrieve it? – we never know. Subversive the film certainly is, in its merciless dissection of the fatuous and decadent aristocracy, but it stops short of actually telling us that Mazzini will get away with it.

The other British cinema of this period is dwarfed by comparison. Anthony Asquith shot *The Importance of Being Earnest* (1952) with much visual flair and poise, and David Lean directed the definitive middle-class melodrama in *Brief Encounter* (1945), where Celia Johnson and Trevor Howard meet and fall in love in a railway-station waiting-room to the strains of Rachmaninov's Second Piano Concerto, but part because both are married. The film is told in flashback, as a confession from the woman to her husband; thus we already know right from the start that virtue will triumph, and it is significant that the woman is shown as the party needing to confess.

The other dominant British studio, Gainsborough, concentrated on period melodrama such as Leslie Arliss's *The Wicked Lady* (1945), for audiences likely to be aroused by Margaret Lockwood in Regency costume. As Brown points out in his article, such films at least recognise the existence of a sexuality usually skirted in Ealing films; but it had to be displaced to the eighteenth century to render it palatable.

The banality of much of the period's output was largely due to a decline in audiences comparable to, though less drastic than, that in the United States. There was a virtual trade war with America. Rank tried and failed to break into the American market, the Labour Government then imposed import duties on films in 1947, with an eight-month ban on British films in America imposed in retaliation. The National Film Finance Corporation was then set up in 1949 to advance loans and guarantees to independent film-makers. Korda maintained his reputation for extravagance by securing £3 000 000 for his British film company, most of which sank without trace, and the result of the crisis, in Britain as in Hollywood, was caution verging on the timorous. One of the more promising ventures was Group 3, overseen by John

Grierson, which made twenty-two features in four years with heavy government support. Their style varied from the neo-documentary to the child-centred adventure. The venture unfortunately lost £444 593, principally because of hostility and consequent bad programming from rival distributors, and was scrapped in 1955. Ealing went on to dominate, not only the output of the decade, but the style of the nascent British television serials and comedies.

The Eastern countries

The aftermath of the war and Nazism ensured that the German industry produced very little, and virtually nothing viewable now, in this period, while the insistence on 'socialist realism' which had thwarted the cinema during Stalin's lifetime remained powerful for some time afterwards. *The Fall of Berlin* (Mikhail Chiaurelin, 1949) is one of the cinema's grossest pieces of hagiography, filmed in quasi-documentary vein although Stalin was played by an actor. 'Socialist realism', ostensibly the depiction of social progress in the workers' state, lapsed into pompous biopics and cosmetic portrayals of heroes of labour and collective farms. It would have been both unfair and unrealistic to expect the Soviet Union to address itself systematically to the complex problem of what constitutes a Marxist or revolutionary cinema, beset as it was by massive under-industrialisation, counter-revolutionary attacks from without, and then the all-consuming demands of the struggle against Nazism. But the humiliations inflicted on the director who made the most serious and sustained attempt to grapple with the problem, Eisenstein, and the sterile prescriptiveness of Central Committee aesthetic directives under Stalin are enough to show that serious researches in this area would almost certainly have been stamped on in the name of a 'realism' whose defining characteristic often seemed to be its tedium. To this day, research into Marxist aesthetics has been more fruitful and sustained in the West than in Soviet bloc countries. Towards the end of our period, signs of the much-trumpeted 'thaw', or liberalisation in artistic expression, became visible, in the work of such young Polish directors as Andrzej Munk and Andrzej Wajda, products of the thriving film-school at Lodz.

The peripatetic film-makers

Right-wing dictatorship extruded its major film-maker (some would say creative artist) when Luis Buñuel left Spain after the Civil War, sinking virtually without trace until he resurfaced in Mexico in 1950 with *Los Olvidados* ('the forgotten ones', translated into English with inapposite theological fervour as *The Young and the Damned*). Raymond Durngat pinpointed the sub-genre within which the film operates when he spoke of it as a 'location melodrama with a liberal social conscience' [7] – concepts familiar from our study of post-war Hollywood but very differently deployed here. The two slum-boys, Jaibo the corrupt and Pedro the innocent, are presented, not as hero and villain, but as different, and in existential terms equally valid, responses to the same brutalising environment. For Buñuel, here as in his other films, this environment is simultaneously internal and external, present as much in Pedro's incestuous dream where his mother appears holding raw meat as in the amoral squalor of the slum where a legless beggar is tipped out of his cart and a blind man is also a child-molester. Such a juxtaposition is clearly what Durgnat had in mind when he wrote:

> 'Again and again in Buñuel, a Freudian awareness of inner reality meets a Marxist awareness of social reality, a rendezvous which is long overdue in Western thought.' [8]

The fifties were a prolific period for Buñuel, though all too many of the films he made are unviewable in Britain. He filmed throughout the period in Mexico (where he still lives), adapting Emily Brontë's *Wuthering Heights* as *Cumbres Borrascosas* (1953), filming *Robinson Crusoe* (1952) as a tale of bourgeois colonialism tempered by his encounter with the native population (Friday floors Crusoe with an atheist argument drawn from the Marquis de Sade), and developing his interest in sexual pathology in *El* (1952), where a forty-year-old virginal idealist finally retreats from the threat of sex into a monastery, and *Essayo de un Crimen* (*The Criminal Life of Archibaldo de la Cruz*, 1955). The latter film, like *Kind Hearts and Coronets* though in a very different way, bears the imprint of Oscar Wilde's *Lord Arthur Savile's Crime*. Archibaldo as a young boy fetichises the assassination of his governess during a revolution, when he saw blood trickling down her thigh, and spends much of his adult life attempting to reproduce that moment via violent sexual crime, only to be constantly thwarted. His 'murder' in the end is perpetrated on a wax dummy of the American tourist-guide whom he selects as a potential victim. Perversion, for Buñuel inevitably linked to both personal and social frustration, here doubles back on itself, its thwarting increasing its intensity.

Those Spanish film-makers who remained under Franco had considerable censorship problems; Luis Berlanga in particular found several of his films intercepted before they were ever screened. His former colleague Juan Antonio Bardem played on the class-barrier with his conflict between motorists and cyclists in *Death of a Cyclist* (1955), and may well have run into trouble as a result. Staying behind and struggling from within proved a very difficult option indeed.

Buñuel and Carl Theodor Dreyer seem at first to have nothing at all in common – the 'professionally irreverent surrealist' and the 'severe Nordic Protestant'. But there are striking parallels between their careers. Both started in the silent era and developed into major sound directors; both managed this despite tremendous difficulties in large part connected to the small size of their countries' film industries (Dreyer made only fourteen films in forty-five years), and both perforce became peripatetic. Buñuel filmed in France and Italy as well as Spain and Mexico; Dreyer's career spans Denmark, Norway, Germany, and France. Both retained an uncompromising intensity more often eulogised than analysed. And both made specific and unique contributions to the development of film language, not least in their juxtaposition of events in the 'internal' and 'external' worlds in such a way as to suggest the transcending of the conventional barrier between them.

Dreyer filmed *Day of Wrath* (1943) and *Ordet* (*The Word*, 1954) in Denmark, around Lutheran subject-matter belied and undercut at every point by the films' construction. *Day of Wrath* begins with one of the most harrowing scenes on record – the discovery, flushing-out, trial, and burning of an old woman suspected of being a witch, punctuated at regular intervals, like the rest of the film, by a relentlessly cool and lucid boys' chorus singing the *Dies Irae*. The pastor's young wife is outraged by this, so much so that when he suspects her (correctly) of adultery she curses him; he drops dead, she is accused of being a witch, and the hideous cycle starts again. . . . Dreyer here extends the close-up technique of *Joan of Arc*, taking scenes almost any other film-maker would have shot as unified tableaux and decomposing or 'deconstructing' them, concentrating on one element at a time and thereby directing our attention to the host of different ways in which it can mesh and interact with other elements. A concept much used in contemporary literary and cinematic criticism is that of the 'open text', the work which does not present itself as a seamless garment of meaning but rather draws our attention to the process by which it is constructed and the ambiguities and resonances within it. Few cinema texts are as dauntingly open as Dreyer's.

Ordet is a study in bigotry and 'true' faith – no more systematically counterposed than Buñuel's 'hero' and 'villain' in *Los Olvidados*, but dissected in their complex relation to each other. Between the two households separated by religious discord strides Johannes, the theological student turned 'religious maniac' (by an excess of devotion, or maybe by the sectarian tensions he unendingly tries to span). At the end, he performs a miracle – the raising of his sister-in-law from the dead. This scene has been criticised for its implausibility but the criticism massively begs the question of the way(s) in which we read the film. Miracles are, by definition, 'implausible' within a realist narrative; but a 'miracle' of some kind is clearly required to bring the two families together, to raise a faith that has become uncharitable and ossified from the dead. . . . Visually too, much of the film's power derives from its juxtaposition of fantastic and realist elements. The location shooting (in the Jutland parish where Munk, author of the play on which the film was based, was pastor – a choice of location reminiscent of Bresson) intensifies the effect of the mother's coming to life. And just about no other director could have thought of signalling resurrection, not through the conventional opening of eyes, but by the movement of a hand.

Dreyer dominates the history of the Scandinavian cinema throughout most of this period, although towards the end of it a young Swedish director called Ingmar Bergman aroused attention with a sombre circus melodrama, *Sawdust and Tinsel* (1953). Bergman was one of a number of European directors who in the fifties and sixties brought about a still more radical transformation of the possibilities of the medium.

9 The Big Movie:
Hollywood, 1955 to 1965

Between 1959 and 1963 Otto Preminger produced and directed four lavish and lengthy spectaculars dealing with 'social-conscience' subject-matter. In 1957, the young television director John Frankenheimer made his cinematic début with *The Young Stranger*. In 1962, Marilyn Monroe committed suicide. These three unrelated items between them distil what is most important about the Hollywood of the late fifties and early sixties – the expansiveness of the films made, the creative osmosis between cinema and television, and the burgeoning and questioning of the star-system. These 'headings' will provide a suitable framework for our exploration of the American cinema of this period.

The blockbuster decade

Wider screens, more sophisticated equipment and techniques, and the decline in regular cinema-going caused by television were instrumental in the move towards spectaculars. De Mille remade his silent *The Ten Commandments* thirty-three years after the original (1956), as a grandiloquent swansong. William Wyler broke into Biblical spectacular three years later with *Ben-Hur*; audiences paid primarily to see the famous chariot-race, and were uplifted by the film's saccharine Christianity (and, if aware enough, maybe scandalised by its repressed homosexual element) as a bonus. Stanley Kramer, after his Columbia misadventures, began directing his own films in 1955 (*Not As A Stranger*), and dealt with such crucial issues as nuclear catastrophe (*On the Beach*, 1959) and war-crimes (*Judgement at Nuremberg*, 1961). Mike Todd, responsible for the Cinerama and Todd-AO wide-screen processes, chartered an all-star cast including Noel Coward, Marlene Dietrich, and Buster Keaton for *Around the World in Eighty Days* (1956), ostensibly directed by Michael Anderson. The result departed considerably from Jules Verne. The musical, disastrously, felt obliged to stretch itself to fill the additional screen-space; Cukor's *My Fair Lady* (1964), based on Shaw's *Pygmalion*, was a major box-office success, but a long way from its director's best. Robert Wise, one of the Val Lewton stable of horror directors, moved into the wide-screen technicolor musical in the sixties with *West Side Story* (1961), whose experiments with colour in the dance-scenes, venturesome at the time, but garish in retrospect, now appear less interesting than its highly-charged ensemble choreography. His major success came with *The Sound of Music* (1965), one of the all-time box-office record-holders. At the beginning, Julie Andrews hurtles full-throatedly into view, belting out the title song, across an Austrian mountain-top – a moment that marks the peak of Wise's career as a horror director.

Vincente Minnelli diversified considerably in this period, turning out the homosexual drama *Tea and Sympathy* (1956), as well as more musicals (notably *Gigi*, 1958) and one of Hollywood's most interesting biopics, *Lust for Life* (1956). Kirk Douglas as Van Gogh and Anthony Quinn as Gauguin sound an unlikely combination, but their tense acting has caused the film to last better than might have been expected.

Preminger and Fred Zinnemann are the best examples of the 'big-movie' trend in Hollywood of this period. Zinnemann became less effective as he became more solemn and literary. Few would now trade *High Noon* for *The Nun's Story* (1959), a protracted melodrama with Audrey Hepburn as a novice, or *The Sundowners* (1960). The Preminger heavyweights work better; *Anatomy of a Murder* (1959) penetratingly demystifies the conventional courtroom drama, fine performances by Lee Remick and James Stewart bringing to light ambiguities often buried in other films. *Advise and Consent* (1962) explicitly tackled the theme of homosexuality and political corruption (like all films of Washington intrigue, it received considerable backdated credibility from the Watergate affair). The other two, attempts to express and resolve the spiritual-cum-political crises of Judaism (*Exodus*, 1960) and Catholicism (*The Cardinal*, 1963), suffer through over-reaching themselves; Preminger is not God, though he has a good try.

These films have probably dated as fast as any others in Hollywood history. Partly this is because it was soon recognised that the distinctive qualities of Hollywood at its best – tension, laconic dialogue, toughness

Voyage dans la Lune, Georges Méliès, 1896. The moon 'weeps' in one of the first-ever trick cinematic effects. (Regent)

The Battleship Potemkin, Eisentein, 1925. A shot from the celebrated Odessa steps sequence. (Contemporary Films)

The Blue Angel, Steinberg, 1930. Marlene Dietrich
begins to fascinate Emil Jannings. (Transit films, Munich)

Gone with the Wind, George Cukor, Sam Wood and Victor
Fleming, 1939. Clark Gable and Vivien Leigh in one of
Hollywood's greatest successes.
(Metro-Goldwyn-Mayer)

Casablanca, Michael Curtiz, 1943. Humphrey Bogart remembers Ingrid Bergman with the aid of a bottle and a tune. (United Artists)

Chikamatsu Monogatari/The Crucified Lovers, Mizoguchi, 1954. The lovers on the run in a characteristically beautiful shot. (Cinegate)

Bus Stop, Joshua Logan, 1956. Marilyn Monroe in one of her best-known roles. (Twentieth-Century Fox)

Blow-up, Michaelangelo Antonioni, 1967. David
Hemmings photographs back at the camera.
(Metro-Goldwyn-Mayer)

Some Like it Hot, Billy Wilder, 1959. Tony Curtis in,
and Marilyn Monroe out, of drag. (United Artists)

A Bout de Souffle/Breathless, Godard, 1959. Jean-Paul
Belmondo as the aspirant gangster. (Connoisseur Films)

L'Année Dernière à Marienbad/Last Year in Marienbad,
Resnais, 1961. Delphine Seyrig in this Robbe-Grillet
scripted film. (Contemporary Films)

8½, Fellini, 1963. Marcello Mastroianni surrounded by
the women he remembers from his past. (Gala)

American Graffiti, George Lucas, 1973. A study of mid-American youth. (Columbia-Warner)

Ai No Corrida/Empire of the Senses, Oshima, 1976. Tatsuya Fuji and Eiko Matsuda in this erotic/political masterpiece. (Cinegate)

– were the very opposite of such big-studio productions. Manny Farber, in a 1957 article, contrasted 'action directors' such as Hawks with 'water buffaloes' such as George Stevens, whose *The Diary of Anne Frank* (1959) and *The Greatest Story Ever Told* (1965) place themselves by their titles alone in the category of Significant Subject-matter. Farber's article, like the theoretical and practical work going on in France at much the same time, stressed the tension, the unforced cynicism, and the exploration of genre that went on in the action directors' movies. Nowadays the work of late-period Zinnemann and Stevens appears by comparison overblown and naïve in its preoccupation with significance.

The influence of television

But it is necessary to understand the particular set of circumstances in which such a cinema was produced. Television had supplanted the regular Saturday or Sunday trip to the movies; for a film to be sure of returning the funds invested in it, it had to be something out of the ordinary (in scale, increasingly equated with quality). Films like *The Ten Commandments* or David Lean's *Lawrence of Arabia* (1962) could take over major cinemas for months at a time, providing the focus for an annual or biannual visit to the movies. The liberal conscience developed in 'problem pictures' carried over into the area of the spectacular, and the results, in their combination of lavish production and unsubtle edification, have palled very rapidly. Frankeheimer's move into the cinema was symptomatic of the rapprochement between film and television in this period. The movies had had to rethink and redefine their place in the popular entertainment system, and once this was done the two worlds coexisted at times very fruitfully. In *The Young Stranger*, a sensitive study of insecure aggression in a small town, and in Sidney Lumet's jury film *Twelve Angry Men* (1957), the smaller scale of television drama was turned to advantage. Frankenheimer's trademark became the 'screen-within-a-screen', television pictures framed within the larger image, reaching its apotheosis in *Seven Days in May* (1964), where the device, though over-used, has the right paranoiac reflexive intensity for its tale of a thwarted military coup against the president.

The star system

Marilyn Monroe's suicide unleashed a massive Hollywood guilt complex about the star system. Her career exemplified that system at its most excessive; early fetichisation as a sex-object who sparked off a host of imitations with neither her sensitivity nor her vulnerability, marriages to America's top sportsman and intellectual (the baseball player Jo DiMaggio and the playwright Arthur Miller), other fraught liaisons, films that played – not to say preyed – on the conflict between sensuous exterior and the craving for warmth and respectability. Wilder's *Some Like It Hot* (1959), his funniest film, is exemplary; as the bibulous, shimmying dance-band singer Sugar, foil to Tony Curtis and Jack Lemmon in drag, her performance is both touching and hilarious, but the hilarity is on the borderline between laughter-with and laughter-at. Curtis (one of two musicians on the run after witnessing a gang killing, whence the drag disguise) pays court to her, while Lemmon is the victim of attentions from Joe E. Brown's rubber-faced millionaire. Lemmon's blurted answer to Brown's proposal of marriage ('I'm a man!') is imperturbably capped with Brown's 'Nobody's perfect' – one of the great curtain-lines. It could also stand as an epigraph for the whole Monroe phenomenon. Perfect physical beauty is not the key – it is the insecurity behind it that inspires in audiences an often predatory fascination.

The breakdown, and the innocence at the root of it, had been fore-shadowed for many years: in the famous scene from Wilder's *The Seven-Year Itch* (1955), where warm air blows up her dress and she gleefully defends her pants, arousing black jealousy from DiMaggio during shooting; in the offscreen problems that marred her later films, the turbulent affairs, drinking, and frantic late-night phone-calls (all of course *enhancing* the films in another, macabre way, particularly for later audiences); above all in her last completed movie, Huston's *The Misfits* (1961), an ambitious drama of the West which suffers from a lack of control and now constitutes a necropolis for the Hollywood of the fifties. Clark Gable, the male lead, died before the year was out; Montgomery Clift, who co-starred with Gable and Monroe, had begun the abuse of pills and alcohol that was to lead to his making only three more films in the six years before his death.

Watching Joan Crawford as Clarence Brown's *Gorgeous Hussy* of 1936, or unlucky in love as one of Cukor's *The Women* in 1939, we need to make an effort of memory to remind ourselves that in 1955, after three failed marriages, she became the wife of the chairman of Pepsi-Cola, and allowed her acting career to tail off as she married a success-ful businessman. She died, peacefully and enormously rich, in 1977. The Monroe–Crawford contrast reveals the make-or-break element inherent in the star system at its most marked. Hollywood's tendency to eat its children also meant that those who survived the banquet were likely to do so in some style.

The Monroe suicide suddenly made the public aware of the traps and risks of stardom. Other Hollywood deaths (Jayne Mansfield's in a car-crash in 1967, after a period of drink and drug abuse; Veronica Lake, the vampish 'peek-a-boo-girl' of the forties, dying penniless and alcoholic in 1973) kept the awareness alive. The booze-happy, bed-hopping image of Hollywood, hitherto evoked with mingled disgust and envy, came to be seen as the manifestation of gigantic collective insecurity. It did not take long for the industry, quite logically, to build this into its own self-image, to use it to add a further layer of gloss to its glamour; as macabre biopics and other items of narcissistic cultivation attest, Hollywood was quite capable of turning to profit the martyrs it produced.

Orson Welles – Hollywood victim if not martyr – produced only four films in this decade (one of them, *Don Quixote* of 1955, never completed) – proof enough of his continuing difficulty in fitting into either of the 'two Hollywoods'. Insufficiently laconic and precise for an 'action director', he appeared in what Farber would doubtless have called 'water-buffalo' films (such as Huston's *Moby Dick* of 1956), but remained determined to direct only on his own terms. The results are often memorable (particularly *Touch of Evil*, 1958), often thwarted by neglect of detail (the abysmal sound in parts of his Falstaff film *Chimes at Midnight*, 1966), or uneasily pretentious (the self-parody of *F For Fake*, 1975). The likening of Welles's career to Kane's Xanadu – a vast congeries of self-obsessed dream, forever and dauntingly inadequate – is none the less apposite for having been often repeated.

The action directors

What of the 'action directors' themselves? Anthony Mann moved away from the West with *El Cid* (1961) and *The Fall of the Roman Empire* (1964), retaining the Western notion of armed battle as a trial between good and evil. Sam Fuller dealt grippingly with a mental hospital in *Shock Corridor* (1963), as well as continuing his police-versus-gangster exploration in equally amoral vein with *Underworld USA* (1961). Nicholas Ray whitewashed the James Brothers in *The True Story of Jesse James* (1957), and was eulogised by the French magazine *Cahiers du Cinéma* for *Party Girl* (1958). Don Siegel, active in the industry since 1945, came into prominence via the gangster drama *Baby Face Nelson* (1957, with Mickey Rooney) and *Invasion of the Body Snatchers*

(1956), about zombies from outer space who penetrate and enslave human bodies – inevitably read as an allegory of totalitarian brain-washing. . . . Robert Aldrich adapted Mickey Spillane in *Kiss Me Deadly* (1955), and in 1962 gloated horrifyingly over the downfall of a star in *Whatever Happened to Baby Jane?* Bette Davis's ex-child star has none of the mummified panache of Swanson in *Sunset Boulevard*; all the more ironic, then, that the film gave her career and that of Joan Crawford a late boost.

This brief catalogue gives some indication of how such directors operated in the period under discussion. They frequently laboured under constraints – not so much the low budgets, on which many of them had precisely learned to thrive, as studio pressures towards significance coupled with the recurrent insecurity of unemployment. There was a tendency to move away from the gangster and the Western, into science-fiction, or more exotic locations, in which the psychological drama often became less laconic and more explicit. But all the directors listed above produced tense, skilful work, emphasing how central to Hollywood cinema the whole 'action director' concept was.

Hawks in this period approached retirement, via films often a long way from his best, but including the extraordinary *Rio Bravo* (1959). No Western can have been shot so largely indoors, indication enough of Hawks's concern with exploring the ways in which men interact under pressure rather than with conventional big-scale action. Where we get this, as in the obligatory shoot-out at the end, it turns almost into a parody of the Western climax – the unlikely posse of four men (Dean Martin's reformed alcoholic, Rick Nelson's teenager, Walter Brennan's toothless cripple, and John Wayne welding them together with customary machismo) operating superbly as a team with some help from chance. The last scene of all brings together the classic Western patronisation/fear of women and Hawks's preoccupation with the ways in which they are perceived as a threat to the male group. Angie Dickinson as the newly-hired barmaid discards her black négligée at Wayne's admission that he doesn't want anybody else to see her in it – the nearest the real Western male can come to a declaration of love. She throws it out of the window, where Walter Brennan picks it up, wraps it around his neck, and walks off cackling. This scene, like the preceding shoot-out, is an incomparably effective development and analysis of an archetypal Western situation. Hawks once again shows his skill at working simultaneously within a myth and against it.

Alfred Hitchcock, along with directors such as Ray and Hawks, became a crucial point of reference for the French *nouvelle vague* during this period. This is not to reduce his work to a pre-text for Truffaut or Chabrol, but rather to emphasise that it shares with the action directors with whom he otherwise has so little in common a concern with *mise-en-scène* or cinematic 'staging', with development of and within the *image* above all else rather than with the humanist significance of subject-matter.

This has led to intense debate on his merit. He has been lauded as one of the cinema's theological poets, sombrely preoccupied with the mechanisms by which some are arbitrarily doomed to madness or violent destruction. He has also been dismissed as a heartless practical joker, whose fish-eyed presence in his own films is an indication of his contempt for actors and audience, and whose stress on madness and violence is diseased and meretricious.

Psycho (1960) was particularly severely criticised, not necessarily for the reasons that make it still chilling today. The murder of Janet Leigh in her shower no longer horrifies nearly so much as it did seventeen years ago (nor, one suspects, would it have horrified so much then without the blast of advance publicity). What makes *Psycho* still effective is the false trail up which Hitchcock leads his audience at the beginning, concentrating on Janet Leigh's theft and absconding until the murder, and the way in which, by acute attention to verbal and visual detail, he never once allows us to suspect that the homicidal mother of Norman Bates (Anthony Perkins) is a corpse in a chair, and that it is Perkins himself who is butchering any woman who comes within reach in posthumous obedience to her jealousy. When the armchair in which 'Mrs Bates' is sitting swivels slowly round to reveal the eyeless cadaver, it is a horrifying instance of the film's power to look back at the spectators – to frighten the audience out of its position of gazing superiority.

Psycho is a film about a pun (Bates's 'mummy' *is* a 'mummy') and about manipulation (the dead mother manipulates her helpless son as Hitchcock manipulates his helpless spectators). Many of his other films can also be read in this way, as *jeux d'esprit* starting from one central conceit or clutch of conceits and manipulating the audience into near-paranoia. *Vertigo* (1958) plays on the fear of heights (ours and James Stewart's), and on the 'vertigo' that is an essential component of cinema-viewing (think how often your head spins when you emerge from the cinema into daylight outside). *The Birds* (1963) gives us its key in a brief Hitch monologue at the beginning about man's cruelty to his feathered friends and how justified they might be in retaliating, which does not make the sexual paranoia induced by the hundreds of jabbing beaks any less intense, nor the ending, when a policeman picks up one among hundreds of dead birds and confidently identifies its species, any less disturbing. Hitchcock is in this respect a more cerebral director than is sometimes thought, closer certainly to a practical joker than to the Bresson of Los Angeles. He has realised the power of the cinema as audience-manipulator, but precisely for this reason is a less important (because less open) director, I would argue, than his most extreme admirers make him out to be.

As for the other established directors, Kazan maintained his reputation as a discoverer of new talent with the intense performance he extracted from Caroll Baker in *Baby Doll* (1956), as a thumb-sucking child bride, and Warren Beatty and Natalie Wood in *Splendour in the Grass* (1961). Wilder followed *Some Like It Hot* with *The Apartment* (1960), a sharp comedy about a clerk forced to pander to his employers by lending them his flat for bachelor evenings; but, as with *The Lost Weekend*, much of the impact was forfeited by a happy ending. *Irma la Douce* (1963) stands with Jules Dassin's *Never on Sunday* (1959) as Hollywood's most unacceptable sentimentalisation of prostitution, presented in both films as a jolly, golden-hearted romp. To this day, the Hollywood movies in which streetwalkers look like streetwalkers and not like glamorised actresses can be counted on the fingers of one hand.

If Stanley Kubrick is included along with American rather than British directors, despite the fact that he has been based in England since 1961, this is largely because his grandiloquent directorial style and emphasis on glossiness of set and photography have more in common with the Hollywood of the Significant Subject than with any indigenous British filmic tradition. Three- or four-year gaps have characterised his more recent work, evidence of how important preparation and sophisticated technique are to him. His first films, the thrillers *Killer's Kiss* (1955) and *The Killing* (1956), bely this later development; the Kubrick we know now appears in his adaptation of *Lolita* (1962), attempting stylistic parodies (as in the long Wellesian shots at the beginning) in analogous vein to Nabokov's novel, but without its unexampled flair. *Dr Strangelove, or How I Learned to Stop Worrying and Love the Bomb* (1963) presents the American officers in charge of the nuclear deterrent as a set of unbridled maniacs to save the world from whom the President has to call upon a former Nazi. The glossiness in both films tended to work against the macabre element, a conflict that becomes more intense in Kubrick's later work.

The cult of youth

Carroll Baker as Baby Doll and Sue Lyon as Lolita were among the more sensationalist examples of the concentration on young people's problems that became more and more marked in post-war American cinema. Richard Brooks in *The Blackboard Jungle* (1955) introduced a naïve schoolmaster (Glenn Ford) into a tough New York college, and provided him with a charged friendship with a coloured boy (Sidney Poitier) to purge him of his illusions. Martin Ritt came from television to make *A Man is Ten Feet Tall* (1956), where Sidney Poitier exercised a calming influence on the overwrought John Cassavetes. More important for the future development of the American cinema than either was Arthur Penn's first feature, *The Left-Handed Gun* (1958), based on an idea by James Dean. Paul Newman as the confused Billy the Kid gave a performance Dean would have had difficulty in bettering; Penn revealed a genuinely original interest in the 'outsider' figure that was to animate his succeeding work, including his study of Helen Keller, *The Miracle Worker* (1962).

But the big studios found the most profitable youth-orientated films to be those capitalising on the success of rock'n'roll, which rivalled more conventional musicals as money-spinners in this period. Bill Haley and the Comets starred in *Rock Around the Clock* (1956) and *Don't Knock the Rock* (1957), both directed by Fred F. Sears for Columbia; apoplexy befell clergymen and cinema managers throughout the world as audiences jived in the aisles and ripped up seats to the rhythm of the music. Elvis Presley regressed from the truculent rebel of *King Creole* (Michael Curtiz, 1958) via Army service to *GI Blues* (Norman Taurog, 1960), *Fun in Acapulco* (Richard Thorpe, 1963), and other identikit vehicles for identikit songs. The level of rock cinema was to remain fairly abysmal until the mid-sixties.

The cut-price, the independent, the underground

What has been said hitherto might suggest that the big studios had it even more their own way in this period than immediately after the war. The financial success and aesthetic acclaim of Kubrick's work shows how far lavish production values were equated by many sections of the public with cinematic value. But there were exceptions to this, of great significance for the development of the medium. Roger Corman performed artificial respiration on the cut-price B-picture with a series of economically-shot horror movies, which he produced himself and turned out at the rate of up to eight a year. The lurid colour and apocalyptic camp of *The Fall of the House of Usher* (1960) and *The Tomb of Ligeia* (1964) make them good entertainment, but Corman's place in contemporary cinematic legend rests more on his use and distribution of time and funds. The profits from Corman's quickies, and the experience gained in working on them, helped to launch directors such as Martin Scorsese and Peter Bogdanovich, who were to become major figures in the seventies. Corman was instrumental in showing that it was possible to sidestep the major studios, as sources of both funds and talent.

There had been a small but flourishing tradition of independent film-making in the United States for several years, notably on the West Coast. Surrealism influenced *Meshes of the Afternoon* (Maya Deren and Alexander Hammid, 1943), a paranoid nightmare culminating in suicide, and the explicitly homosexual work of Kenneth Anger, begun with (allegedly) stolen equipment at the age of fourteen. *Fireworks* (1947) tips sado-masochism over into high camp, when Anger's heart turns into an electricity meter and the penis of his sailor assailant into a spark-ejaculating Roman candle. Also characteristic of surrealism was the use of song and poetry, in Ian Hugo's *The Bells of Atlantis* (1952), as accompaniment to abstract patterns of colour, and the general flight from linear narrative and from the suggestion of interpretable (exhaustible) meaning. The Whitney brothers (James and John) synchronised shimmering kaleidoscopes of colour (computer-produced) with electronically-synthesised music in *Film Exercises* (1943/4) and *Yantra* (1950/5), and techniques such as painting directly onto film, or integrating film into concerts and light-shows, were also widespread.

The above ideas were to gain much currency in the late sixties, with the spread of the 'underground' counter-culture. But, as the above examples suggest, there had in fact been no real interruption between their germination in the surrealist period and their psychedelic resurgence; it was simply that their development was taking place in a very restricted milieu, and with almost no access to international screening and distribution.

Sheldon Renan differentiates avant-garde films of the fifties and afterwards from their predecessors by saying:

'The films of the second avant-garde, being based on literature, or drama, or poetry, or dance, looked like official art. The new films were not so easily identifiable. There were film portraits, mementoes, visual essays, personal documentaries, and many films that didn't have genres.'[1]

The personal note evoked by Renan is manifest in the two major characteristics of the underground films of this vintage: the production of many of them for and about a small audience (friends and family), and the exploration of the potentialities of film as material. Stan Brakhage scratches titles and images onto the celluloid in *Desistfilm* (1954) and *Reflections on Black* (1955); other directors used hand-held cameras, interfered with light-sources, over-exposed, made no attempt to conceal splices, and in a host of ways emphasised and experimented with the materiality of film, treating it not as a transparent membrane but as a medium to be worked on.

Such uses of film – sidestepping or ignoring the conventional requirements of genre, narrative, production, audience, and the transparency of the image – were at the opposite extreme to what was going on in sixties Hollywood. The wider distribution of such films and changes in the American commercial cinema, along with in many ways parallel developments in Europe, were to bring the extremes closer in the next few years. For the moment, though, the work of the experimentalists and that of the big studios went on in mutually ignoring isolation.

10 New Waves:
Europe 1955 to 1965

The first country dealt with in this chapter is France, which during this period replaced Italy as the generally acknowledged centre of cinematic innovation. There were several reasons for this: the financial blockade of 'neo-realist' films mentioned earlier, the unrivalled position of Paris as world capital of film, the theoretical work that went on around the journal *Cahiers du Cinéma*, and, not least, the limits of neo-realism itself. Enough artistic and methodological questions were begged by Zavattini's 'a man eating, a man sleeping, a man crying' for it to be quite plain that – if ever there were to be a last word in cinema – this would not be it. The questions explored in different ways by Eisenstein, Welles, Dreyer, and the underground directors – questions of the status and construction of narrative, of the use of celluloid as a material medium rather than as a window on the world, of the ideology implicit in the visual and narrative strategies directors adopted – needed to be further advanced. So too did the exploration of how far film-makers could emancipate themselves from dependence on the economic and political status quo. Neo-realism had started out, perforce, as a low-budget enterprise, but its end was largely the work of Italian big business.

The French nouvelle vague

We have seen how the cinema had early become an important part of French intellectual life. One of the major influences on the hetero-geneous group of directors linked together under the heading of the *nouvelle vague* was American 'action cinema' of the kind eulogised by Farber, examples of which were regularly to be seen at the Paris Cinémathèque.

Of equal importance was the activity of Claude Chabrol, Jean-Luc Godard, Eric Rohmer, and François Truffaut on *Cahiers du Cinéma*. Theory and practice have always interpenetrated far more, and far more fruitfully, in French than in British (probably than in any other European) cultural and intellectual life. At roughly the same time as these directors began their work, a group of novelists (known as the 'new novelists', though that label is as imprecise as *nouvelle vague*) were working in very different ways to question and extend the scope of the novel, breaking away from accepted notions of character, plausibility, and plot. It is significant that the most prominent figures in this movement – Alain Robbe-Grillet, Michel Butor, Nathalie Sarraute – produced, as well as fiction, theoretical works and essays, re-evaluating the fiction of the past and addressing themselves to the problem of what a contemporary fiction could and should be. There is no sense, in their work or in that of the *Cahiers* group, of a breach between these areas of activity, or of any element of coincidence (so that they were writers or film-makers who also 'happened' to produce theory and criticism). Rather, theory forms an important part of practice, interlinked with and indissoluble from it.

The two main theoretical concepts articulated in *Cahiers* were film-as-writing ('*écriture*') and the concept of the *auteur* as *metteur-en-scène*. Astruc's article (ref. p. 112) suggests how the first of these might be developed. The image was no longer subordinate to a 'literary' scenario as, say, illustrations are to the text of a novel (an extreme example, admittedly, but a philosophy that implicitly underlies most adaptations of literary works to the screen). The cinema was a mode of writing in its own right.

This enables us to understand the related concept of the *auteur*. The director came to be seen as the real 'writer' of the film, the hand that held the camera and ruled the world. This had long been accepted in the European 'art' cinema: Dreyer, Renoir, Pudovkin had always been regarded as the *auteurs* of their films. But Hollywood directors – with certain exceptions such as Welles, whose repeated problems were seen as proof of an artist's integrity – had by and large been submerged in an undifferentiated commercial mass. The *auteur* theory provided a basis for distinction and evaluation.

It did this, as we have seen with Hawks, not on the basis of 'serious' subject-matter, but rather on that of the identification of a series of patterns or motifs that persisted through a body of work, notwithstanding changes in genre. Durability in these motifs was read as evidence of a strong creative individuality, capable of maintaining itself in spite of commercial pressures. This approach has much to be said for and against it. It provided a coherent rationale for saying that *Johnny Guitar* and *To Have and Have Not* were better films than, say, *Ben-Hur*, despite the less 'serious' subject-matter. It emphasised the cinema's claim to parity of treatment with other arts. Its concept of *mise-en-scène* (the way in which actions and scenes are 'staged') made it possible to articulate what was distinctive in a director's *oeuvre*, without unduly privileging the work of either the scriptwriter (as 'literary' critiques had tended to do) or the cameraman (as in praise of 'beautiful' photography). In a word, it made it possible and necessary to speak of 'a Hawks' or 'a Nicholas Ray' as much as of 'a Renoir', and thereby redeemed much great film-making from limbo.

But its strengths were also its weaknesses. Its emphasis on the individual role of the director ignored the dominance of the big studios, and the ideology this represented; Hawks, after all, became 'Hawks' in spite as well as because of the various constraints under which he worked. Auteurism could possibly account for how Losey or Lang retained their distinctive qualities in exile, but not for the reasons – no less important to the film-watcher – behind that exile. Setting out to oppose the canonisation of humanistic subject-matter, auteurism erected in its stead a deification of those 'action directors' seen as the greatest *metteurs-en-scène*. The 'alternative Pantheon' of Hitchcock, Nicholas Ray, Preminger were venerated as uncritically as the old gods such as René Clair or Eisenstein. Auteurism stressed individual explorations within and across genres, and not the social determinants of the genres themselves, so that the different individualisms of the gangster movie and the Western came to be seen as ancillary to the 'genius' of a Hawks working across them. All in all, this critical school was a crucial point in filmic theory, but one that had undoubted, and severe, limitations.

What were its effects on French directors of this period? By rejecting the star-system, the claims of edifying subject-matter, and the Hollywood aesthetic of scale, it emancipated them from a host of restraints. By its emphasis on the individual director's 'authorial' role, it made it appear possible for anybody with sufficient talent and backing to make a film – his or her film. The Hollywood it revered was that of the low-budget feature, a world far more accessible to budding directors than the big studio and the uplifting spectacle.

French films of youth

It is thus not surprising that the directors/critics most affected by it were young, and tended to make films about young people. François Truffaut directed his first feature, *Les Quatre Cents Coups* (*The Four Hundred Blows*, 1959), at the age of twenty-seven. Its 'hero', the adolescent Antoine Doinel, escapes from an unhappy home into petty crime, and, at the end, from a reform school to the sea, beside which we see his face, frozen in mingled ecstasy and apprehension, in the last shot of the film. Much that was new and exciting about the film when it was released (it won the directors' prize at the Cannes Festival) has passed into common currency: the fluid, mobile camera-movements in the street-scenes, the hesitancy and inarticulacy of its central character, the mixture of lyricism, dissection, and humour. Its subject-matter is not dissimilar to that of a 'problem picture', but its mobility and reluctance to draw explicit morals or conclusions are a world away.

Truffaut followed this with *Tirez sur le Pianiste* (*Shoot the Pianist*, 1960), financed by its predecessor's profits. French directors of this period tended to maintain a high rate of production, filming on low budgets and able to support themselves thanks to early critical acclaim. Charles Aznavour plays a mournful night-club pianist who, flashbacks tell us, is an ex-concert pianist with a fraught emotional past. Again, what is important is not the intrigue (a blend of gangster-movie and 'little-man' drama), so much as the rapid alternations of mood and tonality, produced by rapid variations of camera-movement and speed, and the exploration of the possibilities of the medium.

This reached a climax with *Jules et Jim* (1961), applauded for fifteen minutes at its première. Here the *mise-en-scène* produces the film's emotional tensions and ironies. The medium is explored with conscious virtuosity, via dizzying tracking-shots, frozen and accelerated motion, old newsreels blown grainily up to screen size, and rapid cuts and leaps in time and space. The triangular affair between the Frenchman Jim, the German Jules, and Catherine (Jeanne Moreau in a majestically pouting performance), shifts, veers from the tragic to the bitterly ironic, and periodically returns to an exhausted stalemate because of the variety of speeds, angles, and disjunctions of the *mise-en-scène*. At the end, where Catherine drives her car (with Jim as a passenger) off a broken bridge, and we see the shattered Jules leaving the crematorium, we too are shattered, by the double and simultaneous realisation how far it is possible to go with a relationship and a movie camera. It is interesting that *Jules et Jim* became a key work, not only for film-makers in other countries, but, through its consistent turning away from the idea of the conventionally monogamous couple (and, maybe, through the homosexual dimension it hints at but skirts), for the beginnings of the 'new morality' in sex that characterised the sixties. It remains a major work because what is filmed and how it is filmed, the ethical ambiguities of the subject-matter and the variety of ways of filming, are so fluidly yet precisely held in balance.

Truffaut is credited with the 'script' for *A Bout de Souffle* (*Breathless*, 1959), the first feature directed by Jean-Luc Godard. In fact no such script existed before shooting; Truffaut allowed his name, known after *Les Quatre Cents Coups*, to be used to help Godard, in which he succeeded triumphantly. The film, shot cheaply on location in Paris, was an international success. Jean-Paul Belmondo, a small-time gangster who worships Humphrey Bogart (the film is dedicated to the American B-picture company Monogram Pictures), has an indecisive affair with Jean Seberg, an American girl half-studying in Paris. The affair ends with her insecurely betraying him to the police and his gunning-down in the street. Morality is replaced by part-playing; Belmondo and Seberg articulate who they are and communicate through their myths and cultures (he has his Bogie, she her Mozart and Renoir), but it doesn't really work because, though he loves things American and she things European, they operate in totally different registers; an uncertain '*J'sais pas*' (I don't know) is liable to conclude most of their conversations. The film's use of jump-cuts (which skip from one part of an action to another, omitting the middle) was much commented upon when it was released, in tandem with the jumpiness and hesitancy of the characters' behaviour. Nowadays, one is more struck by the long conversation between Seberg and Belmondo that forms the centre of the film – a marathon of indecisiveness, filmed in shot and reverse-shot (the camera focusing on whoever is talking, moving with the dialogue), which may help us to understand the condemnation Godard encountered in many quarters.

Politically committed critics berated *A Bout de Souffle* and its follow-up, *Le Petit Soldat* (*The Little Soldier*, 1960), for a nihilism they saw as tantamount to neo-fascism. In the light of the later politicisation of Godard's cinema, this accusation appears far-fetched; but it may not always have been so easy for critics of the time to disentangle Godard's interest in his 'little soldier' Bruno's rootlessness and his involvement with the paramilitary colonialist OAS, to which Godard emphatically did not subscribe.

A related criticism – made especially by critics connected with the journal *Positif* – was of a total, narcissistic absorption in the cinematic medium to the total exclusion of all other considerations. Watching Godard's *Une Femme est une Femme* (*A Woman is a Woman*, 1961), with its seemingly interminable flow of Hollywood musical parody, or reading at several years' distance some of the more peremptory and oracular affirmations of the auteurists, this too becomes comprehensible. But the related emphasis on *mise-en-scène* was of immense practical utility to Godard and his contemporaries, both for the way in which it allowed them to produce individual films on low budgets and for the possibilities it opened up for investigation within and parody of the various genres, and hence within the institution of cinema itself – possibilities whose ideological implications were to be developed later.

Les Carabiniers (*The Sharpshooters*, 1963) took the picaresque framework of the Western or the war picture and transposed it to the urban wasteland of outer Paris. Two gulls join the King's army in return for promises of riches untold, but discover that these riches come only in the form of photographs, and are shot at the end of the film. The suburban samurais' willingness to accept the image for the object can be seen as a warning not to equate film with transparent, objective reality.

The dangers as well as the delights of film are plain too in his next feature, *Le Mépris* (*Contempt*, 1963), in which the break-up of a marriage is counterpointed with the making of a cinematic adaptation of the Odyssey, directed by Fritz Lang (who plays himself). Godard's work of this period appears profoundly ambiguous, adumbrating but not developing to the full conceptions that did not come into their own until his *annus mirabilis* of 1965.

The dangers and delights of cinema as of any *mise-en-scène* are nowhere more rigorously or excitingly explored than in the work of Jacques Rivette, *Cahiers* critic and sometime assistant to Renoir, whose *Paris Nous Appartient* (*Paris Belongs to Us*) was made between 1958 and 1960, as funds permitted. A group of actors rehearse a production of *Pericles*; some of them come into contact with an alleged totalitarian conspiracy to overthrow society. The production is never staged, the conspiracy turns out to have been a figment of the (collective) imagination. The predictable anti-climax of the two strands of plot is secondary to the reflections they provoke on the interplay of spectacle and everyday existence – only Renoir and (later) the Japanese director Oshima (ref. p. 178–80) have gone so far in this direction – as well as on the urban paranoia that was to be a major concern of sixties cinema, and on the film-watching process as a trap to whose illusion of reality we willingly succumb. Five years were to pass before Rivette's next film, *La Religieuse*

(*The Nun*), which made his name through a ban on the film, ill-advised even by Gaullist standards, imposed by the then Minister of Culture André Malraux.

The new-wave films mentioned so far paid relatively little attention to the French bourgeoisie which figured so prominently in much of Renoir's work. Two directors were to make this preserve their own, the Catholic Eric Rohmer and Claude Chabrol. Rohmer's major work was to come after 1966, though he had already made his mark with *Le Signe du Lion* in 1959. Chabrol attempted to marry a sardonic portrayal of the French provincial middle-classes with many of the stylistic ironies of Hitchcock, so that it is now very difficult to remember, for instance, whether the continual eating that goes on in both director's films was initially a Hitch- or a Chabrolism. *Le Beau Serge* (1958), his feature début – full of snow, depression and drunkenness in a small village – set a tone that was to become less fatalistic and more acerbic with the increased concentration of his later work on the bourgeoisie. *Les Bonnes Femmes* (1960) focuses on four girls working in a record-shop, each pursuing a fairly modest dream of happiness. The least stereotyped is strangled in a forest by a sex-maniac – first in a long line of perverse Chabrol murders, here crisply and unblinkingly shot in black-and-white. The dreams of the other three are anatomised in all their mediocrity. The effect is rather like watching the wings being pulled off flies; in his later work, Chabrol was to turn to larger, and nastier, insects.

On the left Bank

Richard Roud has established a useful distinction between the *Cahiers* group and what he dubbed the 'Left Bank' directors: Alain Resnais, Chris Marker, and Agnès Varda. The latter were distinguished in the period under discussion by explicitly left-of-centre political views, and a clear involvement with literary developments. Alain Resnais remains unique among major directors in never having contributed or altered a line of script; the screenplays for his films were always commissioned from prominent authors, and filmed in their entirety, almost as though in polemical assertion that the director *is* the *auteur* of the film however little he has been involved with the script. His move from documentary to feature came with *Hiroshima Mon Amour* (1959), scripted by the novelist Marguerite Duras. Its major thematic preoccupations dominate his *oeuvre*: the now corrosive, now creative effect of memory, places as repositories of emotion, love as the reactivator, like psychoanalysis, of buried trauma. All are present in this tale of a Japanese businessman and a French actress reliving and catharting their wartime experiences in fifties Hiroshima.

The use of varied speeds to effect the transition from past to present, the haunting music, and the disjunction between image and soundtrack (the scream when the woman's wartime lover is killed is the only sound we hear from the past) are amplified and multiplied in *L'Année Dernière à Marienbad* (*Last Year in Marienbad*, 1961), scripted by Alain Robbe-Grillet. Here, despite the precision of the title, time and place in the conventional narrative sense are abolished, existing only as the duration of the film and the 'place' on the screen. A man and a woman (the latter superbly played by Delphine Seyrig) meet in an echoing baroque château; the man attempts to persuade her that they had an affair the previous year, and that she agreed to go away with him; she resists, but leaves the château with him at the end. The film can be, and has been, read as:

– an allegory of persuasion (Robbe-Grillet informally subtitled it *Persuasion*)

– the account of a psychoanalysis (the trauma being exorcised at the end)

– a variant of an old Breton legend in which Death comes to claim his victim after a year and a day

– an exploration of the gulf between the 'subjective' time constituted by our sensations and memories and the 'objective' time of the clock.

It is also, perhaps most importantly, a film about seduction, and particularly about the seduction which persuades us to accept a celluloid film as 'reality'. Each image in the film has equivalent status; there is no clear visual or narrative dividing-line between 'real', 'past', and 'imaginary' events, between the actual and the hallucinated or remembered, so that, along with *Orphée*, it is probably the most dreamlike of all films. The mirrors that abound in the château evoke and undercut the process by which we watch a film as a 'mirror of reality'. In this respect the film comes close to the unattainable goal of the Surrealists, the point 'at which life and death, the real and the imaginary, the past and the future . . . cease to be perceived as opposites' (André Breton).

The hysterical masochistic emotional power of the film's décor of feathers, statues, mirrors, and corridors opening onto contradictory perspectives is unsurpassed, notably in the one passage Resnais has ever altered from a published screenplay. This is where the man bursts into Delphine Seyrig's room two-thirds of the way through, not as in the script for violent rape, but for us to see her coming ecstatically forward to him, arms outstretched, in over-exposed repeated shots. Cinema as ecstasy has gone no further.

Chris Marker also worked in the field of the documentary, until his *La Jettée* of 1963. Like *Marienbad* this is a film in which conventional boundaries of time and reality are transcended, innovatory in being composed almost exclusively of still photographs. More effective is *Cuba Si!* (1961), a documentary that makes no attempt to disguise its left-wing *parti pris* (most commercial documentaries attempt to ignore their right-wing bias), and is consistently exciting to watch. Marker's movement from documentary to feature was paralleled by Jean Rouch, whose *Chronique d'un Été* (*Chronicle of a Summer*, 1961) edited twenty hours of Paris street interviews down to a feature-length narrative which is then commented upon by those who edited and participated in it.

Agnès Varda reversed stereotyped ideas of male and female roles by experimenting with narrative in *Cléo de 5 à 7* (1961), whose running time corresponds to two hours in the life of her central character – a rare coincidence of 'filmed' and 'filmic' time – while her husband, Jacques Demy, made lyrical musicals set in the seaports of Normandy and Brittany (*Lola*, 1961; *Les Parapluies de Cherbourg/The Umbrellas of Cherbourg*, 1964). The variety of films lumped together as *nouvelle vague* should now be plain. The label rapidly acquired a polemical force that helpfully dispensed its users from the need to refer to anything precise.

Other French directors

Not all French cinema development of this period was confined to 'new-wave' directors. Louis Malle directed *Les Amants* (*The Lovers*, 1958), whose unambiguously ecstatic ending – Jeanne Moreau elopes happily with her lover – continues to perplex audiences accustomed to a greater degree of irony, and *Le Feu Follet* (*Will o' the Wisp*, 1963), the bleak account of a suicide. It may well be the absence from these films of the ambiguities and openness of a *Breathless* or a *Jules et Jim* that has caused them to date considerably.

Neither of Bresson's two films of this period counts among his best. *Pickpocket* (1959) refines his austerity to the point of self-parody, and is overschematic in its reversal of conventional values (the pickpocket is the saint, his respectable foil the villain). *Le Procès de Jeanne d'Arc* (*The Trial of Joan of Arc*, 1961) invites, and suffers by, comparison with Dreyer. The rhetoric of Dreyer's close-ups is manifest and self-dissecting, compelling the viewer to concentrate upon his own sadism as the camera stays on Joan's harrowed countenance beyond the point of endurance; that of Bresson's is more covert and less analytical (as in the use of a heavy echo-effect on the soundtrack, producing a melo-dramatic dimension that the scrupulous fidelity to contemporary records of the trial appears to disavow).

Renoir was less prolific and less influential in this decade (the mis-conceived science-fiction of *Le Déjeuner sur l'Herbe*, 1959, is arguably his worst film); Cocteau bade the movies farewell with *Le Testament d'Orphée* in 1960; and, just as Loren and Lollobrigida had been the major money-spinners of Italian cinema, so Brigitte Bardot, directed by her then husband Roger Vadim in *Et Dieu Créa la Femme* (*And God Created Woman*, 1956) was thereafter unstoppable.

Bardot succeeding Françoise Arnoul, Godard and Resnais instead of Clouzot and Cayatte; the changes French cinema underwent in this decade were certainly great.

Italy

New developments also began to make themselves felt in the Italian cinema. De Sica and Rossellini were both far less influential after the mid-fifties (though Rossellini did some interesting work for television, including a coldly perfect series of tableaux on *La Prise du Pouvoir par Louis XIV* (*Louis XIV's Seizure of Power*, 1966)). Visconti's out-standing work of the period was the three-and-a-half hour *Rocco and his Brothers* (1960), which took off from a neo-realist base – the dissolution of a Sicilian peasant family in the big city – towards meta-physical and operatic heights. The scene where Rocco, the 'good' brother, Bressonian in his combination of saintliness and inarticulacy, surrenders the girl he loves to his brother who has raped her, acquires immense power from the way in which Visconti plays on our sense of Rocco's moral force and at the same time on a whole series of constrict-ing fundamentalist-Catholic assumptions about sex. The realist base is never forgotten even at the film's most melodramatic moments.

Michelangelo Antonioni became internationally famous after *L'Avventura* was screened at the Cannes Festival in 1960. One anomaly of this institution is that it is at once an international exhibition of cinema and a vehicle for the civic pride of an extremely reactionary town. At the showing of *L'Avventura*, the second element triumphed, as the Cannes bourgeoisie in all its finery kept up a raucous barrage of heckling indignantly disowned by the critics the next day. Ironically for one who had worked as assistant on *Les Visiteurs du Soir* eighteen years before and turned out five previous features, Antonioni was an overnight celebrity.

In *L'Avventura*, we never know what happens to the girl who disappears during a boat trip to an island, and for whom the others search. Antonioni is interested in the shifting and developing relationships between the characters during the search. Difficulty of communication, alienation from environment, necessary and significant silences – Antonioni's central concerns seem a distillation of those of the sixties, but we should not forget that he was the first film-maker to develop them with such an eye for landscape and ear for the 'sound of silence'. It is usually easier for his characters to talk than to feel, and periodically impossible for them to do either.

The landscape of *L'Avventura*, as in many Bergman films, is both a physical setting and a signifier of the characters' isolation. For Antonioni, no man, still less any woman, still less Monica Vitti (his former lover and leading actress in most of his films), is anything but an island. These concerns are transposed to the town in his next two films, *La Notte* (*The Night*, 1961) and *L'Eclisse* (*The Eclipse*, 1962). The titles, obvious references to emotional prostration, have also a literal narrative application; *La Notte* details a night in which Marcello Mastroianni and Jeanne Moreau traverse a crisis in their marriage, ending with ambiguous embraces on a golf-course at dawn, *L'Eclisse* ends with a solar eclipse after Monica Vitti has left indecisively to meet her lover (a sequence strangely reminiscent of Delphine Seyrig's leaving the château at the end of *Marienbad*). The films are kept visually stimulating through Antonioni's control of setting and townscape, in Jeanne Moreau's solitary walk through the city in *La Notte* or in the extraordinary final sequence of *L'Eclisse* where darkness descends, frame by frame, on a town almost bereft of human presence.

Antonioni's first use of colour, in *The Red Desert* (1964), which again uses Monica Vitti in a sensually highly-strung role, ranks among the most imaginative in cinema. Naturalistic and metaphorical use of colour coexist in the same frame, as where a stall in the gloomy industrial environment is selling grey apples, and the dominance of dull pastels is challenged only in the scene where Vitti tells her child a fantasy-story illustrated in brilliant Mediterranean hues. The derisive reception accorded by many critics to these aspects of the film when it was released is a damning indictment of how narrowly literal the approach to colour in film can be.

It was quite fashionable to be decadent in the Italy of that period, as the history of Federico Fellini's *La Dolce Vita* (1959) shows. When word spread that Fellini – an established director since *La Strada* of 1954 – was proposing a vast exposé of the corruption and self-indulgence of high Roman society, its leading names fell over one another in the rush for bit-parts. This crystallises the paradox of the film; it is as sprawlingly self-indulgent as the society it purports to castigate, as much the dupe of the striking appearance (witness the helicopter-borne statue of Christ at the beginning), and as oblivious of the need for a rigorous approach.

This makes the triumph of *Eight and a Half* (1963) all the more surprising. Here, Fellini transcends the flaws of his earlier films – the sentimentalisation of women evident in *La Strada*, the difficulty in bringing rich visual detail under organised control – within (?) the narrative framework of a director working on his ninth film (like Fellini, whence the title), under pressure from colleagues and backers to structure an autobiographical riot of detail that is to be the raw material for his definitive filmic statement. Incapable of doing so, he disappears under a table during the press conference at the end and shoots himself, whereupon the figures from the past that have haunted his imagination and the sets of the film return to perform a joyous, circus-like dance upon which the film closes. Closes . . . only to reopen endlessly upon itself. The narrative status of the 'suicide' is ambiguous; is it a metaphorical abdication of the organising responsibilities of 'art' in favour of some higher principle of 'life' (whatever that may be); a ritual gesture by the director (Marcello Mastroianni) to inaugurate the film he can now make; or a 'real' suicide that liberates Mastroianni from the presences that then parade before us? The only answer is that it is none of these; the movie Mastroianni is supposed to be making leads back into *Eight and a Half* itself, it is vain to look for any 'explanation' of the ending in terms of a conventionally hierarchised narrative discourse. Like *Marienbad*, like *Paris Nous Appartient*, the film moves beyond the old 'realist' canons towards a qualitatively new exploration of the narrative and the dreamlike possibilities of cinema conjoined. It also demonstrates a worrying complicity with not only Romantic notions of the creative genius, but also the allied view of the 'art cinema' as a closed and privileged area; the 'dance of life' at the end reads almost like a polemical assertion that the cinema of the individual creative auteur puts him – by extension, Fellini himself and us his audience – into a position of unique familiarity with and access to 'real experiences' and his/our personal histories, whose implications vis-à-vis cinema as an institution can certainly be seen as reactionary.

Antonioni's bleakness and Fellini's garrulous ripeness dominated the Italian art cinema for most of our period, polar opposites that yet had in common an awareness of the need to evolve new narrative strategies to match changing ethical norms and social conditions. Pier Paolo Pasolini, well-known as poet and novelist before his entry into the cinema, was to take this awareness still further, and become a leading innovator in film structure. His début, *Accattone* (1961), operated within a superficially neo-realist framework (the violent life and death of a small-time Roman pimp), but the preoccupations he was to develop are evident in embryo: an enquiring interest in language (the dialogue is in the Roman equivalent of Cockney), crime and, by extension, 'evil' as forms of the transgression necessary if the tyranny of the old social order is to be vanquished, the perennial Italian polarisation between Catholicism and Communism. This last is most evident in his adaptation of *The Gospel According to Matthew* (significantly, no 'saint' in the Italian title, 1964), with its savage photography and working-class Christ.

The growth of an international 'art-house' circuit helped to emancipate the Italian industry from the financial constraints that had aborted the neo-realists. Towards the end of our period, young directors such as Marcho Bellocchio gave further evidence of new ideas in the Italian cinema.

The return of the exile

Spain, meanwhile, remained under-industrialised and dogged by censorship. Buñuel's major Mexican work of this period, *Nazarin* (1958), may well have been instrumental in deciding the Franco government to allow him to return; its sympathetic account of a young priest in a poor village has Bressonian overtones in its inversion of conventional Christian norms. Franco could hardly have been expected to recognise the subversive implications of this, so Buñuel spelt out his impenitent anti-clericalism with tremendous force in *Viridiana* (1961), made on his return to Spain. The film's account of the merciless disabusing of a former religious novice who attempts to rescue sinners by kindness was reinforced by its constant references to the under-industrialisation that was strangling the Spanish economy as a direct result of Franco's anachronistic and repressive methods. The Government, scandalised, ordered all copies of the film to be seized; a pirate print fortunately survived. The film's power derives, not only from an anti-clericalism that appears rather dated outside a Spanish context (the notorious scene where the drunken beggars parody Leonardo's 'The Last Supper', and a beggar-woman takes a 'photograph' by flinging up her skirts – an aggression that rhymes in many ways with the slit eye at the beginning of *Un Chien Andalou* thirty-three years before), but from the ambiguity of its portrayal of the practical landowner cousin with whom Viridiana at the end settles down to a game of cards, and maybe more (interpretable as feudalism recognising the inevitability of capitalist industrialisation). Her naïve spirituality and his coarse pragmatism are poles between which no synthesis is suggested in the film (perhaps because none would have been possible in Spain at that time). Both may hold part of the truth about the country's situation, but both are stunted and thwarted. The film castigates Franco's Spain in more ways than through its clergy-bashing.

Buñuel's hasty return to Mexico, after this memorable piece of effrontery, produced *The Exterminating Angel* (1962), about a group of people at a society reception who find themselves mysteriously unable to leave. Buñuel's subsequent work was increasingly to rejoin, not only his old Surrealist antecedents, but his increasing concern with the politics of narrative, the way in which how a story is told (from what position, and in what relation to what an audience is likely to expect) has strong ideological and political connotations.

Angry young men

The very end of our period marked the end of thirteen years of Conservative government in Britain – years marked by a progressive upsurge of discontent with, and rebellion against, what became imprecisely stigmatised as 'the Establishment'. It was the time of beatniks, of the Campaign for Nuclear Disarmament, of the boom in press, theatre, and television satire, of 'Angry Young Men' (usually cut-price imitations of Orwell) railing against High Culture, of 'kitchen-sink' novels and plays dealing with provincial working-class life. If almost everything in this list is now embarrassingly obsolete, it is only because it is still relatively recent history (nothing is more out-of-date than yesterday's fashions). A reason at least as important is the British pragmatism (and thus *de facto* conservatism) that underlay the various movements: no coherent political project behind CND; no serious consideration of how one could tell a story, and what a story was (as opposed to what kind of story one should be telling), in the theatrical and literary worlds; and, not surprisingly, no committed work on formal and ideological elements in the 'New British Cinema'. The 'establishment' cinema was, no question about it, sterile and hidebound; the 'alternative', launched by Lindsay Anderson and Karel Reisz in the 'Free Cinema' of 1956 (an umbrella label for mid-fifties British documentary cinema), moved away from London to the provinces, from Ealing flirtation to supposedly earthy sex (nipples and pudenda of course beyond the pale), from good chaps to bad lads. It was not easy, in the stultifying 'intellectual' climate of late fifties Britain, to do much else, and the success of many of the films is proof enough of how desperately regeneration was needed.

Albert Finney became a cult figure of almost Bogartian proportions for his performance as Arthur Seaton in Reisz's *Saturday Night and Sunday Morning* (1960). Laurence Harvey beat the bourgeoisie at their own game in Jack Clayton's adaptation of John Braine's *Room at the Top* (1958). Richard Harris's fraught and sweaty affair with Rachel Roberts, as his landlady, in Lindsay Anderson's *This Sporting Life* (1963), Rita Tushingham's bitter-sweet pregnancy in *A Taste of Honey* (Tony Richardson, 1961), Richard Burton's original 'angry young man', Jimmy Porter, in Richardson's adaptation of John Osborne's *Look Back in Anger* (1959), certainly widened the scope of a cinema which had hitherto tolerated little that was more emotional than the stiff upper lip. But the dependence of the 'New Cinema' on stage and literary adaptations, the stodgy visual puritanism of its main exponents, and its failure to mount any real challenge to received notions of what the cinema could do ensured its rapid demise, or rather assimilation via television into the very cultural establishment against which it had ridden forth to do battle.

The aftermath of Stalin

Pragmatism (and its political ally Labourism) inhibited the British counter-culture; post-Stalinism did likewise, far less covertly, in the Warsaw Pact countries. The 'thaw' announced by Khruschev gave rise to films like Grigori Chukrai's *Ballad of a Soldier* (1959), and Mikhail Kalatozov's *The Cranes are Flying* (1957), in which the camera experimentation that had been taboo in the Stalin era resurfaced. More interesting was work in the Polish cinema. From the Lodz film school came Andrzej Wajda and Andrzej Munk. Wajda first brought Polish cinema to the attention of the international audience with his trilogy: *A Generation* (1954), *Kanal* (1956), *Ashes and Diamonds* (1958) – the first two set during the war and the last on the first day of peace, although at the time Wajda had not been twenty. This is some indication of the war's continuing traumatic effect and of its convenience for the government as subject-matter, diverting attention as it did away from problems and inadequacies in contemporary society.

The sewer chase in *Kanal*, and the performance of Zbigniew Cybulski, the 'Polish James Dean', in *Ashes and Diamonds* remain memorable; but the most influential Polish director of this generation, unlike Wajda, early turned his back on indigenous subject-matter. This was Roman Polanski, who from 1964 has worked in France, Britain, and the United States, a leading propagator of the fashionable 'international-director' life-style. Polanski views sex as an oscillation between the macabrely menacing and the hysterically humorous, so that his best films have been those in which this polarisation has been most successfully maintained – *Repulsion* (1965, shot in South Kensington), where Catherine Deneuve's sexual horrors teeter unnervingly on the dividing line between the unbearable and the hilarious, and *Cul-de-Sac* (1966, shot on an island off the Northumberland coast), in which the sexual insecurities of Donald Pleasence are flushed grotesquely to the surface when gangsters on the run break into his *ménage* with Deneuve's sister, Françoise Dorléac.

Scandinavia

The Scandinavian industries began to make a considerable amount of money from pornographic movies for export in this period. Sweden was intelligent enough to impose a tax on each seat sold at a porn cinema, ploughing the proceeds back into the film industry – a pattern not followed by other European governments whose often ineffectual attempts to censor or suppress meant that customers paid more money to porn-traders for having to go underground, while the serious cinema benefited not at all.

Dreyer's death in 1968 may well have been advanced by the disgraceful reception accorded to his last film, *Gertrud* (1964), at its Paris première. Critics who doubtless thought themselves highly discriminating branded the work as 'non-filmic', which would be a hilarious piece of ineptitude if it were not also tragic. The extreme slowness with which Dreyer lays before us Gertrud's relationships with her husband and younger lover, and her decision at the end to live on her own, cut off from the masculine world, are in one sense at least the filmic at its most achieved – in the anatomy of emotional detail, the stress not only on the details of each image, but on the way in which they work together, combine and conflict, to produce the process of decision for Gertrud and meaning(s) for us, the formal accomplishment of the ensembles throughout. Dreyer had always been deeply concerned with the feminine point of view and the ways in which women can be oppressed (as *Joan of Arc* and, even more with its stress on female sexuality, *Day of Wrath* demonstrate). His final film is the culmination of this concern. Perhaps that is why the ever-chauvinistic French felt so uneasy about it.

The Scandinavian director who during this period symbolised (the verb is singularly appropriate) the art cinema in Europe, Ingmar Bergman, directed his first film in 1945. After 1953's *Sawdust and Tinsel* (ref. p. 118), *Smiles of a Summer Night* (1955), *The Seventh Seal* and *Wild Strawberries* (both 1957), and *The Virgin Spring* (1959) established him as *the auteur* of the international art-cinema circuit – a reputation that was to decline as quickly as it had risen. The reasons for this are sound, not merely modish, and connected with his fundamentally static and literary use of symbolism. Robin Wood[1] has criticised the medieval odyssey of *The Seventh Seal* precisely because it is a series of beautifully-designed stills placed end to end; *mise-en-scène*, and the openness and ambiguity of the articulation between one shot and the next, are minimal. Similarly, in *Wild Strawberries*, Professor Borg's twofold journey, towards a supreme academic award and a chastened understanding of his own past, aligns its symbols (the handless clock and the hearse that loses a wheel in the dream-scene near the beginning) with a solemnity at once too literary and too literal, leaving the viewer little room for participation in the production of the film's meanings.

The more open cinematic texts of such as Antonioni and Godard changed ideas of what cinema-as-art could do, in a direction unfavourable to Bergman. He began to leave the world of heavily closed symbolism behind in the trilogy of 1961/1963: *Through a Glass Darkly*, *Winter Light*, and *The Silence*. Emotional tensions within small groups are his subject-matter, filmed sparingly and with self-conscious austerity. Each film is articulated around one or more sexual taboos defied within it (incest in *Through a Glass Darkly*, adultery between priest and parishioner in *Winter Light*, implicit Lesbian incest and pick-up copulation between two partners neither of whom can speak the other's language in *The Silence*). If Dreyer is concerned with women, Bergman is obsessed; the pastor in *Winter Light* inveighs against his mistress for her chilblains, her eczema, and other 'feminine' complaints, a disgust which is one of the hysterically extreme points of his obsession. Woman is seen as either purifying saint (the young girl raped and killed in *The Virgin Spring*, paradoxically the incestuous and mentally-disturbed girl in *Through a Glass Darkly*), or polluting and polluted (Anna's first action in *The Silence* when she returns to her hotel after copulation with a pick-up in a church is to rinse out her pants). In his films of the next decade, Bergman was to move away from this split fascination with Woman towards a deeper concern with women; the results were to be his best work.

Conclusion

Developments in this decade were arguably in many ways the most revolutionary for the European cinema since the advent of sound. The low budgets of the French *nouvelle vague*, the Swedish porn tax, and the development of an international art-house circuit provided crucial financial support; theoretical developments in France integrated and articulated the importance of the American cinema for work in Europe; the themes tackled broadened in scope considerably. Above all else, the 'art-cinema' extended its audience and made a deeper mark than in the more financially-cramped post-war years.

11 Cinemas of the East: India and Japan up to 1965

The absence up to now of any reference to the cinema outside the United States and Europe is not an indication of chauvinism; rather, it reflects the relatively late development of the cinema in Asia (and still later in Southern America), and the belated discovery by Western audiences that there were non-white audiences that had heard of the movie camera.

Japan

There had been film-makers active in Japan for thirty years before Akira Kurosawa's *Rashomon* won the Grand Prix at the 1951 Venice Film Festival and alerted the West to the existence of the Japanese cinema. Teinosuke Kinugasa's haunting *A Page of Madness*, a Caligari-like tale of a sailor's attempts to retrieve his wife from an asylum, dates from 1926; forty-five years later, it was re-released to immense acclaim. But it was after the war that the industry really began to expand, on a scale beyond Hollywood's wildest dreams.

Ruthlessly efficient organisation of production, shooting, and distribution was the main reason for this. Six major companies carved up the market between them, each catering for a particular stratum or section of opinion, so that housewives, businessmen, reactionaries nostalgic for feudal glory, and the rest would be assured of a steady stream of generally low-budget and rapidly but competently produced films to their assumed liking. The process was of course a circular one; the various groups had put before them what they were going to like, and thus had little choice but to like what was put before them (a variant of the process described in the American automobile industry by J. K. Galbraith in *The New Industrial State*). The results were unlikely to reach a very high standard; but they made money at a time when much Western cinema was losing heavily.

Many of these films relied on Japanese adaptations of established Hollywood genres, such as the 'Godzilla' horror movies and the samurai films, which dealt with events from feudal Japanese history after the manner of an American Western. It was these latter films, via their most accomplished exponent, Kurosawa, that were for the fifties and most of the sixties to be Japanese cinema, for British art-house viewers at least. Only in the very recent past have other, more important bodies of work received anything like their due attention, and then as often as not via the printed word rather than in cinemas.

Rashomon is alleged to have been made specifically for Western consumption. Whether this is so or not, it certainly could be true; the film's use of subjective narrative points of view (so that we hear the story of the attack on a merchant's wife by a vagrant successively from the standpoint of each of the parties involved, before a woodcutter who witnessed it gives his 'objective' account, casting maximum discredit on everyone else) was a device familiar from experiments in the European novel, and there was little in the photography or *mise-en-scène* to suggest a conception of cinema radically different from what the West was used to.

Kurosawa came closer to this in some of his subsequent films, including *Ikiru* (*Living*, 1952), where a disillusioned civil servant spends his dying months helping to advance the building of a children's playground, and *Throne of Blood* (1957), a Japanese version of *Macbeth*. But he remains best known in the West for the curious 'samurai Westerns', from *The Seven Samurai* (1954), to *Sanjuro* (1962). Epic outdoor photography reminiscent of John Ford here merges with traditional Japanese styles of acting (including the Kabuki theatre whose stylised grimaces and codes of emotion had so impressed Eisenstein), and elements of grotesque humour. A good example of the last-named is *The Hidden Fortress* of 1958, where the heroic Toshiro Mifune is accompanied as he chaperones a princess to safety through civil war by two peasants, clodhoppers worthy of a Shakespeare history play.

Kon Ichikawa probably came a poor second to Kurosawa in the list of Japanese directors whose films were periodically shown in Britain; his documentary *Tokyo Olympiad* (1965) was assured of fairly wide distribution, and the startling transvestism of *An Actor's Revenge* (1963) predated serious treatment of this theme by Western directors. But the two Japanese whose contribution to the development of film language can rank with that of any director of the sound era remained largely neglected. Towards the end of his life, the films of Yasujiro Ozu began to make the odd appearance at film festivals, whose audiences were programmed to expect a cinema so quietistic as to be boring, and so 'Japanese' as to be incomprehensible to a European audience. Such a reading is a cop-out. As little (or as much) 'happens' in *Une Partie de Campagne* or (until the very end) *Le Journal d'un Curé de Campagne* as in Ozu's *Tokyo Story* (1953); and audience difficulty with this, his best-known film, certainly cannot be attributed to any inherent 'Japanese-ness' in its subject-matter, the varying gulfs that reveal themselves between the elderly parents in Tokyo on a visit and their children and children-in-law. The problem is rather that often experienced with Dreyer, with whose use of film language Ozu has much in common; the various elements of the screen discourse are separated out and closely analysed, so that a space can often be presented to us before it is occupied by a character, or after it has been vacated. Watching his work requires a rigorous and sustained effort. Its meanings are not given to us predigested, we have to participate actively in their construction.

It is as though Ozu encouraged the impression that his films are all interchangeable, with such titles as *Late Spring* (1949), *Early Spring* (1956), *Late Autumn* (1960), and *Early Autumn* (1961). This may well be a deliberate strategy, playing down the expected sharp differences in title and plot the better to concentrate on the passage from moment to moment that is fundamental to cinema (a comparison with the plots of the Sternberg/Dietrich melodramas may be helpful here). It is a mistake to think of his visual style as a series of static leitmotifs, like the family photographs that recur so often in his work; the most beautiful moment in *Tokyo Story* is the journey the elderly couple take through the city, shot from inside the tramcar with great subtlety and vivacity – structurally not dissimilar to the dodgem-car scene in Bresson's *Mouchette*.

A straw poll conducted among film fans for the title of greatest director of women would probably find George Cukor and Ingmar Bergman running neck and neck, with maybe a few serious votes for Dreyer and a few sexist ones for Vadim. Such a result would reveal the considerable ignorance of the Eastern cinema that still exists. Kenji Mizoguchi's treatment of women is more profound than Cukor's and less hysterical than Bergman's – a judgement that the National Film Theatre's early 1978 retrospective has made it possible to confirm.

His best-known work is *Ugetsu Monogatari* (translated as *Tales of the Pale and Silvery Moon after the Rain*, 1953). Two potters leave their village during wartime in search of riches and glory, which turn out to be illusory. One enjoys a romantic idyll with Lady Wakasa, who is revealed to be a ghost, and returns to 'real life' to find his wife murdered; the other refinds his wife in the brothel into which she has been forced. This cursory summary does serve to highlight some of Mizoguchi's major preoccupations: the use of a historical epoch both as a specific historical setting and as an allegory for social turmoil; the awareness that in times of social stress men and women are likely to suffer in different, complementary ways, and women rather more than men; the transcendentally calm filming of suffering and despair, not callous or resigned any more than a concentration-camp diary need be; the concern for a flexible, supple composition that remains formally satisfying from moment to moment. The feudal oppression of women in Japanese society is eloquently protested against throughout his work.

Sansho Dayu (1954), with its overwhelmingly moving final scene where the dispossessed bailiff's son meets and recognises his old blind mother by the sea, and *Chikamatsu Monogatari* (1954), whose sound-track marries 'natural' sound-effects and Japanese music, and whose tale of illicit and finally crucified lovers is as great a love-film as *You Only Live Once* or *Pierrot le Fou*, work on and deepen the same preoccupations. Many of Mizoguchi's films are lost; but it is fortunate that the efforts of distribution companies and the National Film Theatre are restoring to this giant among directors the attention his work deserves.

India

The Indian industry developed later, and in a more haphazard way, than the Japanese. Problems of physical distribution, of funding, and of language worked together to inflict almost insuperable handicaps on it. If I mention only one director here, it is because he is (with the exception of his California-born disciple James Ivory) the only India-based film-maker to have acquired any degree of recognition in the West.

Again, as with *Rashomon*, one festival revealed the existence of a new industry to Europe: Cannes, 1956, and Satyajit Ray's first feature, *Pather Panchali*. The film took five years to make, and was only completed at all thanks to West Bengali help. The film and its two successors in the 'Apu Triology', *The Unvanquished* (1957) and *The World of Apu* (1959), delineated, with precise attention to detail, the life of the young

Apu from childhood, through arranged marriage, widowhood, and literary aspirations, to a hinted-at but not shown reconciliation between himself and the son he has rejected because his wife died in childbirth. Truffaut walked out of the film at Cannes, and one can understand why its concern with humanist values and subject-matter would have irritated the rising star of the brash French industry; it was left to *Sight and Sound* to dress the balance with an article, *Ray or Ray?*, praising Satyajit Ray's work at the expense of Nicholas Ray's supposed lack of choice in the field of subject-matter.

Satyajit Ray's subsequent work, largely freed from the financial problems that blighted his early career, has been prolific and varied. *The Music Room* (1958), about a faded aristocrat under the British Raj who takes aesthetic refuge from the crumbling of his class, retains great interest, and his more recent work – notably *Company Limited* (1972), about industrial unrest in Calcutta – has shown signs of the more radical political commitment absent, or at best hinted at, in his earlier work.

Interest in cinemas of the East – the Japanese industry in particular – has expanded considerably thanks to wider availability of films in London over the past few years. It is to be hoped that this will prove to be the tip of the iceberg.

12 The Last Ten Years

Long before its institutionalisation in festivals and art-houses, there had existed a separation between 'commercial' and 'art' cinema. The mass French audience of the late thirties went to watch Pagnol comedies or the early Fernandel, not *La Grand Illusion*. But the competition from television, the obsession with scale, and the increasing costs of making a film all acted to intensify the division. From the fifties onwards you had to know precisely for whom you were making a film to stand any real chance of getting backing. Resnais got his 450 000-franc advance for *L'Année Dernière à Marienbad* because the French Government was concerned about cultural prestige and knew that there was a network of cinemas catering to the public who would be interested in the film. It has never been a film that would fill the vast Leicester Square Odeon for weeks on end, but over the years it has probably been seen by as many people as the major CinemaScope blockbusters.

Cinema as an art-form, in other words, became institutionalised, under economic pressures, in the fifties, and it was against this institutionalisation that major late sixties and early seventies developments were later to define themselves. The American underground tried to escape the constraints of the 'traditional' art cinema via formal experimentation and a political radicalisation that (not unsurprisingly) reached a peak in about 1968; Godard's work on revolutionary cinema aimed at being a simultaneous analysis and demolition (a 'deconstruction') of established filmic institutions; Bergman's move into what he called 'chamber' cinema also represented a rejection of many of the conventions his earlier work had implicitly accepted; and much intensive theoretical work went on, in France, the United States, and – *mirabile dictu* – Great Britain, along analogous lines.

Madness and language

Godard's two 1965 films are as good a place as any to begin the exploration of these new developments. *Alphaville* works within a combined private-eye and science-fiction framework; Lemmy Caution is the name of the American detective who rescues Anna Karina from the computerised Alphaville tyranny, in which expression of emotion ('acting illogically') is treated as a criminal offence. The film has been read as a rather simplistic allegory of feeling-versus-technology (Karina's 'I love you' at the end signalling the triumph of the former), but its reverberations – particularly concerning the way in which our thoughts, and hence also our emotions, are linguistically determined – go far further and deeper.

They become plainer if *Alphaville* is read alongside *Pierrot le Fou*, Godard's masterpiece. The central male character, a disaffected intellectual played (in a conscious reference to *A Bout de Souffle* though the sex-roles are reversed) by Jean-Paul Belmondo, is obsessed with in his own words 'what goes on between people, in space . . . like sound and colours'. This is a clear allusion to Godard's own obsession with cinema, but also to the inescapable ambiguity of language as our only means of articulation as well as communication. Marianne (Anna Karina), with whom Belmondo runs away from a constipated Parisian existence to the South, is impatient with such concerns. Her unanalytical spontaneity is what attracts him, but she persists in addressing him as 'Pierrot' (a clown), instead of by his real name Ferdinand – a simultaneous denial of his seriousness and denunciation of his madness in running off with her. She complains to him:

'. . . you talk to me with words and I look at you with feelings.'

If Ferdinand were merely 'Ferdinand', he would deliver a Parisian intellectual admonition on the impossibility of severing words and feelings (language and emotion) which is one of the things he is in flight from. As it is, being 'Pierrot' as well, he kills Marianne (ostensibly because of her treacherous involvement with a band of gun-runners), paints his face blue (accepting the Pierrot identity), and, uttering the primal shrieks of one forced back to the point before language, blows himself up with dynamite.

The film is laceratingly beautiful – in its death-filled Mediterranean landscape, in the matchless performances of Karina and Belmondo, in the songs that mark their idyllic moments together, and in Godard's success in producing a work that is, precisely, about 'what goes on between people, in space'. The concerns of conventional narrative are rejected for a fragmented, juxtapository discourse, in which lyricism and analysis are *not* mutually exclusive.

Where was Godard to go after making the greatest of all films about being in love? The stultifying clichés of the cocktail-party at the beginning of *Pierrot*, and that film's experiments with narrative, between them provide the answer: into a 'deconstruction' of both cinematic form and Gaullist and post-Gaullist French society. The precise moment of his political radicalisation is difficult to date, but an overt concern with contemporary social issues becomes plain with *Deux ou Trois Choses que je Sais d'Elle* (incorrectly Anglicised as *Two or Three Things I Know About Her* – the 'elle' refers to 'l'agglomération parisienne', Greater Paris, not to the central female character), of 1966. Here Godard takes and reworks Brecht's view of prostitution as a metaphor for all life in a society dependent on the profit-motive. Juliette Jeanson (Marina Vlady) is a housewife living in a tower-block outside Paris, who supplements the family budget by part-time prostitution. The most alarming thing about the film is her passive acquiescence; the only values explicitly recognised are those of the glossily-packaged consumer goods across which the camera tracks at the end.

The passivity of a society in which consumption is stressed the better to disguise the relations of production was seen by Godard as a crucial element in the 'conventional' cinema, produced by big corporations and consumed by spectators like any other commodity. In reaction against this, he worked intensively on narrative forms which involved his audiences much more in the production of the film, and mounted a two-pronged attack on Western capitalist society and on the aesthetic and ideological norms that are an integral part of it.

But this dual politicisation led Godard into some paradoxical situations. *Le Gai Savoir* was commissioned by French television in 1968, but its combination of experimentation and occasional blatant abuse of the politico-cultural establishment led to its being banned. *British Sounds* (1969), first of the 'Dziga-Vertov' films on which he worked with Jean-Pierre Gorin, was likewise turned down by Thames Television – because of its use of female nudity and because it was deemed too 'difficult' (?subversive). To blame Godard for 'obscrurantism' (the conditioned reflex of the Establishment and of much of the Left) is unfair; new historical conjunctures inevitably demand new artistic forms, and these forms are inevitably – to begin with at least – difficult of access. *Le Gai Savoir* is one of his least successful films, but the criteria by which ORTF (the French broadcasting authority) rejected it are unlikely to have taken much account of that. Had the film's agitational content been plainer, as the example of *British Sounds* shows, suppression would have followed just as quickly.

Among the works of Godard's 'committed' periods (it would be over-simplifying to speak just of one), the two that stand out immediately precede and follow his work with the Dziga-Vertov group. *Weekend* (1968) uses the Friday-night motorised exodus from Paris as a metaphor for capitalist greed, selfishness, and cannibalistic competitiveness. It is often forgotten how funny Godard's films can be, especially at their most grimly serious. *Weekend* is a sustained *tour de force* of black comedy, whose use of stars from more 'popular' cinema (Jean Yanne and Mireille Darc) is an index of its greater accessibility.

Numéro Deux (*Number Two*, 1975), made with Anne-Marie Miélville after Godard had forsaken Paris for Grenoble, is outstanding for several reasons. It is his most overtly feminist film to date; it addresses itself to problems of generation (in both senses), in its scrutiny of a working-class family (grandparents, parents, and children), all living under the same block, and all labouring under various sexual problems; and its use of split-screen (two or more separate images within the same frame) extends the resonances and combinatory possibilities of the narrative. The blank obtuseness of the film's reception by establishment critics when it opened in London in 1977 is sufficient indication of the difficulties that beset progressive film-makers.

The suicide of narrative

Jacques Rivette also extended his experimentation with the bounds of narrative to the point of exploding them, in a series of films whose (by modern standards) extraordinary length has hampered their distribution. All rework the concern with spectacle and 'reality', and the paranoia ever-present on screen or just off it, of *Paris Nous Appartient*.

Céline et Julie Vont en Bateau (*Céline and Julie Go Boating*, 1974) is the only one to have been at all widely shown. Its eponymous heroines, a magician and a librarian, become involved with a mystery going on in a (haunted?) house, to which they gain access by swallowing a (psychedelic?) sweet. The mystery, which turns out to involve a plot to murder a child whom they manage to spirit away into 'reality', is shot in the dark, constricting tones of fifties Hollywood, or even of

Chabrol. There is a wearing zaniness to many scenes, but the flawless parodying of the old-school cinematic style and the insistence on cinema as dream-spectacle are extraordinary.

Out One: Spectre (1973) is a four-and-a-quarter condensation of the never-shown thirteen-hour *Noli Me Tangere* (1971). The themes of theatrical production and paranoid conspiracy in *Paris Nous Appartient* are here spun out to a length which eventually forces narrative to admit its own defeat. The paranoia runs itself to exhaustion, only cinema is left. . . . Rivette's two 1976 films, *Duelle* (*Twhylight* [*sic*]) and *Noroit* (*Nor'West*), revert to more average length, but the dreamlike element is no less powerful. 'Everything is clear when you don't ask yourself questions' (an interview in the *Figaro* in 1976) – in the cinema of Rivette as in a dream. Both, by the same token, simultaneously elicit and elude hermeneutic, 'ultimate' analysis.

New names were rare in the post-1965 French cinema; among the most significant were the novelists Marguerite Duras and Alain Robbe-Grillet, who moved from scriptwriting for Resnais into directing their own films. Resnais himself, after *Muriel* (1963), set in a post-war Boulogne-sur-Mer, and the over-lengthy *La Guerre est Finie* (1966), with Yves Montand as a Spanish Civil War veteran who cannot admit to himself that 'the war is over', went off the rails into an embarrassing piece of science-fiction hokum, *Je t'Aime, Je t'Aime* (1968), rather as Renoir had done with *Le Déjeuner sur l'Herbe*. *Stavisky. . . .* (1974), counterpointed the French swindler's rise and fall with Trotsky's exile. *Providence* (1976), scripted by the English playwright David Mercer, was a return to form, both artistically and commercially.

Truffaut's development post-1965 shows how far he had deteriorated in this period, with the exception of *L'Enfant Sauvage* (*The Wild Child*, 1969), about the integration of a boy found running wild in eighteenth-century France into 'civilisation' – though even this looks pretty feeble beside Herzog's *The Enigma of Kaspar Hauser*. For the rest, the distance between *Les Quatre Cents Coups* and *Antoine Doinel*, Jean-Pierre Léaud's third adventure, *Baisers Volés* (*Stolen Kisses*) of 1968, measures the decline in Truffaut's work. From a director who had so transformed our sense of the possibilities of the medium with *Jules et Jim*, the return to what remained glossily conventional film-making and the rejection of analytical rigour were a sad anti-climax.

Catholic directors

1967 saw Bresson's last black-and-white film, *Mouchette*, like *Au Hasard, Balthazar* of the year before finding sanctity in squalor. Mouchette is a sullen, rebellious peasant-girl whose moments of quasi-religious ecstasy come on the dodgems at a fun-fair and when, arms extended in the shape of the Cross, she submits to rape from the village tramp. Bresson is careful not to present her suicide as a choice pondered and led up to by the rest of the film. It is only when a passing tractor-driver fails to return her wave of greeting that (as most people would probably shrug their shoulders) she rolls, at the third attempt, down the bank into the river, and Monteverdi's *Magnificat* fills the sound-track. . . . Suicide is equated with the truly saintly deed that comes as a spontaneous movement of the soul rather than as a crisis of ethical commitment.

Suicide both begins and ends Bresson's first colour feature, *Une Femme Douce* (*A Gentle Creature*, 1969). The mass slaughter that concludes *Lancelot du Lac* (1974) marks, not spiritual force like these suicides, but utter spiritual exhaustion; the Grail story according to Bresson takes up when the knights return, exhausted, from their unavailing search, and fall apart into internecine factions. The film extends remarkably Bresson's use of parts of the body (hands and feet in particular) as vehicles of the soul (talk of personality in his work is meaningless). In the tournament-scene, armour-cased extremities cross-cut with the reactions of the crowd tell us all we need to know about what is happening, and who it is happening to. It is as though Bresson believed that it were possible to film the tip of a man's mail-shod foot in such a way as to show whether he is saved or damned.

Salvation and damnation have little to do with the Catholicism of Eric Rohmer. In *Ma Nuit chez Maud* (translated as *My Night with Maud*, though given the absence of copulation *My Night at Maud's* would have been more appropriate, 1968), Pascal's existential bet on the existence of God is the starting-point from which the teacher, played by Jean-Louis Trintignant, talks himself out of the divorcee Maud's bed and into marriage with a young student (Françoise Fabian). This is the most successful of Rohmer's series of six 'moral tales', largely because the monotony of winter life in a French provincial university town is subtly and tellingly enough evoked for Trintignant's intellectual pirouettes around his sexual insecurity and guilt to appear as comprehensible ways of passing the time. Elsewhere, in *La Collectionneuse* (1966) and *Le Genou de Claire* (*Claire's Knee*, 1970), Rohmer's habit of talking his characters towards, around, and away from bed with one another appears as tedious and limited as the small-town life in *Ma Nuit chez Maud*, and hypocritically reactionary in its substitution of a sanctimonious pleasure in righteous evasion for the joys of sex.

The indiscreet charmlessness of the bourgeoisie

Chabrol's entomological delight in the nasty ways of the French middle-classes continued unabated through this period. *Que la Bête Meure* (*Killer!*, 1969) and *Le Boucher* (*The Butcher*, 1969) centred on role-reversals, to which many critics attributed a metaphysical dimension; the determined avenger of his son's killing by a hit-and-run driver finds himself acquiring paternal feelings towards his prospective victim's son, the village schoolmistress who has ever so courteously made the local butcher realise that his passion is unrequited comes to feel a confusedly participatory guilt in his sex-murders. . . . But there is a perverse glee in Chabrol's insistence on bloodlust that works against the viability of such readings. His camera spies upon the provincial bourgeoisie in their bloated and meretricious splendour, like Claude Piéplu's Gaullist mayor in *Les Noces Rouges* (*Blood Wedding*, 1972), knowing that it will sooner or later catch them in some grotesquely compromising pose because it is more intelligent and sharper than they are. Chabrol the malignant voyeur is an altogether more persuasive persona than Chabrol the perverse metaphysician.

The camera of Louis Malle turned itself upon two cherished French bourgeois assumptions: that the family is a bulwark against precocious sexuality in *Le Souffle au Coeur* (1971) (misbaptised for some reason *Dearest Love*, though it means 'heart murmur' – the illness from which the central character is suffering); that the French were all heroic resistants in *Lacombe Lucien* of 1973. Lucien, turned down by the Resistance, signs up with the Germans as unquestioningly as he might have signed for his second-choice football club after rejection by his first. The logic of this decision is not explored so rigorously as it might have been, and Malle's best film remains *Le Souffle au Coeur*, where a young mother's sexual initiation of her son is presented, not as guilt-ridden trauma nor as ecstatic Oedipal transgression, but as a tender act of friendship which enables him to overcome sexual hesitancy with girls of his own age. The film finally shows him rejoining his family after his first experience with a teenager, and his unknowingly cuckolded father leading the chorus of laughter that is a sexist sign of his newly-acquired manhood.

Run-of-the-mill French comedy has always appeared even more

excruciating than its British 'Carry On' equivalents, which has not prevented the antics of Bourvil and Louis de Funès from grossing consistently large sums at the box-office. Tati has remained an exception to
this, though not so dazzling a one as Noël Burch claims when he refers
to *Playtime* (1967) as 'the first [film] in the history of cinema that not
only must be seen several times, but also must be viewed from several
different distances from the screen – the first truly "open" film'[1]. The
problem with Tati's films post-*M. Hulot* (only three in twenty years)
is that the intricacy of their crafting tends to work against the humour
rather than with it, blunting the cutting edge that we find in the work
of an even greater comic director, Buster Keaton.

Theory and practice – the open text

Tati, Bresson, Truffaut, Godard – the names that led French cinema
in this period were practically the same as in the previous decade. The
'new wave' had lost such coherence as it had once had, and the best
films of this period had moved from the early confidence in the cinema
as a means of solving problems to an awareness of how it needed to be
used to pose and articulate them. The disillusionment this inevitably
entailed is a crucial component of Jean Eustache's *La Maman et La
Putain* (*The Mother and the Whore*, 1973). Jean-Pierre Léaud, more
compulsively voluble than ever, and the two women in his life – the
fashion-designer with whom he lives (the 'mother') and the unhappily
promiscuous nurse he picks up outside a café (the 'whore') – talk and
talk, for three-and-a-half hours and with the consumption of portentous
amounts of alcohol, through, about, and around their relationships.
The gradual erosion of their and our confidence in words as a means
of solving problems, their inability to break free from the archetypal
Catholic polarisation of femininity in the title, their expansion to
Rivettian length of the ironies and ellipses of much *nouvelle-vague*
cinema, the nurse's vomiting in the final moments of the film, as though
simply unable to digest and process all that has gone before – all appear
to lead back to a defeatism and an exhaustion reactionary in their
implications. But Eustache here, like Godard in *Numéro Deux* and
Rivette in *Out One: Spectre*, goes beyond the view of cinema as an art-
form whose ebullient youthfulness is its own justification, to an involvement with the problems of narrative and cinematic meaning which the
medium could not for long have avoided. A London critic's judgement
that the film even demanded heckling surely adds a new dimension to
the notion of the open text.

There was a corresponding shift in theoretical perspective in this period. Existentialism, concerned with problems of freedom and individual respectability, had been the philosophical basis for the work of André Bazin, herald of the *Cahiers* critics, and (implicitly) for the *auteur* theory, with its stress on the film-maker as individual free to develop his own stylistic and thematic preoccupations within the various studio-systems and genres just as the citizen within a social-democrat system was supposed to be able to develop himself freely by choosing from the various possibilities that the groupings within that system created for him. This was displaced in the theoretical work of the sixties and seventies by a greater (often Marxist-influenced) insistence upon the political and linguistic elements of narrative. 'Realist' storytelling came to be seen as a perpetuation of ideas about man and society that recent work on linguistics, psychoanalysis, and political theory had rendered obsolete and thus reactionary. The film, as much as the novel, needed to modify and evolve new narrative methods to meet changed ideas and conditions. Christian Metz attempted an examination of cinema as a language, a system for producing meanings, a set of signs whose laws of production and combination needed to be ascertained. Noël Burch (like Metz a writer for *Cahiers*) saw the central dynamic of film as dialectical, though in a very different way from Eisenstein (ref. p. 18). Burch's dialectics involved interplay and alternation – between planning and chance, on- and off-screen space, viewer identification and non-identification with the perspective from which the camera films a scene. Notions of the *auteur* creating for a passively consuming audience gave place to the view, influenced by Brecht and the Marxist philosopher Louis Althusser, of film-maker and film-audience as complementary participants in the production of a film's meanings. The notion of the 'open text', as one which did not close itself off within a predefined space of meaning, was crucial in literary and cinematic theory. The work of Godard, Rivette, and Eustache ranks among the outstanding recent examples of open text.

Germany

The German cinema, as it belatedly emerged from the darkness of Nazism and the war, also played an important part in the evolution of cinematic language. Ironically, two of its major directors, the wife and husband Danièle Huillet and Jean-Marie Straub, are French, but Straub left France to settle in Germany in order to avoid call-up for the Algerian War. Straub's conception of textual openness is at the opposite extreme to Rivette's, so far as length goes; *The Bridegroom, the Actress, and the Pimp* (1968) condenses a normal-length stage-play into a ten-minute 'module', inserted into a short film using some of the same actors in roles which can only be understood by reference to the play, so that the two texts interact. Neither 'has the meaning' of the film; both contribute to its meanings.

Straub and Huillet had become internationally known through *The Chronicle of Anna Magdalena Bach* (1967, and ten years in the making), which focuses on the material problems under which Bach laboured and his dual status as artist and practising professional musician in eighteenth-century Germany. Their transposition of Brecht's text *History Lessons* (1970), about Julius Caesar, to a contemporary Roman context enables us to understand who Caesar's pillaging equivalents in our own time are, as well as what Caesar historically stood for, through its alternation of quasi-documentary interviews with former colleagues and soldiers of Caesar and film of the streets of modern-day Rome, shot from a moving car. What we hear in the interviews and what we see from the car have interacted to produce each other, in the film and in the social universe to which it relates.

There have been enough film-makers experimenting with new material in the Germany of the past ten years for there to be talk of a 'German new wave' – a tenable expression only if used as loosely as in reference to France. Many of the new film-makers (notably Werner Herzog and Rainer Werner Fassbinder) formed themselves into a production/distribution collective, but at the time of writing word is that this is falling apart under commercial pressures.

Like Straub/Huillet, Herzog became known outside Germany only when he had already been making films for several years. He returned late to any sort of narrative cinema, after a feature début with *Signs of Life* in 1967; his films for several years thereafter can loosely be characterised as 'documentary', though not the least valuable feature of *Fata Morgana* (shot in the Sahara, 1970) is the way in which it evades any kind of categorisation other than the unacceptably vague 'poetic'. . . . The two films that secured his reputation as one of the most important of modern cinematic innovators, *Aguirre, Wrath of God* (1972) and *The Enigma of Kaspar Hauser* (1974), both call our contemporary assumptions about what constitutes 'civilisation' devastatingly into question (not unlike what Nicholas Roeg attempts in *Walkabout*). *Aguirrre*'s sixteenth-century Spanish conquistadores fall apart under the pressures of the very greed that has led them to embark on the search for Eldorado; Kaspar Hauser, deaf-mute from birth and abandoned in the marketplace unable to speak, becomes a real threat to Nuremberg society through his devastatingly lucid manipulation of his newly-acquired language. The lyrical power of Herzog's filming in the scenes where Kaspar relates his dreams reinforces our sense that the so-called 'primitive' has perceptions more subtly and acutely organised than those prevailing in the society into which he is forced.

Fassbinder's indefatiguable turning-out of 'left-wing' cinema might legitimately arouse suspicions that underneath it all he subscribes to bourgeois criteria of hyper-productivity. He has dealt with such social problems as marriage between black and white (*Fear Eats the Soul*, 1973), Lesbian possessiveness (*The Bitter Tears of Petra von Kant*, 1974), and under-age sex (*Wild Game*, 1975), perhaps too omnivorously; the period distanciation and restrained black-and-white of his adaptation of the novel *Effi Briest* (1974), about the oppression of women by the social codes of nineteenth-century Germany, reveals a different, less self-imposing and more thought-provoking Fassbinder. But, in his more modern films, the platitude of the narratives, and the tedium of his sub-Brechtian attempts at stylisation, can have the effect of largely neutralising the political content, which comes increasingly to appear as grist to the mill. Neither good agitprop-documentary nor major film art (and a look back to Dziga Vertov shows how little incompatible those two are), his films subscribe more than Fassbinder would perhaps wish to norms they purport to subvert.

Italy

Avowedly left-wing film-makers also made up the majority of the younger Italian directors in the art cinema of this period. The industry laboured under difficulties after major production companies shut down in 1963, but Pasolini could still afford to engage Terence Stamp for *Theorem* (1968). Stamp's mysterious stranger, in his brief stay in a bourgeois household, seduces all its members, and the film delineates what happens to them as a result. The daughter (Anna Wiazemsky, Godard's second wife) goes into a catatonic trance, the capitalist husband tears off his clothes and charges naked across Mount Etna, the son abandons his job, the mother becomes compulsively promiscuous, and only the peasant maid, who levitates above the house and is promptly revered as a saint, avoids (in her own terms) disaster. Pasolini's uneasy fusion of Marxism and Catholicism works out its implications in his castigation of the bourgeoisie (interesting to compare with Buñuel's), corresponding canonisation – literally – of the peasantry, and view of Terence Stamp's 'stranger' as an almost Lawrentian erotic Messiah.

Pasolini's theoretical work – like that in France much concerned with linguistic aspects of the cinema – and his heterodox Marxism combined to produce his rather questionable notion that cinematic language was both the most truly material (because it supposedly transcribes 'reality', things-in-themselves, not labels for reality), and the most universally accessible – a conception that overlooks the fact that the 'real objects' on the celluloid in front of us have been selected and arranged in a specific way, and that a celluloid image is not a 'real object' any more than a printed word is a live voice, to say nothing of the cultural factors which mean that many tribes are unable to decipher filmed images until trained to do so.

It was precisely in the decade when both the extreme Left and the Communist Party became more powerful forces in Italy than for a very long time before, that Pasolini's exercise of this theory took him back into the feudal past. *Oedipus Rex* (1967) and *Medea* (1969, with Maria Callas), had reworked classical mythology; *The Decameron* (1971), *The Canterbury Tales* (1972), and *The Arabian Nights* (1974) declared themselves as attempts to reinvent the epoch of pre-capitalist innocence, in which to quote Geoffrey Nowell-Smith:

'What counts is the possibility of attributing to the past, in the imagination, the values that are so strenuously negated in the present.'[2]

The films become successively less absorbing, enhancing the view that they represent unvailing escapism rather than terrain for experiment.

Pasolini's murder in 1976 by a homosexual pick-up, and the release shortly afterwards of his Marquis de Sade adaptation *Salo, or the One Hundred and Twenty Days of Sodom*, followed so close on each other that they have inevitably been read together, and *Salo* seen as a 'last testament' of bitter disillusionment. The coldness of its images of torture and humiliation is what makes it shocking – a point clearly lost on the authorities, who crassly seized a print shortly after its opening in London; any film less calculated to excite sadistic urges in its audience it is difficult to imagine. Its explicit equation of torture and fascism (Salo was a Northern Italian Fascist puppet republic) is given rather than stated, asserted rather than developed, and Pasolini's camera flinches from the logical conclusion of his film, showing the final agonies only in part and without sound. The film is not perfect, but it is shattering, and almost no other European director could have made it.

Bernardo Bertolucci's *succès de scandale* with *Last Tango in Paris* in 1972 is cold tea by comparison. Marlon Brando and Maria Schneider meet and couple savagely without knowing each other's name, but Gunnel Lindblom and Birger Malmsten had done the same in *The Silence* nine years before without even speaking each other's language. Brando's buttering of Schneider's anus as a preliminary to buggery is tepid compared to the genital eating-scenes in Oshima's *Empire of the Senses*, and their erotic frenzy cold and stagey beside that in Buñuel's *L'Age d'Or* (1930). The film was an unhappy confirmation of the self-conscious artiness of *The Conformist* (1970), whch substituted art-deco references and virtuoso camera-tilting for any really innovative use of film language or penetrating critique of fascism. Bertolucci's precocious facility (*The Conformist* was made when he was not yet thirty) is turning out to be his worst enemy.

Two other directors to apply themselves with some degree of conscious commitment to problems of contemporary Italy were Marco Bellocchio, whose *Fists in the Pocket* (1966), like Bertolucci and earlier Visconti influenced by grand opera, uses epilepsy as a metaphor for the decadence of the ingrowing family, and Francesco Rosi, whose series of tightly-constructed 'thrillers' are also political explorations of a variety of contemporary themes (the Mafia in *Salvatore Giulliano*, 1962: the oil industry and CIA involvement in *The Mattei Affair* ten years later).

Antonioni and Fellini, in different ways, both turned their attention away from contemporary problems. Antonioni filmed in swinging London (*Blow-Up*, 1966) and spaced-out California (*Zabriskie Point*, 1970); the real 'blow-up' in these films comes at the end of *Zabriskie Point* in a brilliantly-coloured explosion of material goods, visually striking enough but nowhere near so probing as Godard's epiphany of consumer goods at the end of *Deux ou Trois Choses*. *The Passenger* (1975), with Jack Nicholson as a reporter who assumes a dead man's identity, has a line which could stand as an epigraph for the de-Italinised Antonioni, with his almost pathological rootlessness: 'I used to be somebody else, but I traded him in.'

Fellini's journey into the past with *Satyricon* (1969) is radically different from Pasolini's political escapism. The polymorphous sexual and gastronomic excesses of ancient Rome, satirised by Petronius, are deployed by Fellini in a gigantesque fresco that appears as an extension of the *mores* of its time rather than an escape from them. The bulk of critics found *Roma* (1972) tedious and self-indulgent, showing themselves oblivious not only to its dazzling set-pieces (such as the ecclesiastical fashion-parade), but also, more seriously, to Fellini's production of a film which, without any narrative thread and remarkably little dialogue, was as coherent, through wealth and organisation of visual detail, as any of his other, better-received work.

Fellini more than most other directors has gone out of his way to endorse and reproduce the reactionary Romantic myth of the director as larger-than-life individualist creator. The final reel of *Roma*, in which Anna Magnani fends off questioning with a weary: 'Ciao, Federico', is ambiguous in this regard. Are we to suppose that the wonder-boy, after two hours' sustained self-production as *auteur*, has succeeded only in wearying his entourage with his egoism? Or is Magnani's comment but an inverted homage to Fellini's presumed mischievous insatiability? The latter appears the more plausible reading, but the possible coexistence of the other brings into focus an important ambiguity in Fellini's work.

Marco Ferreri's *La Grande Bouffe* (*Blow-Out*, 1972) uses gluttony as an express metaphor for bourgeois *ennui*. Just as Pasolini's four torturers in *Salo* are a judge, a banker, a general, and a bishop, pillars of respectable society each one, so the four men who shut themselves away in a country-house for a weekend and literally gorge themselves to death occupy well-paid middle-class jobs. The film works because of superb performances (notably by Marcello Mastroianni and Michel Piccoli) and because of the progressively more baroque quality of the dishes, culminating in a veritable Royal Pavilion of pâté, the apotheosis of what the French critic Roland Barthes talks about in reference to French women's magazines as 'an openly dream-like cookery . . . whose consumption can perfectly well be accomplished by looking'[3]. For daring to ingest it as well, the penalty, clearly, is death.

Surrealism: real and not so (sur-)real

The director to whom Ferreri is most often compared, Buñuel, displayed in all his films of this period a concern to undercut any belief his audiences might have had in an 'objective' reality which goes back to his surrealist roots. *Belle de Jour* (1967) leaves in doubt the status of Catherine Deneuve's erotic fantasies, though I question whether its hour-and-a-half achieves much more than Mireille Darc's brief 'orgy' monologue in *Weekend*, at the end of which her 'friend' (psychiatrist, lover) asks whether it really happened and she replies, with a listlessness only Deneuve could have matched: 'I don't know'. *Le Charme Discret de la Bourgeoisie* (1972) and *Le Fantôme de la Liberté* (1974) tease us by constantly making as if to unfold a narrative, but abruptly moving on to another short sketch; *Le Charme Discret* in particular, a mirror-image of *The Exterminating Angel* with its bourgeois dinner-party that never manages to get started, could appropriately have been sub-titled (after the Monty Python film to which it is structurally similar) *And Now For Something Completely Different*.

A mutedly surrealistic influence also became evident in the British cinema, in the work of Lindsay Anderson. *If. . . .* (1968), a conscious homage to *Zéro de Conduite*, veers insecurely between 'realist' elements (the acute delineation of public-school life), and the half-baked surrealism of, for example, the scene where the Chaplain, shot by the school revolutionaries, is produced alive and well from a drawer in the headmaster's desk. *O Lucky Man!* (1972) is a sour hangover from the 'rise of. . . .' school of the fifties, a *Nothing but the Best* or a *Room at the Top* that tries to be far more ambitiously scathing about its hero's rise and in so doing over-programmes its audience so much that many of them must have felt like administering to Anderson the slap he gives the film's star, Malcolm McDowell, towards the end.

It is a sorry condemnation of the British cinema that Anderson's modishness passed for a long time as its most exciting experimentation. The recent re-release of *Performance* (codirected by Donald Cammell and the former Corman and Truffaut cameraman Nicholas Roeg in 1968, first released in 1971), billed as 'the film that was ten years ahead of its time', has done something to redress the balance. James Fox's gangster and Mick Jagger's retired rock sybarite are forced into contact when Fox, on the run from the mob for whom he has been working, rents a room in Jagger's mansion as a hideaway. Blurring and exchange of identities, an LSD-trip scene, group sexual romps in the obligatory four-poster – such a summary of stock sixties themes might make the picture sound ominously dated. What gives it a far greater staying quality than, say, *Blow-Up* is Roeg/Cammell's careful development of the notion of performance. Turner, the rock star, recognises an alter ego in the gangster Chas because both are performers, who do not exist (as Turner in his refuge pretends to have ceased to exist) unless they are putting on some kind of show. It is this that links the ever-present mirrors and the allusions to the South American writer Borges into a coherent text on seeming and being.

Walkabout (1971) and *Don't Look Now* (1973) increased Roeg's reputation as the most interesting of British directors – not that the competition was particularly hot. Richard Lester's anglicisation of the *nouvelle vague* in *The Knack* (1965) was less successful than his *A Hard Day's Night* (1964), because it attempted a structured story-line and lacked the superb Beatles songs. Not even a further clutch of these could save *Help!* (1965) from fatuous zaniness. The Lester/Beatles films and John Schlesinger's *Darling* (1965) now appear as the tip of the 'swinging sixties' iceberg – which produced many atrocious films and lost a good deal of money in the process.

Screen

One of the most exciting recent British developments is almost alone in springing from a sustained theoretical project. This is the work of Laura Mulvey and Peter Wollen (author of a seminal work on *Signs and Meaning in the Cinema*) – *Penthesilea* (1975) and *Riddles of the Sphinx* (1977). Both films are explicitly feminist; both operate as 'open' montages rather than by closed linear narrative; and both draw on many of the concepts elaborated by the magazine *Screen*, without question the foremost British contribution to film theory.

Screen articulated concepts drawn from French developments (notably the work of the psychoanalyst Jacques Lacan, and of the already-mentioned Louis Althusser, Christian Metz, and Noël Burch). Its work is at times dauntingly difficult, but represents one of the most serious and sustained attempts to think through, conjointly, the political implications of film form and the psychological structures that determine our pleasure in it – to think, in other words, at once film-as-revolution and film-as-dream. The charges of obscurantism levelled against it are sometimes justified, but more often than not betray in their hysteria a combined mistrust and fear of theory and of cinema – the plentiful source of *Film Night* tittle-tattle and whippersnapper among art-forms – as a domain in which to apply it. The British cinema of the seventies may well be the only period in British intellectual life when theoretical developments at least kept abreast of developments in artistic practice.

Marx and cinema

Brecht, another major text for *Screen*'s aesthetics, is also one of the dominant forces behind Theodore Angelopoulos's *The Travelling Players* (1975), whose shooting during the last days of the Papadopoulos dictatorship in Greece ranks with Rossellini's making of *Rome, Open*

City as a major cinematic coup. The post-war history of Greece is filtered through the lives of a troupe of itinerant actors, which fuse and overlap with the plays they stage. The film plays for well over three hours, but not because (as with *Out One: Spectre*) its director's awareness of the limits of narrative makes it virtually impossible to stop; its length is a necessary concomitant of the period of history it embraces and its scrupulous concern to give an adequately dialectical account of it.

We have seen how important for film-making (Godard, Straub, Angelopoulos) and for cinematic theory (Godard, Pasolini, Straub, *Screen*) Marxism has been. The Eastern European countries, where aesthetic freedom has (to put it mildly) always been at a premium, appear to have produced very few film-makers who share (or are permitted to) their Western contemporaries' concerns. Czechoslovakia threw up a belated, and often rather twee, *nouvelle vague* with the work of Jiri Menzel (*Closely Observed Trains*, 1966) and Milos Forman (*A Blonde in Love*, 1965) before the intervention of Moscow. The effects of the 'thaw' percolated tardily through to the Russian cinema to produce results rather more substantial than the *Ballad of a Soldier* vintage; Andrei Tarkovsky's lengthy science-fiction *Solaris* (1972), and Gyorgy Shengelaya's film about the Georgian primitive artist *Pirosmani* (1971) are examples.

Poland remained the most cinematically advanced of the Warsaw Pact countries, though by the end of the sixties her two outstanding directors were working abroad. Polanski's *oeuvre* is as ineradicably marked by the barbaric murder of his wife Sharon Tate as Pasolini's is by his own violent end. The Satanism of *Rosemary's Baby* (1968) and the parade of sexual deviation in *What?* (1972) found Polanski at his most flamboyantly perverse. In *Chinatown* (1974), he directed Jack Nicholson, Faye Dunaway, and John Huston in what many critics praised as the greatest of all private-eye films. It was less than that, for it lacked the pace and crackle of the great Hawks/Bogart originals or the out-of-focus black humour of Robert Altman's *The Long Goodbye*; but its dialogue was striking, and its organisation tighter than that of much of Polanski's other work.

Walerian Borowczyk's *Contes Immoraux* (*Immoral Tales*, 1973), four episodes all focusing on eroticism from a feminine standpoint, was the culmination of the fetichisation of objects and décor apparent in the totalitarian fantasies *Goto, Ile d'Amour* (*Goto, Island of Love*, 1968) and *Blanche* (set in the Middle Ages, 1971). From the harsh, Swiftian contours of his feature-length cartoon *Le Théâtre de M. et*

Mme Kabal (1967), his movement has been in the direction of a much greater luxuriance – overreaching itself in *The Streetwalker* of 1976, but diffusing itself across the landscape of *Immoral Tales* in such a way that there is not a photograph or a blade of grass on screen but becomes erotically fetichised. This working beyond the conventional bounds of eroticism (whereby it is what is filmed rather than how it is filmed that determines the libidinal charge) is Borowczyk's most important contribution to date, though a growing sexism has marred his later work.

Chamber cinema

Bergman's concentration of style in this period produced his major work. *Persona* (1966) marks an emancipation, at least in part, from the 'angel-or-whore' view of woman, and its treatment of what amounts to an exchange or fusing of identities between two women – Elizabeth (Liv Ullmann), an actress who has become catatonic on stage, and Alma (Bibi Andersson), the nurse charged with supervising her recovery – reaches a stunning visual climax when the two women's faces join. The film also operates a constant critique of its own position as film, via blank frames, the celluloid burning, sprocket-holes becoming visible. Identity is not transparent, far from it; why, Bergman asks, should we expect film to be so?

Bergman's 'island' films, *The Shame* (1968), perhaps the cinema's most harrowing evocation of the effect of war on non-combatants, and *A Passion* (1970), concentrate on the interaction of small groups of people on the island of Faro. His 'chamber-cinema' work culminates in *Cries and Whispers* (1972), where two women come together round the bed of their dying sister, to whom only her old nurse can provide unambiguous comfort.

America – new developments

Narrative experiment, the questioning of social and cultural institutions, the concern with following character, to quote Antonioni, 'beyond the moments conventionally considered important' – such preoccupations, central to the European cinema, were also important to many sixties and seventies American directors. The work of Bob Rafelson, indeed, has often been described as a 'Europeanisation' of the American cinema. *Five Easy Pieces* (1970) reworks that quintessential American genus, the journey movie, transforms it into a journey to anywhere (or nowhere), and in its eye for landscape and oblique, fragmented presentation of character justifies comparison with *Pierrot le Fou*. Two-and-a-half minutes at the beginning showing Jack Nicholson's drop-out pianist (shades of Truffaut's second feature) sitting at home with his 'wife' Raylette tells us all we need to know about the trapped complexities of their relationship with minimal dialogue – facial expression and the country-and-western song 'Stand by Your Man' are sufficient. Nicholson's Bobby Dupea, however, lacks Pierrot's 'European' capacity for anything so self-dramatisingly conclusive as suicide; an affair with his brother's wife and the abandonment of his own, on impulse, outside a filling-station leave his odyssey open. It is better to travel hopelessly than to arrive.

This theme likewise underlies Nicholson's journey in *The King of Marvin Gardens* (1972) – the title derives from a position on the American Monopoly board – to help his brother (Bruce Dern), desperately enmeshed in emotional and speculative-financial trouble in Atlantic City. Why Dern's 'middle-aged kewpie doll' finally shoots him is less important than the shifting balance of family relationships, and the contrasting styles of hopelessness. Nowhere else does the Great American Dream so conclusively reach the end of the road.

The late-sixties disillusionment with traditionally acquisitive American values, expressed in the 'campus revolt' of the New Left and the parallel 'life-style revolt' into psychedelic drugs and rock music, favoured the emergence of a number of directors who worked initially on low budgets and at once within and against traditional genre formats. D. A. Pennebaker's documentary *Don't Look Back* (1967), focusing on Bob Dylan, was among the first major films to make extensive use of rock music. The help and encouragement of Roger Corman gave Francis Ford Coppola, Monte Hellman, Martin Scorsese, and the critic Peter Bogdanovich their first directorial chances. The enormous success of *Easy Rider*, shot by Dennis Hopper in 1969, brought Jack Nicholson to public attention and showed what it was possible to do on a shoestring budget. Henry Fonda's son Peter costarred with Hopper in the film, a coast-to-coast odyssey on motorbikes and hallucinogens that ends with their being gunned down by rednecks.

'Anti-journey' movies soon became the rage. *Five Easy Pieces* was certainly the best, John Schlesinger's *Midnight Cowboy* (1969) one of the most commercially successful, despite its coy handling of bisexuality. Arthur Penn's *Bonnie and Clyde* (1967) fused most of the ingredients which were *de rigueur* for a movie of this type to succeed: 'anti-hero' central characters, played by leading young performers (Warren Beatty's and Faye Dunaway's bank-robbers), an element of sexual ambiguity (Clyde's impotence), location filming that increased *verismo* and decreased budgets, comic grotesquerie in the supporting cast, a tragic end seen as inevitable almost from the beginning. It has probably dated faster than most of the others because of its derivative visual style (which owes much to early Truffaut and Godard), and heavy reliance on the tomato-sauce bottle at violent climaxes.

Nostalgia and the cinema

French *nouvelle-vague* influences were also apparent in the career of Peter Bogdanovich, beginning with his shift from critical writing into direction. Boris Karloff owed Corman a few days' work which he passed on to Bogdanovich, who had helped him with *The Wild Angels*. The result, *Targets* (1968), juxtaposed two kinds of horror, the monster movies in which Karloff's retired actor ('Byron Orlock') used to star and the psychosis of the young killer he helps to capture in a drive-in cinema – a rich commentary on changing notions of the horrific in cinema which Bogdanovich was to have difficulty in surpassing. *The Last Picture Show* (1971) was one of the most significant of the nostalgia movies that flooded the decade, shot in black and white as a conscious homage to Ford and Hawks. Bogdanovich, as he showed in the screwball *What's Up, Doc?* of 1972, has understood that admiration of an *auteur* and tribute to him entail a rethinking and resituation of his work rather than simple derivativeness. Too much the victim of the limits of auteurism, he nevertheless occupies a considerable place in modern American cinema.

Dissatisfaction with contemporary America found an outlet in retreat into an often very recent 'golden age', tending to coincide with the film-makers' (and their hypothetical audience's) teens. *The Last Picture Show* is situated exceptionally early (country-and-western rather than rock forms the soundtrack). Far more typical is *American Graffiti* (George Lucas, 1974), with its elegiac 'Rock-an'-roll's never been the same since Buddy Holly died', and its compendium of stock late-fifties types (bespectacled weed, couple insecurely going steady, freewheeling blonde, motorcycling hoodlums) and situations (final school dance, car-races round the streets, petting in the rushes). A sombre political dimension is at once implied and evaded by the final titles, which tell us that one of the characters was killed on active service and another is living in Canada (presumably to avoid the draft). Revulsion from the America that had given rise to the Vietnam war here takes the form of regression into nostalgia.

Blockbusters and genres

Lucas's *Star Wars* (1977), an elaborate science-fiction extravaganza, bids fair to become the most lucrative film ever made – an illustration of how young directors can nowadays move from low-budget features (like *American Graffiti*, shot with a previously unknown cast and immensely remunerative) to international blockbuster status. The path had previously been trodden by Steven Spielberg, from *Duel* (1972), a tense thriller about a driver on a freeway pursued by a (driver-less?) truck of motiveless malignity, to *Jaws* (1975), ostensibly about a beach community terrorised by a giant white shark. I say 'ostensibly' because what *Jaws* was really about was being the most successful film of all time. It was conceived, made, publicised, attended (by millions all over the world), criticised, and analysed as such, the ultimate example of how Hollywood could manipulate a self-fulfilling prophecy.

Apart from its self-constituted unique status, *Jaws* was a not parti-cularly imaginative reworking of the monster movie – yet further evi-dence of the tenacity of the institutionalised genres, even when self-consciously updated (*Bonnie and Clyde*) or subverted (*Targets*). The Western might well have been thought obsolescent, a straitjacket of racist and imperialist values which even its (and their) high priest John Wayne found himself able to express more offensively elsewhere, in the Vietnam drama *The Green Berets* (1968). But the Western still managed to produce the sanguinary work of Sam Peckinpah, whose *The Wild Bunch* (1969) and *Pat Garrett and Billy the Kid* (1973) make powerful use of violence in explicit slow-motion, as well as Arthur Penn's *Little Big Man* (1970), whose central character is half-white, half-Red Indian, and Mel Brooks's parody *Blazing Saddles* (1974), featuring a Yiddish-speaking Indian chief and cowboys eating baked beans round the traditional camp-fire and farting raucously.

The thriller, whose leading exponent Hitchcock was below top form for most of this period, had demonstrated its adaptability to political content with *Seven Days in May*. This was widely seized upon in the aftermath of Watergate, notably by Alan J. Pakula, whose *All the President's Men* (1976) was a skilful piece of work marred only by the fact that its star reporter-heroes looked far too much like Dustin Hoffman and Robert Redford. . . . Pakula had first come to prominence with *Klute* (1971), in which Jane Fonda's 'only truly liberated woman' – the prostitute Bree Daniels – and Donald Sutherland's mournful detective were played off against each other. There was no overt political dimension to the film, but its implications about the status of women, urban paranoia, and the connection between authority and sexual violence made of it a far more subversive work than *All the President's Men*.

The most extensive exploration and subversion of genre in this period was carried on by Robert Altman. He has worked within the war movie (*M.A.S.H.*, 1970), the Western (*McCabe and Mrs Miller*, 1971), the gambling film (*California Split*, 1974), and the bank-robber movie (*Thieves Like Us* of the same year), exploring simultaneously cinema genres and social institutions, seeing the two as interwoven to a greater extent than any other director in the American industry at least. This is plainest in *Nashville* (1975), where country music is seen as a metaphor for the whole American entertainment industry, and beyond that for a whole American style of life. In *The Long Goodbye* (1972), Altman works within the detective-story again to produce a world in which there is no secure point of knowledge, a cinematic universe both blackly funny and nightmarishly convoluted.

Underground

The shift away from the secure narrative conventions of forties and fifties cinema had the effect of narrowing the stylistic gap between 'mainstream' and 'underground' film. Economically, though, the gap was still there. Stan Brakhage moved from 16 mm to 8 mm film not out of conscious artistic choice, but because his camera was stolen and 8 mm was all he could afford as a replacement. He has continued, in both 8 mm and 16 mm, to concentrate on his family and friends, producing 'diary' films of startling beauty and inventiveness; *Scenes from Under Childhood* (1966/70) uses a variety of superimpositional and distorting techniques to give a child's-eye view of life.

Many directors dispensed with live actors altogether. Robert Breer uses paintings, drawings, and filmed frames edited together into high-speed collages (*Blazes*, 1961; *Fistfight*, 1964); Tony Conrad's *The Flicker* (1965) consists simply of the stroboscopic alternation of black-and-white frames (one viewer in 15 000 will suffer an epileptic fit); the Whitney brothers continued their computer experiments. The most important of 'non-actor' directors is Michael Snow, whose *Wavelength* (1967) calls into question established notions of narrative evolution and space. The camera tracks unremittingly for forty minutes across a loft, finally focusing on a picture of some waves on the far wall. The space of the 'action' is traversed from time to time by people, fragments of whose conversation we hear, but they never distract the camera from its movement. The result is not boring (other than episodically, as almost every film is); it compels us to an awareness of the tyranny of the camera, and to a close scrutiny of the space the camera is scrutinising (and of our relationship to its scrutiny), whose effect is hypnotic without ever being numbing.

The concept of the actor-as-star is, with one notorious exception, anathema to underground cinema. Those film-makers who do not dispense with actors completely tend, like Brakhage, to rely on their own entourage, elevating the home-movie to an aesthetic statement. Gregory Markopoulos produced thirty three-minute sketches of friends and artistic influences (*Galaxie*, 1966) after his *The Iliac Passion* (1964/66), which he describes as a 'sum total of the human passions'. Jonas Mekas, best known as an intensely polemical defender of the underground film, has kept a film diary since 1950, released in episodes of varying length, as well as winning the best documentary award at the 1964 Venice Festival for his adaptation of Kenneth Brown's play about the sadistic logic of an American Army prison compound, *The Brig*.

Andy Warhol began almost as a 'non-actor' director before evolving into the notorious exception described above. *Sleep* (1963) simply shows a man sleeping for six hours, and *Empire* (1964) is a prolonged view of the Empire State Building. These films are the most extreme examples of 'realist' cinema; the camera merely observes (it was even rumoured that Warhol would simply set it up and leave it running, abdicating all directorial control), and *mise-en-scène* is minimal. In about 1965, he moved into working with sound and actors, producing films about (as they rapidly became part of) the New York *demi-monde*. These were heralded by much sensationalist publicity which must have produced some pretty disappointed voyeurs; bisexuality, drug-addiction, and transvestism were there all right, but presented in an unblinking manner (carried over from the silent films) that refused to find them surprising enough for titillation. *Chelsea Girls* (1966) marks the height of this period, two three-and-a-half-hour movies projected on parallel screens about life in the Hotel Chelsea, focus for the world that preoccupied Warhol at about this time.

Warhol's 'stars' – Nico, Viva, Baby Jane Holzer, and later the underground's king camp clown Taylor Mead – came more into prominence with the Western parody *Lonesome Cowboys* (1968), and the films Warhol went on to make in collaboration with Paul Morrissey. The police seizure of *Flesh* (1968) in London was a clear case of the right thing (in their terms) for the wrong reason; what is truly shocking to bourgeois mores in the film is not the 'depravity' depicted (homosexual prostitution, lesbian love-play, protracted fellatio), but the camera's utter unwillingness (or inability) to see it as depravity. When the girl says after sucking off Joe Dallesandro: 'I got a frog in my throat', her tranquil good humour and the bland indifference of the other characters show quite clearly that sex does not bite if you are not afraid of it. That is the most subversive import of Warhol's documentary calmness.

Exports and exiles

More and more European directors worked in America during this period, attracted by the more generous backing and facilities available. The British John Boorman enjoyed far more box-office success with the urban thriller *Point Blank* (1967) and with *Deliverance* (1972), about four town-dwellers' attempt to return to nature, than with the British-shot *Leo the Last* (1970). Yet the latter film is most suggestive and imaginative, in its use of Mastroianni's defeatist langour as a European prince who moves into a poor area and is appalled by what he sees, and in its variety of shots through windows, telescopes, and other frames-within-the-frame. As an oblique commentary on the problems of revolutionary political action in the Britain of its time, the film is unsurpassed. Its commercial failure, and Boorman's subsequent Americanisation, say much about the British industry.

Joseph Losey, however, adapted himself remarkably well to it after his McCarthyite expatriation. *The Servant* (1963) was a fruitful collaboration with Britain's leading playwright, Harold Pinter, and established Dirk Bogarde as an outstanding serious actor. His subsequent films have often tended towards an allegorical portentousness that has found it all too easy to pass itself off as high seriousness, in the Oxford drama *Accident* (1967) and especially in *The Go-Between* (1971), a would-be fraught drama of tension in the lush countryside summer whose manipulativeness, via snatches of music and visual Atmosphere with a capital A, is as gross as that of the Swedish Bo Widerberg's *Elvira Madigan* four years before. Kubrick, likewise continuing to work in Britain, produced his most visually striking work, *2001: A Space Odyssey* (1968), which brought psychedelia to the mass circuits, and *A Clockwork Orange* (1971), whose study of violence and aversion therapy was secondary to its hard glossiness of texture. A comparison of the careers of Boorman and Losey or Kubrick, the British expatriate in America and the Americans in Britain, sheds much light on the two industries.

Many of the most trenchant cinematic critiques of American society were the work of Eastern European directors. Polanski's *Rosemary's Baby* (1968) can be read in this way, as can *WR: Mysteries of the Organism* (1971), by the Yugoslav Dušan Makavejev. Makavejev relies heavily on a collage technique, both here and in *The Switchboard Operator* of four years earlier. *WR* counterposes the psychiatrist Wilhelm Reich, advocate of political-through-sexual liberation (hence a previously neglected influence on the New Left), and Joseph Stalin, through a mixture of newsreel clips and loosely-structured feature filming. The film, for all its apparent openness, does not so much suggest as impose that the forces that hounded Reich to the brink of madness during his exile in America and those that Stalin wielded were one and the same, that sexual liberation is the most important kind, and that, in capitalist and Communist societies alike, the results are likely to be catastrophic. The liberating female in the Yugoslav feature sections of the film is butchered by her lover, as Reich is psychologically butchered by the forces of redneck capitalism. Makavejev, unlike the middle-period Godard to whom he has often been compared, is most easily readable as a defeatist director.

The most frontal assault on American values by a European director came in 1975, with Milos Forman's *One Flew Over the Cuckoo's Nest*. Forman had left Czechoslovakia for America in 1971, to make *Taking Off*, a brittle and brutal comedy of the generation gap that gave little hint of the power of *Cuckoo's Nest*. Jack Nicholson as McMurphy, fomenter of rebellion in a tyrannical mental hospital, gave the most forceful performance of his career. The novel by Ken Kesey on which the film was based adopted the narrative point of view of the Indian patient Chief, forced into feigned muteness, who at the end smothers McMurphy out of compassion after he has been lobotomised. Forman's shift of perspective diminishes the impact of the story, relegating the character whose oppression is cultural and racial as well as medical to a secondary role.

The American dissidents: a summary

Almost every film-maker of note in the United States of this period implicitly or explicitly denounced American society as oppressive. The denunciation may slur over the essential issues (*American Graffiti*), in one way or another blunt their impact (*One Flew Over the Cuckoo's Nest*), be overdependent on the star and studio system that is one facet of the oppression (*All the President's Men*), adopt a stance of nihilistic, hedonistic detachment (the entire Warhol *oeuvre*), glamorise individual revolt (*Bonnie and Clyde*), or – often most fruitfully – articulate itself around contrasts and contradictions between cultures (*Targets*, *Deliverance*, the Rafelson/Nicholson films). The revulsion aroused by the Vietnam war, and the counter-culture it spawned, dissipated itself with astonishing rapidity, largely due to the non-emergence of any coherent revolutionary (as opposed to radical) political strategy. This had its effect in the cinema too, as witness the variety of reactions outlined above and the failure to produce any reappraisal of film politics along the lines of such as Pasolini, Godard, or Straub/Huillet.

South America

The South American cinema made tremendous progress in this period, though more subject than any other to often brutally dictatorial interventions. The Marxist régime of Salvator Allende in Chile encouraged a variety of artistic experimentation brought to an abrupt stop by the military coup of 1973. The Brazilian director Glauber Rocha worked under frequently immense difficulty to produce *Antonio das Mortes* (1969) and *Terra em Transe* (1967), both films about political commitment and changing sides which made considerable use of stylised theatrical elements. But all too often the initiative of what became known as the Cinema Nuovo movement was stymied or broken by political repression; many of South America's leading cinematic talents are now languishing in jail.

Japan: the future of cinema?

Along with Godard and Straub/Huillet, Japan produced the most important living revolutionary (in both a political and an aesthetic sense) director, when Nagisa Oshima made his *Death by Hanging* in 1968. Few films have functioned on so many different levels at once. It is an 'absurdist' comedy about the obscenity of capital punishment. It is an existentialist drama of identity (R., the central character, insofar as such a term has meaning, is accused of murder, forgets who he is, and has to be brought 'back to life', so that it will really be he who is hanged). It is an indictment of the oppression of minorities (R. is a student – the film coincided with the major Japanese student uprisings of 1968 – and a Korean, occupying a place in Japanese society analogous to that of coloured people in Britain or the USA). It is, above all, a constant disruption of our complacent position as spectators within the cinema; from the perennial 'derealisation' of the narrative to the organisation of camera angles, all these levels or codes are articulated in such a way that we can never say which is on top, what the film 'really means'.

Oshima's subsequent work has expanded the already colossal revolutionary potential of this film. *Diary of a Shinjuku Thief* (1968) draws on the stylisation of the Kabuki theatre that had so fascinated Eisenstein, on the connections between theft and sexuality (explored by writers such as Freud and Jean Genet), on the relations between sexual and political liberation, between student and revolutionary politics. . . . *The Ceremony* (1971) is on the level of subject-matter a conscious homage to Ozu, focusing as it does entirely on the ceremonies (weddings, funerals, tea-parties, even a hara-kiri) around which his films, like so much of Japanese society, are organised. Not readily apparent at a first viewing is the ambitious political/allegorical dimension; characters represent political figures and parties, and each severance or union in the various ceremonies corresponds to a precise crisis – feud, coup, or alliance – in contemporary Japanese history.

The two poles of Oshima's cinema – the erotic/psychoanalytical and the revolutionary/political – reveal themselves to have been one all along in *Ai No Corrida/Empire of the Senses* (1976). A former geisha and a restaurant-owner make unceasing love until she, with her lover's consent, strangles him with a scarf at the moment of orgasm; she wanders the streets of Tokyo for four days with his severed genitals in her pocket, in a state of intense ecstasy. The last line of the film is: 'This happened in 1936' – year of an abortive military coup in Japan, harbinger of the Nazi alliance to come; year too of the first showing of a sound film in the country, attended by a minister who was assassinated in the attempted coup on the very next day . . . . As with *The Ceremony*, it is easy to miss the density and complexity of the film's political references.

As *Empire of the Senses* progresses, the sexual roles are reversed; the man, physically and otherwise 'on top' at first, comes to accept, physically and otherwise, a subordinate position, even to strangulation and castration. The male codes of sexual dominance even stronger in Japan than in other societies (and against which Mizoguchi's cinema had represented a powerful protest) are inverted with the most shattering effect. The erotic scenes are sustainedly exciting and inventive (what censorship mechanisms must have been at work in the unconscious of the critics who found them boring!) As well as (and part of) its synthesis of the psychoanalytical and the political, the film is (after *Pierrot*) one of the greatest documents of the *amour maudit* ('accursed love') extolled by the surrealists, in which the connection between love and death (the death of the dominant male, the death of the phallus, and hence for psychoanalysts too the death of language) is supremely explored.

Empire of the Senses is virtually banned in its native Japan, has been subject to prosecution and harassment in Germany, and had immense problems in reaching Britain because the Customs alleged that it contravened the law against gross indecency (one feature of which is that it admits no evidence about the artistic worth of the allegedly infringing text). If the cinema has a future, *Empire of the Senses* is the most dramatic pointer to it – to its capacity to articulate complex social, political, and psychoanalytic considerations, to the way in which it can constantly stretch the bounds of what is possible (in subject-matter and filming alike), to its ability (perhaps the acid test of an art-form) to produce and at the same time work against its own codes and conventions. But it also acts as an example of the cinema's subjection to grubby-minded restraints from which literature did not rid itself until the *Lady Chatterley* trial (and which even now are in danger of recrudescing), to harassment in the name of 'civilised morality' and of the profit-motive alike.

The cinema is a young art that has matured immensely fast, and whose capacities for constructive change still appear limitless. Our adjustment to it, couched in the answers to questions such as what we can view, how we can view it, what considerations guide our viewing, and how what we view influences us, have a very long way still to go to catch up with the fact of cinema.

Glossary

auteur   the director seen as overall creatively responsible for a film or body of films

biopic   a film dealing with the life-story of a well-known figure

caméra-stylo   the camera regarded (literally) as a 'pen', a means of writing on a par with the written word

chiaroscuro   heavy contrast of light and dark – a visual style much beloved of the German Expressionists

ciné-vérité   'cinema-truth' – the camera observing people as they naturally behave, instead of filming a scripted and staged scene

deep focus   the illusory third dimension of the screen deepened and intensified (by lighting and/or elaborately constructed sets), so that action can often take place on two or more levels at once

écriture   in French, 'writing' – a term much used to accentuate the linguistic nature of apparently non-verbal activities, including the cinema (cf. *caméra-stylo*)

film noir   loosely applied to many Hollywood films of the forties and fifties, characterised by gloomy urban locations, pervasive cynicism, and often a sense of existential exhaustion

genre   label to cover a class of film (examples: Western, thriller, *film noir*)

leitmotif   a recurrent theme or pattern in a body of film work (examples: foot-fetichism in Buñuel, the director always appearing in a small part in his own films in Hitchcock)

mise-en-scène   in French, theatrical term for production and staging. Used by the *Cahiers* critics to draw attention to how a film was produced and staged rather than what it ostensibly talked about

montage   the production of cinematic meaning by the juxtaposition of individual shots (or elements within a shot)

neo-realism   loosely applied to post-war Italian movement that moved away from elaborate studio staging to concentrate on location shooting that gave the impression of behaviour spontaneously observed (cf. *ciné-vérité*)

nouvelle vague 'new wave': loosely used, in reference to French film-makers of the fifties and sixties who reacted against stories with a moral slant, filmed within the studio, in favour of an often American-influenced conciseness, location-shooting, and abstention from overt moral judgement

open text a term borrowed from recent French critical work on literature, to denote a work which does not fix its own boundaries of meaning. The reader (or viewer) is required to play an active part by sorting out meanings for himself

subjective flashback a past event recollected and represented through the point of view of one of the participants

tracking shot one where the camera moves sideways, across an immobile space or one peopled with moving characters

Filmography

This lists the most important directors mentioned in the text, and a selection of their major films, in chronological order.

Altman, Robert   1970: *M.A.S.H.* 1972: *The Long Goodbye.* 1975: *Nashville*

Anderson, Lindsay   1968: *If. . . .* 1973: *O Lucky Man!*

Anger, Kenneth   1947: *Fireworks.* 1964: *Scorpio Rising*

Antonioni, Michelangelo   1960: *L'Avventura.* 1961: *La Notte.* 1962: *L'Eclisse.* 1964: *The Red Desert.* 1966: *Blow-Up.* 1970: *Zabriskie Point.* 1975: *The Passenger*

Bergman, Ingmar   1953: *Sawdust and Tinsel.* 1955: *Smiles of a Summer Night.* 1957: *The Seventh Seal, Wild Strawberries.* 1959: *The Virgin Spring.* 1961: *Through a Glass Darkly.* 1963: *Winter Light, The Silence.* 1966: *Persona.* 1968: *The Shame.* 1970: *A Passion*

Bertolucci, Bernardo   1970: *The Conformist.* 1972: *Last Tango in Paris*

Boorman, John   1967: *Point Blank.* 1970: *Leo the Last*

Borowczyk, Walerian   1967: *Le Théâtre de Monsieur et Madame Kabal.* 1971: *Blanche.* 1974: *Contes Immoraux*

Bresson, Robert   1945: *Les Dames du Bois de Boulogne.* 1950: *Le Journal d'un Curé de Campagne.* 1966: *Balthazar.* 1967: *Mouchette.* 1974: *Lancelot du Lac.* 1977: *Le Diable, Probablement*

Buñuel, Luis   1928: *Un Chien Andalou.* 1930: *L'Age d'Or.* 1950: *Los Olvidados.* 1958: *Nazarin.* 1961: *Viridiana.* 1962: *The Exterminating Angel.* 1970: *Tristana.* 1973: *Le Charme Discret de la Bourgeoisie.* 1974: *Le Fantôme de la Liberté.* 1977: *Cet Obscur Objet du Désir*

Capra, Frank   1936: *Mr Deeds Goes to Town.* 1939: *Mr Smith Goes to Washington*

Carné, Marcel   1937: *Drôle de Drame*. 1938: *Quai des Brumes*. 1939: *Le Jour se Lève*. 1945: *Les Enfants du Paradis*

Chabrol, Claude   1958: *Le Beau Serge*. 1960: *Les Bonnes Femmes*. 1969: *Le Boucher*. 1974: *Une Partie de Plaisir*

Chaplin, Charles   1925: *The Gold Rush*. 1931: *City Lights*. 1936: *Modern Times*. 1940: *The Great Dictator*. 1947: *Monsieur Verdoux*

Clair, René   1924: *Entr'acte*. 1931: *Le Million*. 1932: *A Nous la Liberté*. 1941: *The Flame of New Orleans*. 1955: *Les Grandes Manoeuvres*

Clarke, Shirley   1960: *The Connection*. 1967: *Portrait of Jason*

Cocteau, Jean   1930: *Le Sang d'un Poète*. 1946: *La Belle et la Bête*. 1950: *Orphée*

Cukor, George   1936: *Camille*. 1949: *Adam's Rib*. 1952: *Pat and Mike*

Curtiz, Michael   1936: *The Charge of the Light Brigade*. 1943: *Casablanca*. 1944: *Passage to Marseille*

de Mille, Cecil B.   1923: *The Ten Commandments*. 1956: *The Ten Commandments* (remake)

de Sica, Vittorio   1948: *Bicycle Thieves*. 1952: *Umberto D*

Dmytryk, Edward   1945: *Farewell My Lovely*. 1947: *Crossfire*

Dovzhenko, Alexander   1929: *Arsenal*. 1930: *Earth*. 1935: *Aerograd*

Dreyer, Carl Theodor   1928: *The Passion of Joan of Arc*. 1932: *Vampyr*. 1943: *Day of Wrath*. 1954: *Ordet/The Word*. 1964: *Gertrud*

Eisenstein, Sergei   1924: *Strike*. 1925: *The Battleship Potemkin*. 1927: *October*. 1929: *The General Line*. 1938: *Alexander Nevsky*. 1944/45: *Ivan the Terrible*

Fellini, Federico   1954: *La Strada*. 1959: *La Dolce Vita*. 1963: *Eight and a Half*. 1969: *Fellini Satyricon*. 1972: *Fellini Roma*

Ferreri, Marco   1973: *La Grande Bouffe*. 1975: *La Dernière Femme*

Feuillade, Louis   1913/14: *Fantômas*. 1919: *L'Homme sans Visage*

Flaherty, Robert   1922: *Nanook of the North*. 1926: *Moana*

Ford, John   1935: *The Informer*. 1939: *Stagecoach, Young Mr Lincoln, Drums along the Mohawk*. 1940: *The Grapes of Wrath*. 1945: *They Were Expendable*. 1956: *The Searchers*

Franju, Georges   1949: *Le Sang des Bêtes*. 1959: *Les Yeux sans Visage*

Frankenheimer, John   1962: *The Manchurian Candidate*. 1964: *Seven Days in May*

Fuller, Samuel   1952: *Pickup on South Street*. 1955: *House of Bamboo*

Gance, Abel   1922: *La Roue*. 1926: *Napoléon*

Godard, Jean-Luc   1959: *A Bout de Souffle*. 1963: *Les Carabiniers*. 1964: *Une Femme Mariée*. 1965: *Alphaville, Pierrot le Fou*. 1967: *La Chinoise*. 1968: *Weekend*. 1969: (with J. P. Gorin) *British Sounds*. 1971: (with J. P. Gorin) *Vladimir and Rosa*. 1975: (with A. M. Miéville) *Numéro Deux*. 1978: (with A. M. Miéville) *Comment Ça Va?*

Grierson, John   1929: *Drifters*

Griffith, D. W.   1915: *The Birth of a Nation*. 1916: *Intolerance*. 1921: *Orphans of the Storm*

Hamer, Robert   1949: *Kind Hearts and Coronets*

Hawks, Howard   1932: *Scarface*. 1938: *Bringing Up Baby*. 1939: *Only Angels Have Wings*. 1945: *To Have and Have Not*. 1946: *The Big Sleep*. 1948: *Red River*. 1959: *Rio Bravo*

Herzog, Werner   1972: *Aguirre, Wrath of God*. 1974: *The Enigma of Kaspar Hauser*

Hitchcock, Alfred   1929: *Blackmail*. 1938: *The Lady Vanishes*. 1940: *Rebecca*. 1948: *Rope*. 1951: *Strangers on a Train*. 1958: *Vertigo*. 1959: *North by Northwest*. 1960: *Psycho*. 1963: *The Birds*. 1964: *Marnie*.

Huston, John   1941: *The Maltese Falcon*. 1948: *Key Largo*. 1953: *Moulin Rouge*. 1961: *The Misfits*

Ichikawa, Kon   1956: *The Burmese Harp*. 1963: *An Actor's Revenge*

Jennings, Humphrey   1943: *Fires Were Started*. 1945: *A Diary for Timothy*

Kazan, Elia   1954: *On the Waterfront*. 1955: *East of Eden*. 1961: *Splendour in the Grass*

Keaton, Buster   1924: *Sherlock Junior, The Navigator*. 1926: *Battling Butler, The General*

Kramer, Stanley   1959: *On the Beach*. 1961: *Judgement at Nuremberg*

Kurosawa, Akira   1950: *Rashomon*. 1954: *The Seven Samurai*. 1961: *Yojimbo*. 1970: *Dodeskaden*

Lang, Fritz   1924: *The Nibelungs*. 1927: *Metropolis*. 1931: *M*. 1932: *The Testament of Dr Mabuse*. 1936: *Fury*. 1937: *You Only Live Once*. 1944: *The Ministry of Fear*. 1953: *The Big Heat*

Losey, Joseph   1951: *M*. 1963: *The Servant*. 1971: *The Go-Between*

Lubitsch, Ernst   1934: *The Merry Widow*. 1937: *Angel*. 1942: *To Be or Not to Be*

Lumière, Louis and Auguste   1895/96: shorts including *La Sortie des Usines, L'Arroseur Arrosé*

Mackendrick, Alexander   1948: *Whisky Galore*. 1955: *The Ladykillers*

Makavejev, Dušan   1967: *The Switchboard Operator*. 1961: *WR – Mysteries of the Organism*

Malle, Louis   1958: *Les Amants*. 1963: *Le Feu Follet*. 1971: *Le Souffle au Coeur*

Mann, Anthony   1950: *Winchester '73*. 1955: *The Man from Laramie*. 1964: *The Fall of the Roman Empire*

Marker, Chris   1961: *La Jetée, Le Joli Mai*

Mekas, Jonas   1961: *Guns of the Trees*. 1964/69: *Diaries, Notes, and Sketches*

Méliès, Georges   1902: *Le Voyage dans la Lune*. 1903: *Le Royaume des Fées*. 1906: *Les Quat' Cents Farces du Diable*

Melville, Jean-Pierre   1950: *Les Enfants Terribles*. 1965: *Le Deuxième Souffle*. 1970: *Le Cercle Rouge*

Menzel, Jiri   1966: *Closely Observed Trains*

Minelli, Vincente   1951: *An American in Paris*. 1954: *Brigadoon*. 1956: *Lust for Life*

Mizoguchi, Kenji   1939: *The Story of the Last Chrysanthemums.* 1952: *The Life of O-Haru.* 1953: *Ugetsu Monogatari.* 1954: *Sansho Dayu, Chikamatsu Monogatari*

Murnau, Friedrich   1922: *Nosferatu.* 1924: *The Last Laugh.* 1925: *Tartuffe*

Ophuls, Max   1932: *Liebelei.* 1947: *Letter fron an Unknown Woman.* 1949: *The Reckless Moment.* 1953: *Madame de . . .* 1955: *Lola Montès.*

Oshima, Nagisa   1968: *Death by Hanging, Diary of a Shinjuku Thief.* 1969: *The Boy.* 1971: *The Ceremony.* 1975: *Ai No Corrida/Empire of the Senses.* 1977: *Empire of Passion.*

Ozu, Yasujiro   1941: *The Brothers and Sisters of the Toda Family.* 1949: *Late Spring.* 1951: *Early Summer.* 1953: *Tokyo Story*

Pabst, G. W.   1925: *Joyless Street.* 1931: *The Threepenny Opera, Kameradschaft*

Pasolini, Pier Paolo   1961: *Accattone.* 1964: *The Gospel According to Matthew.* 1967: *Oedipus Rex.* 1968: *Theorem.* 1969: *Medea.* 1971: *The Decameron.* 1975: *Salo, or the One Hundred and Twenty Days of Sodom*

Peckinpah, Sam   1965: *Major Dundee.* 1973: *Pat Garrett and Billy the Kid*

Penn, Arthur   1958: *The Left-Handed Gun.* 1967: *Bonnie and Clyde*

Polansky, Roman   1962: *Knife in the Water.* 1966: *Cul-de-Sac.* 1968: *Rosemary's Baby.* 1974: *Chinatown*

Preminger, Otto   1955: *The Man with the Golden Arm.* 1960: *Exodus.* 1963: *The Cardinal*

Pudovkin, Vsevolod   1927: *The End of St Petersburg.* 1928: *Storm over Asia*

Rafelson, Bob   1970: *Five Easy Pieces.* 1972: *The King of Marvin Gardens*

Ray, Nicholas   1948: *They Live by Night.* 1955: *Rebel without a Cause.* 1958: *Party Girl*

Ray, Satyajit   1955: *Pather Panchali.* 1958: *The Music Room.* 1970: *Days and Nights in the Forest*

Renoir, Jean   1931: *La Chienne.* 1932: *La Nuit du Carrefour, Boudu sauvé des Eaux.* 1935: *Toni.* 1936: *Le Crime de M. Lange, Une Partie de Campagne.* 1937: *La Grande Illusion.* 1939: *La Règle du Jeu.* 1945: *The Southerner.* 1962: *Le Caporal Épinglé*

Resnais, Alain   1959: *Hiroshima mon Amour.* 1961: *L'Année Dernière à Marienbad.* 1963: *Muriel.* 1966: *La Guerre est Finie.* 1976: *Providence*

Riefenstahl, Leni   1936: *The Triumph of the Will*

Rivette, Jacques   1961: *Paris nous Appartient.* 1969: *L'Amour Fou.* 1973: *Out One: Spectre.* 1974: *Céline et Julie Vont en Bateau.* 1976: *Duelle, Noroît*

Roeg, Nicholas   1968: (with Donald Cammell) *Performance.* 1971: *Walkabout.* 1973: *Don't Look Now*

Rohmer, Eric   1968: *Ma Nuit chez Maud.* 1970: *Le Genou de Claire*

Rossellini, Roberto 1945: *Rome, Open City*. 1946: *Paisà*. 1966: *La Prise du Pouvoir par Louis XIV*

Siegel, Donald 1954: *Riot in Cell Block 11*. 1968: *Madigan*

Sirk, Douglas 1955: *All That Heaven Allows*. 1956: *Written on the Wind*

Sjostrom, Victor 1913: *Ingeborg Holm*. 1917: *The Outlaw and his Wife*. 1926: *The Scarlet Letter*

Stiller, Mauritz 1917: *Thomas Graal's Best Film*. 1924: *The Atonement of Gosta Berling*

Straub, Jean-Marie (with Danièle Huillet) 1965: *Not Reconciled*. 1967: *The Chronicle of Anna Magdalena Bach*. 1968: *The Bridegroom, the Comedienne, and the Pimp*. 1975: *Moses and Aaron*

Truffaut, François 1959: *Les Quatre Cents Coups*. 1960: *Tirez sur le Pianiste*. 1961: *Jules et Jim*. 1968: *Baisers Volés*. 1976: *L'Histoire d'Adèle H*

Varda, Agnès 1961: *Cléo de 5 à 7*. 1964: *Le Bonheur*

Vertov, Dziga 1929: *The Man with a Movie Camera*. 1934: *Three Songs of Lenin*

Vidor, King 1928: *The Crowd*. 1929: *Hallelujah!*

Viconti, Luchino 1942: *Ossessione*. 1947: *La Terra Trema*. 1960: *Rocco and His Brothers*. 1971: *Death in Venice*

Von Sternberg, Joseph 1930: *The Blue Angel*. 1932: *Shanghai Express*. 1934: *The Scarlet Empress*. 1935: *The Devil is a Woman*. 1941: *The Shanghai Gesture*

Von Stroheim, Erich 1921: *Foolish Wives*. 1923: *Greed*. 1928: *The Wedding March, Queen Kelly*

Wajda, Andrzej 1956: *Kanal*. 1958: *Ashes and Diamonds*

Walsh, Raoul 1939: *The Roaring Twenties*. 1941: *High Sierra*

Warhol, Andy 1966: *Chelsea Girls*. 1968: *Lonesome Cowboys*

Welles, Orson 1941: *Citizen Kane*. 1942: *The Magnificent Ambersons*. 1948: *Macbeth, The Lady from Shanghai*. 1955: *Confidential Report/ Mr Arkadin*. 1958: *Touch of Evil*

Wiene, Robert 1919: *The Cabinet of Dr Caligari*

Wyler, William 1941: *The Little Foxes*. 1946: *The Best Years of our Lives*. 1959: *Ben-Hur*

Zinnemann, Fred 1952: *High Noon*. 1953: *From Here to Eternity*

Notes on text

Chapter One
1. *A Biographical Dictionary of the Cinema*, Secker and Warburg. 1975.

Chapter Two
1. In *The Film Sense* (tr. Leyda), Faber. 1943.
2. In *The Film Sense* (tr. Leyda), Faber.
3. Yon Barna, *Eisenstein*, Secker and Warburg (Cinema Two). 1973.
4. In *Kino*, Allen and Unwin. 1960.
5. In *A Biographical Dictionary of the Cinema*, Secker and Warburg.
6. In *Luis Buñuel*, Studio Vista. 1967.
7. v. infra, p. 154.

Chapter Three
1. In *The Long View*, Paladin. 1974.
2. In *Buster Keaton*, Secker and Warburg (Cinema One). 1969.
3. In *A Biographical Dictionary of the Cinema*, Secker and Warburg.

Chapter Four
1. In *The Film Till Now*, Jonathan Cape. 1949.
2. In *Essais sur la Signification au Cinéma*, Klinksieck (my own translation). 1968.
3. In *What is Cinema?* (tr. Gray), University of California Press. 1971.
4. In *The Contemporary Cinema*, Penguin. 1963.
5. In *What is Cinema?* (tr. Gray), University of California Press.
6. Celia Britton in *Film Form*, issue no. 1.
7. In *Brecht/Diderot/Eisenstein* (tr. Heath), in *Screen*, summer 1974.
8. Quoted by Basil Wright in *The Long View*, Paladin.

Chapter Five
1. In *Signs and Meaning in the Cinema*, Secker and Warburg (Cinema One). 1969.
2. In *Hollywood in the Thirties*, Zwemmer. 1968.
3. In *A Biographical Dictionary of the Cinema*, Secker and Warburg.

Chapter Six
1. In *Humphrey Jennings: A Tribute*. 1950.
2. Quoted by Penelope Houston in *The Contemporary Cinema*, Penguin.
3. In *Humphrey Bogart*, Pyramid Illustrated History of the Movies. 1973.
4. In *A Biographical Dictionary of the Cinema*, Secker and Warburg.
5. Quoted in André Bazin, *Jean Renoir*, W. H. Allen. 1974.
6. Quoted in Penelope Houston, *The Contemporary Cinema*, Penguin.
7. In *Sight and Sound*, autumn 1976.

Chapter Seven
1. In *A Biographical Dictionary of the Cinema*, Secker and Warburg.
2. From John Osborne's *Look Back in Anger*. 1957.
3. In *The Contemporary Cinema*, Penguin.

Chapter Eight
1. In *What is Cinema?* (tr. Gray), University of California Press.
2. In *The Immediate Experience*, New York. 1962.
3. In *French Cinema since 1945*, Zwemmer. 1966.
4. In *The Films of Robert Bresson*, Studio Vista. 1969.
5. Quoted by Penelope Houston in *The Contemporary Cinema*, Penguin.
6. In *Sight and Sound*, summer 1977.
7. In *Luis Buñuel*, Studio Vista.
8. In *Luis Buñuel*, Studio Vista.

Chapter Nine
1. In *The Underground Film*, Studio Vista. 1968.

Chapter Ten
1. In *Ingmar Bergman*, Studio Vista. 1969.

Chapter Twelve
1. In *Theory of Film Practice*, Secker and Warburg (Cinema Two). 1973.
2. In *Pier Paolo Pasolini*, British Film Institute. 1977.
3. In *Mythologies*, Paladin. (tr. Lavers), 1972.

Index

This includes the individuals and main movements and ideas mentioned in the text, but not (for reasons of space) titles of individual films.